Nailed to the Crossbar

Nailed to the Crossbar:

From the NCAA-Penn State Consent Decree to the Joe Paterno Family Lawsuit

Ronald A. Smith

Mt. Nittany Press
Lemont

Published by Mt. Nittany Press, an imprint of Eifrig Publishing,
PO Box 66, Lemont, PA 16851.
Knobelsdorffstr. 44, 14059 Berlin, Germany

For information regarding permission, write to:
Rights and Permissions Department,
Eifrig Publishing,
PO Box 66, Lemont, PA 16851, USA.
permissions@eifrigpublishing.com, 888-340-6543.

Library of Congress Cataloging-in-Publication Data

Smith, Ronald A., 1936-
 Nailed to the Crossbar: From the NCAA – Penn State Consent Decree to the Joe Paterno
Family Lawsuit / by Ronald A. Smith.
       p. cm.
       Includes timeline and index

Paperback: ISBN 978-1-63233-409-1
Hardcover: ISBN 978-1-63233-174-8
Ebook: ISBN 978-1-63233-175-5

     1. Pennsylvania State University-Sports. 2. Pennsylvania State University-Football
          3. NCAA 4. Sports-Administration. 5. College sports-Corrupt practices-
          Pennsylvania-University Park. 6. Educational history-Joe Paterno
     I. Smith, Ronald A. (Ronald Austin), II. Title.

22 21 20 19 2018

5 4 3 2 1

Printed on acid-free paper in the USA. ∞

CONTENTS

Dedication

To Jackie Esposito and her Penn State archival team, and all those professionals who work to protect our institutional legacies and history.

R.A.S.

Preface and Acknowledgments

I spent 28 years as a Penn State professor teaching sport history in the Department of Kinesiology. That department, known as the Department of Physical Education when I was hired, was ranked as the top department in the field for four decades. The professors doing research in exercise physiology, biomechanics, motor learning, and history and philosophy of sport were rated at the top of their fields, and often were elected into the prestigious Academy of Physical Education and Kinesiology. As I have written a number of books on the history of sport, particularly the history of intercollegiate athletics, I was open to criticism of being either pro-intercollegiate athletics or anti-intercollegiate athletics. This is particularly true with college athletics, unlike a study of physiological fast twitch or slow twitch muscles, because winning and losing in athletics carries strong emotional ties to individual institutions. My relationship to Penn State, being pro-Penn State or anti-Penn State, is not an exception to this proposition. I have acquired loyalties to Penn State since arriving in 1968. Anyone who has attended many Penn State events, as I have, knows that the chant "We Are . . . . Penn State" is an emotional statement at a woman's volleyball contest of 4,000 spectators or at a football game in the 107,000-seat stadium. As I have more recently done research on Penn State athletics, looking at its history, I have looked at both the positives and negatives in its development.

Famed jurist Learned Hand put it succinctly, "Keep an open mind to every disconcerting fact, or an open ear to the cold voice of doubt." As an historian I have attempted to keep an open mind with a kind of detached skepticism, and base my writing on historical evidence. What I have endeavored to do in *Nailed to the Crossbar* (and my previous *Wounded Lions*) is to use my Penn State experience and my background of researching college sport for over a half-century to tell an accurate story resulting from the Sandusky Scandal. I have based my writing about the Penn State situation on factual material that I have gathered during the period following the largest scandal in Penn State history. In my search for the truth, as close as I can come to it, I have placed emphasis in *Nailed to the Crossbar* on the failure of the NCAA to carry out the American emphasis on due process and the NCAA's lack of justice to Penn State.

I want to acknowledge a number of individuals who read parts of the manuscript. I have used many of their suggestions in an effort to improve this volume. These include Alex Black, Darwin Braund, Richard Crepeau, Bob Downs, Rosa Eberle, Jackie Esposito, Drew Hyman, Tom Jable, Joel Myers, Dan Nathan, Mike Poorman, Ken Pyle, Bob Reising, Vic Russo, Karl Stoedefalke, Lee Stout, and Jere Willey. Kudos to six individuals who read the entire manuscript and made lengthy responses: Bob Barney, Mike Bezilla, Frank Deutsch, Art Glenn, Piet van Ogtrop, Jack Selzer, and John Swisher. No one did more reading and commenting than my wife of over a half-century, Susan Fernald Smith. I am indebted to three individuals, Mike Bezilla, Mike Poorman, and Jack Selzer, who spoke at my Penn State-connected Osher Lifelong Learning Institute (OLLI) class on the legacy of Joe Paterno, an important focus at the close of *Nailed to the Crossbar*.

Introduction

Accusation is not proof and that conviction depends
upon evidence and due process of law.[1]
Edward R. Murrow, CBS (1954)

The Jerry Sandusky child abuse scandal, blown open on November 5, 2011, morphed from a crisis for Penn State University into a disaster. Penn State administrators and Board of Trustees members made plenty of mistakes following the Pennsylvania grand jury presentment against Sandusky and Penn State administrators. However, the NCAA under its president, Mark Emmert, using the insupportably written Freeh Report about the scandal, bullied Penn State's Rod Erickson into signing a damaging Consent Decree. The "illegal" Consent Decree of July 2012 not only damaged Penn State athletics, but also more importantly put the mark of Cain on Penn State with costs that would approach a billion dollars.

This is a story of Penn State being nailed unjustly by leaders of the National Collegiate Athletic Association who bypassed NCAA Bylaws and without due process. It emphasizes what crisis manager Steven Fink has stated about both the head of the NCAA and the author of the Freeh Report—"Mark Emmert and Louis Freeh are grandstanding past masters."[2] Mark Emmert was out to castigate "lily white" Penn State and its athletics for his own personal glory and NCAA redemption. Louis Freeh—a second antagonist in this sorry tale—offered defective conclusions castigating Penn State officials. There are, unfortunately, no protagonists, unless it is a female psychologist, Alycia Chambers, who early on suggested that Jerry Sandusky's action with a young boy in a Penn State shower room was that of "a likely pedophile."[3] Her report was dismissed by local governmental officials in May of 1998, and 13 unlucky years later, and many more abused children, the Sandusky Scandal exploded.

Following a number of lawsuits and their depositions and informative documents, it has become clear that to the end of the field of play where Penn State was once nailed, two individuals should have been firmly attached to the crossbar. One was Mark Emmert, head of the NCAA; the other was Louis Freeh, author of the disputed Freeh Report. Emmert was aided and abetted by the NCAA Counsel, Donald Remy, who should have advised his boss that the NCAA Constitution and Bylaws were being violated. Rather, Emmert took punishing Penn State into his own hands rather than following the due process rules that were clearly written for the NCAA Committee on Infractions to deal with any violations that may have occurred.[4] What Emmert did to Penn State reminded me of the demagoguery and lack of due process in the 1950s by Senator Joe McCarthy. Coming from my home state of Wisconsin, McCarthy made false claims and exploited prejudice, as did Emmert over a half-century later. McCarthy did his witch hunting of communists based on false claims and exploiting prejudice. In that case, a journalist, Edward R. Morrow, stood tall and helped destroy McCarthy, his demagoguery, and his lack of due process.[5] Emmert, in his own way, used false claims and exploited prejudice about the Sandusky Scandal as he bypassed the NCAA's own due process.

Unfortunately for Penn State, the institution was led by a new and uninformed, but well liked, president, Rod Erickson, who didn't know the first thing about the NCAA or how it operated. All he wanted to do was to "MOVE FORWARD" from the scandal, but it is almost impossible for any prisoner to move forward with a ball and chain tied around his leg.[6] That was the Consent Decree, signed hours after removing from campus the iconic Joe Paterno statue to be hidden away for years. Signing the most damaging punishment ever given out by the NCAA and at the same time concealing the bronze likeness of Paterno a half year after his death, was a stab in the back to many who supported Penn State and probably the best known individual in Penn State's history.

Living only two miles from campus for over four decades, I was strongly affected by the announcement by the Pennsylvania Attorney General's office of the charges against Jerry Sandusky in early November 2011. I knew most of the individuals directly involved in the scandal, but not intimately or socially. I had known Jerry to some extent since he joined the faculty and was an assistant coach in the Department of Physical Education in 1969. That was a year after I joined the same faculty in the professorial role as a sport historian, emphasizing the history of college athletics.[7] Jerry, along with Jim O'Hora, appeared to me to be the friendliest members of the football coaching staff whom I often saw in Recreation Building and in the coaches-physical education locker room. Two others often in my building were Tim Curley and Joe Paterno. I had been around athletic director Tim Curley since he was an undergraduate in the 1970s. It was difficult for almost anyone not to like Tim who was cordial and accommodating. Joe Paterno was more difficult to be around, for as one-time athletic director at Penn State Jim Tarman (1982-1993) once pronounced, Joe "isn't as abrasive as he once was."[8] And that was from a friend.

Before President Graham Spanier was ousted because of the scandal and eventually sentenced to prison, I frequently saw him in our locker room as he often played racquetball in Recreation Building. Previously, I had a lengthy talk with Graham in 1995 when he was still provost at the University of Nebraska, though he had been elected to the presidency of Penn State. There, while I was researching for a history of the influence of radio and TV on college sport, he told me that at Penn State his administration would be "more open," a change in style for the university.[9] He also said that his biggest problem at Nebraska was his hiring an outsider, Bill Byrne, as athletic director rather than the insider, Al Papik, favored by outgoing AD Bob Devaney and football coach Tom Osborne.[10] When that hiring controversy erupted, Spanier responded in a statement, "You won't find a chancellor around as supportive of intercollegiate athletics as I am."[11] So he was at Penn State, attending many sport events such as women's volleyball and basketball, and always at the Penn State football games, where the President's glassed-in special box held nearly 400 spectators.

Almost as soon as the Sandusky Scandal arose, I wanted to know more about how the history of athletic administration at Penn State may have contributed to the scandal. As I was a college athlete in both baseball and basketball at Northwestern University, I was aware of a number of issues in college athletics. In addition, I was on the physical education faculty at Penn State and in the same building housing all of the men's coaches, including head coach Joe Paterno. I had also spent my entire career researching intercollegiate athletics with a particular interest in the administration of big-time athletics. Being skeptical, a trait of most historians, I began researching the background of the Jerry Sandusky scandal by going through the massive historical records in the Penn State Archives—more than a century of papers and texts of presidents, board of trustees, faculty, students, alumni, coaches, athletic directors, and sports information individuals among others.[12] My findings resulted in a book titled, *Wounded Lions: Joe Paterno, Jerry Sandusky, and the Crises in Penn State Athletics*. This book began with a short history of life in Happy Valley, as this region is called. It ended with the grand jury presentment against Sandusky and two Penn State administrators and the signing of the Consent Decree.[13]

The writing of the current volume was the next logical step in this sorry saga. The Consent Decree that was foisted on Penn State, revealed a great deal about how NCAA officials used the Penn State scandal for their own purposes. Lawsuits abounded, including the two most important for understanding the questionable legality of the Consent Decree. The first was a court case by Pennsylvania State Senator Jake Corman against the NCAA, including Mark Emmert and Edward Ray, head of the NCAA Presidents' Council. It was settled out of court.[14] The other was a long-simmering suit of the Paterno Family against the NCAA. It was principally initiated to try to reestablish Joe Paterno's good name.[15] But, more important to Penn State, it showed how the NCAA never followed due process when it imposed the Consent Decree on the state's land grant institution. This, then, is that story of Penn State and football being unjustly "nailed to the crossbar."

As my age may give me some added insight into the nature and motivations of human beings, it may also tend to harden personal opinion about individuals and institutions. I am quite conscious of biases that confront all of us at whatever age. For as British author and historian, J. A. Froude, stated long ago, "The first duty of an historian is to be on the guard against his own sympathies." Yet, Froude believed "We cannot wholly escape their influence."[16] It is true as it pertains to my interpretation of the Sandusky Scandal and the NCAA's reaction to it.

I have tried, in this volume and others that have been published, to follow the dictum found on a plaque attached to the principal administrative building at the University of Wisconsin, Madison, where I achieved two advanced degrees. "Whatever may be the limitations which trammel inquiry elsewhere," the Bascom Hall brass reads, the researcher "should ever encourage that continued and fearless sifting and winnowing by which alone truth can be found. "Truth" about the Sandusky Scandal and Penn State's and the NCAA's reactions to the revelations, remains rather elusive. This volume is my best effort to "sift" and "winnow" and let the historical chips fall where they may. There will be others to follow with their own interpretation of the facts.

A lifetime leading to the status of octogenarian has led me to agree with the English novelist, Charles Dickens, who, early in life, recognized hypocrisy in human activity with individuals who have "affection beaming in one eye and calculation shining in the other."[17] The Sandusky Scandal evolved into more "calculation" than "affection." Pointedly, NCAA president Mark Emmert "shining" his hypocrisy, two months after the Sandusky Scandal broke, told those at the NCAA annual convention that the NCAA could not do anything about the father of Cam Newton, the star football quarterback, attempting to sell his son to Mississippi State University for over $100,000 by saying "We don't have a rule that makes that clear."[18] At about the same time, Emmert said that the Penn State Scandal was a criminal case, not a violation of specific NCAA Bylaws. Then, a half year later, Emmert would violate the NCAA's own rules, infringe its own due process provisions, and direct the punishment of Penn State with the most stringent penalties ever given by the NCAA. This volume is the sad tale of the ill-devised NCAA-Penn State Consent Decree—violations of NCAA Bylaws, lack of due process, and hypocrisy of leaders of the National Collegiate Athletic Association. It is the saga of the NCAA nailing Penn State to its football crossbar. It is also the story of the NCAA being challenged, not by Penn State but by outsiders, in an attempt to redress the wrongs inflicted upon Penn State and the wider community.

Chapter 1

From Home Rule to Emmert Bullying:
How the NCAA Came to Enforcement

The question of justice only enters where there is equal power to enforce it, and that the powerful exact what they can, and the weak grant what they must.[19]

Thucydides, ca. 411 B.C.E.

Twenty-four centuries before the 2011 C.E. Jerry Sandusky Scandal broke at Penn State University, Thucydides, the father of "scientific" history, wrote in 411 B.C.E. about the Greek island of Melos not willing to join Athens in its fight against Sparta in the Peloponnesian War. Because Melians were militarily weak relative to the giant Athens, the island's population was eliminated, its men killed by the Athenians and its women and children sold into slavery. The powerful Athenians had exacted what they could, and the vulnerable Melians, unwilling to bend to the power, were destroyed.[20] Thucydides had it right about power, "the powerful exact what they can, and the weak grant what they must." A successor nineteen centuries later, Niccolò Machiavelli, was more cunning in his political advice than Thucydides was in his history. He instructed: "A prince, especially a new one cannot observe all those things for which men are esteemed, being forced, in order to maintain the state, to act contrary to faith, friendship, humanity, and religion."[21] Surely twenty-first century president Mark Emmert, the "prince" of the National Collegiate Athletic Association, came across both the writings of Thucydides and Machiavelli as he received graduate degrees in political science and public administration at the University of Washington and Syracuse University. The Machiavellian-deceiving Emmert and a few leaders of the NCAA mirrored the negative aspects of humanity over the millennia as they dealt with the Penn State crisis. The result of the powerful over the weak at that time resulted in the athletic nailing of Penn State to the cross by the NCAA Consent Decree of 2012.[22]

In order to attempt to severely harm if not destroy Penn State athletics, especially football, the NCAA cabal, led by Emmert and his counsel Donald Remy, deceived a new and uninformed president of Penn State, Rod Erickson, and Stephen Dunham, less than one week into his new position as Penn State counsel. The NCAA's two power brokers, Emmert and Remy, used bullying tactics while violating the NCAA's own Constitution and Bylaws in order to boost the tenuous position of Emmert and inept NCAA leadership. The story of the signing of the Consent Decree on July 23, 2012 is one of Machiavellian deception by an organization that claimed, for over a century, national leadership of intercollegiate athletics. Emmert, unlike a brilliant NCAA leader, Walter Byers (1951-1987), made policy by circumventing the NCAA Bylaws for dispensing institutional penalties and taking power unto himself. As former president of the NCAA and author of the definitive history of the NCAA, Joseph Crowley, has written, Byers and his "staff did not make policy. They implemented it."[23] Mark Emmert turned that guiding principle on its head, and in the process attempted to doom Penn State athletics with a Consent Decree a quarter century after Byers retired.

From NCAA Home Rule to Post-World War II Enforcement

How did the NCAA receive the power to punish bad behavior by its member institutions? The NCAA had no power when it began in 1905 with no power other than moral suasion over any institution, except to set the rules for football. The year 1905 is pivotal to understanding the role of a new national organization to have any influence over men's intercollegiate sport. It all began with football, the sport around which the crisis in Penn State athletics evolved. Football had dominated American college athletics since the 1880s when Harvard, Yale, and Princeton set the standard for big-time college athletics. The 1905 season, when Penn State was a second tier football school at best, saw President Teddy Roosevelt of the United States, call a meeting of the dominating Big Three of big-time college athletic institutions. The brutality of college football that year and previous years, as well as questionable ethics, influenced President Roosevelt to bring the leaders together, challenging his own alma mater Harvard and the other two schools to be principled leaders for the lesser schools to follow. After an October meeting in the White House, athletic leaders of the three institutions drew up an agreement for clean and ethical football. The memorandum of Harvard, Yale, and Princeton read:

> It was agreed that we consider an honorable obligation exists to carry out in letter and in spirit the rules of the game of football, relating to roughness, holding and foul play, and the active coaches of our universities being present. . . pledge themselves to so regard it and to do their utmost to carry out that obligation.[24]

Yet, the Big Three failed to follow their own agreement—as did other teams throughout America. At the season's end, a group of eastern teams met to discuss the banning or reform of football. The outcome was the formation of a national conference and the creation of the NCAA. Soon new football rules were drawn in an attempt to do away with brutal play and open up the game with the creation of the forward pass.[25]

However, the NCAA only revised football rules, forsaking any national rules for eligibility, recruiting, limiting the number of years any individual could participate, or upholding a commitment to amateurism. Consequently any rules would have to come from individual institutions or conferences, then coming into existence. Keeping control on a local or regional basis was known as "home rule," with the NCAA passing no legislation or enforcement of rules.[26] There were no police powers at the national level. The NCAA would thus remain primarily a debating society for institutional faculty athletics representatives with no legislative and executive function until after World War II. Only then did "home rule" weaken and enforcement authority come into being as the NCAA passed its first eligibility and recruiting rules, and at the same time it passed national legislation to control the telecasting of football contests.[27]

With the passage by the NCAA of the so-called "Sanity Code" for eligibility and recruiting in 1948 came the first Constitutional Compliance Committee and Fact-Finding Committee for investigations of wrongdoing. The Compliance Committee had a meager budget of $5,000, hardly enough to be effective in bringing wayward institutions before the law of the NCAA.[28] The only penalty for violators, however, was something akin to the "Death Penalty"—expulsion from NCAA membership, which would mean that only a NCAA vote could allow regaining membership.[29] Leader of the reform movement and president of the NCAA, Iowa's faculty representative Karl Leib, announced, "conform or get out."[30] Out of a plethora of institutions violating the recruiting and payment of players under the Sanity Code, including Penn State, the 1950 NCAA convention voted not to oust the charged "seven sinners," who, among many sinners, were illegally providing financial aid to players to participate in athletics.[31] At that time, only one of the seven could be considered a big-time football school, the University of Maryland. There were four other Southern schools, The Citadel, Virginia, Virginia Military Institute, and Virginia Polytechnic Institute, and two Northern institutions, Boston College and Villanova. The vote to oust did not carry. With the vote, the Sanity Code, which one president said "will make liars of us all," was dead.[32] However, the idea of enforcement was not abandoned.

Soon after the defeat of the abortive Sanity Code, the NCAA voted 135-14 to create a somewhat more practical enforcement arm with a Subcommittee on Infractions of the Membership Committee.[33] Suspension of play, or what might be called the "death penalty," was high on the list of punishments. The first case under the new regulations was a crucial one for the existence of the NCAA as an enforcement agency. The University of Kentucky's dominant basketball team under iconic coach Adolph Rupp, winner of several national championships and the 1948 Olympic basketball gold medal with his Kentucky team, was charged with providing illegal financial aid to its players. This came shortly after some of Rupp's players had been found guilty of being bribed by gamblers and throwing games or shaving points to meet the point spread in the 1951 scandal, centered primarily in New York City. New York City judge Saul Streit, after sending several gamblers and players to prison, wrote a 63-page report on the basketball scandals, including Kentucky, and the shame of intercollegiate athletics.[34] First, the Southeastern Conference took action by completing a thorough study of Kentucky athletics. The SEC first banned Kentucky from conference basketball competition.

The NCAA at its annual conference then voted 122-1 to extend the ban by issuing a boycott of Kentucky for any NCAA institution competing against coach Adolph Rupp's team during the 1952-53 season.[35] This came after the Subcommittee on Infractions ruled that because of the continual excessive payment of Kentucky basketball players (and using Judge Saul's indictment of Kentucky) the entire season must be cancelled. The University of Kentucky did not challenge the penalty, an action similar to that by Penn State when it signed the Consent Decree without administrative opposition six decades later.[36] Kentucky even penalized itself by prohibiting recruitment of basketball players outside of Kentucky, limiting the number of athletic scholarships to five for non-Kentuckians, banning post-season games except for the SEC tourney, playing all games on campuses, and officially reprimanding coach Adolph Rupp.[37] The first national "death penalty" had succeeded, and enforcement on a national level would continue. Stated a member of the NCAA committee, Howard Olson of Colorado College: "The gradual development of the NCAA in the field of legislation after an initial abortive effort [of the Sanity Code], is of real significance. . . . We are making slow but positive progress."[38]

What Followed the Kentucky Case

For the next two decades following the 1952 Kentucky death penalty, the newly named Committee on Infractions moved to stem the number of violations. Enforcement, especially in the area of recruitment and payment of athletes, was advanced in 1955 with the NCAA hiring of the first person for enforcement duties. There were checks and balances for NCAA penalties. Charges of wrongdoing went through not only the Committee on Infractions but also the Membership Committee, the NCAA Council that ran the NCAA between annual conference meetings, and finally the entire membership at the annual convention.[39] In the first four years of successful NCAA enforcement, 77 cases were investigated and 25 institutions were found to be in violation of NCAA rules.[40] Penn State was not among them.

Even in this early period of NCAA enforcement, the Committee on Infractions, not the president of the NCAA, directed any investigation and filed an official inquiry of the cited institution. That process was evaded by the NCAA President Mark Emmert in the 2012 Penn State case over a half-century later. The Committee on Infractions would hold hearings and then report the case to the governing NCAA Council, which would impose any penalty.[41] There was no evidence that NCAA employees, such as Executive Director Walter Byers (1951-1987), bypassed the Committee on Infractions and bullied any investigated institutions as did Emmert and NCAA counsel Donald Remy in the Penn State Consent Decree case.[42] But, in the early period there was no provision to appeal a NCAA Council decision as occurred shortly after a due process controversy in the Jerry Tarkanian case toward the end of the twentieth century.[43] Following the important Tarkanian case, the NCAA came somewhat closer to meeting the American due process clauses of the 5th and 14th amendments to the U.S. Constitution when the NCAA created the Infractions Appeal Committee.[44]

A major change in NCAA investigative and enforcement procedures came about in the early 1970s when the enforcement arm was expanded with an increase in the number of NCAA staff investigators who, on behalf of the Committee on Infractions, were charged with gathering evidence of infractions. The staff would then give its findings to the Committee on Infractions, which would hand out any penalties. The NCAA Council would only become involved if the institution appealed the penalties. Thus, the staff would provide information, and eventually the Committee on Infractions would make a decision for any violations. The disciplinary measures available to the Committee on Infractions had been expanded to include the possibility of a reprimand and censure, probation, ineligibility for a NCAA championship, banning of a postseason participation, ineligibility for TV appearances, reduction of athletic scholarships, removal of team or individual records, and banning of outside participation. A "show cause" provision allowed further penalties if the penalized institution did not take disciplinary action against individuals guilty of wrongdoing.[45]

At about the same time that an expanded list of possible penalties was created, the NCAA decided to do away with its basic academic standard for eligibility that had been developed in the 1960s. With the elimination of the so-called 1.600 grade point average legislation, high school graduates could enter college with the most limited academic qualifications.[46] Illiterates among high school graduates could and did come to college to participate in athletics, leading to not only low graduation rates but also to what appeared to be an unusual number of violations of NCAA rules. In a convention discussion over the structure of the NCAA, the Rev. J. Donald Monan of Boston College stated that "the problems of dismal academic achievements and of questionable degree programs and of lower graduate rates among athletes. . . have much more to do with changing admissions practices and divergent education philosophies and social policies of our individual campuses than the organization structure of the NCAA."[47] It was assumed, erroneously, that presidential involvement would solve major problems.

When institutional presidents gained some power with a new NCAA Presidents Commission in the mid-1980s, the presidents called for a special convention, in which the passage of tougher penalties would be a major solution to violations among NCAA schools. Yet, there was little consideration by presidents for reinstituting freshman ineligibility or raising academic standards that had existed until the late 1960s and early 1970s. Bringing the traditional freshman ineligibility back would help those academically unprepared athletes (whom presidents were allowing into their institution as specially admitted students) to concentrate on academics rather than to make the varsity team in the first year. An NCAA study showed that freshmen who were awarded athletic scholarships were far below the academic standard for non-athletes.[48] Droves of presidential special admits of athletes (what Penn State called "presidential admits"), from the 1970s until well into the twenty-first century, contributed greatly to lower academic standards for athletes. The same presidents who came to power in the NCAA were themselves contributing greatly to NCAA problems.

From the SMU Death Penalty Through the Tarkanian Case

The athletic violations in the 1980s were such that the newly created NCAA Presidents Commission directed that a special convention be convened in 1985 to address certain athletic evils. Participants of the special conference were convinced that a prime deterrent to athletic violations was the lack of a major penalty for repeat violators. Those in attendance voted overwhelmingly to institute the so-called "death penalty" to repeat violators. Southern Methodist University was a prime target. SMU had shown corrupt athletic tendencies since the 1920s and during the 1980s was in the midst of activities that would produce the worst scandal since the early 1950s collegiate gambling scandals. Individuals associated with SMU were paying signing bonuses and providing monthly pay to such players as star running backs Eric Dickerson and Craig James. Moreover, officials, including the coaches, athletic director, president, and members of the board of trustees were covering up these activities.[49] Previously granted only two years before with the possibility of a "Death Penalty," the Committee on Infractions decided in 1987 to punish SMU football for repeat violations with a one-year death penalty.

Since the SMU death sentence, that athletically impacted the Texas institution for several decades, the NCAA discussed the possible use of the death penalty for other violations.[50] Yet, while the death penalty was discussed, it was never threatened to be used by NCAA officials for an institution with no major violations of NCAA regulations until the Penn State Sandusky Scandal a quarter-century later. The fact that it has never been used in big-time sports since 1987 may well be due to what former University of Miami president, John V. Lombardi, once stated: "SMU taught the committee that the death penalty is too much like the nuclear bomb. . . . We'll do anything to avoid dropping another one."[51] It nevertheless did not mean the NCAA wouldn't threaten using the death penalty to further other ends by individuals, such as Mark Emmert, or for the perceived benefit of the NCAA.

The SMU case and others that followed were all violations of specific NCAA Bylaws, painstakingly outlined in its Division I Manual that had grown to several hundred pages from a 25-page pamphlet in the 1950s. Most violations had to do with recruiting and payment of athletes, and the penalties were an attempt to keep the playing field level for all competitors. It was made explicit by a leader of the NCAA in the mid-1980s, Auburn University professor and Secretary-Treasurer of the NCAA, Wilford Bailey. Speaking at a NCAA conference, Bailey said the NCAA's "primary responsibility for the membership is [to create] equity of competition"—a level playing field.[52] The Committee on Infractions spent most of its time attempting to punish institutions that attempted to unlevel the playing field and by so doing to warn others to play by the rules or be penalized. Nevertheless, lacking due process procedures, the NCAA and the Committee on Infractions came under attack for questionable investigations. That was about to be altered.

Some important changes occurred in the way the NCAA and the Committee on Infractions carried out its investigations following the quarter-century long Jerry Tarkanian inquiry and legal cases. The NCAA eventually won its U.S. Supreme Court case in 1988 against the successful basketball coach but lost a decade later when its $2.5 million out-of-court settlement vindicated Tarkanian.[53] He had charged the NCAA with harassment and conspiring to remove him from coaching at the college level, and the likelihood of winning a court case in the local jurisdiction of Las Vegas was a "home court advantage" for Tarkanian.[54] The NCAA was embarrassed for not better "understanding of one another's positions," according to NCAA Executive Director Cedric Dempsey. The Tarkanian case pressured the NCAA to study its own due process standards. A generation later, when the Paterno Family brought suit against the NCAA, the legal staff at the NCAA denied it had "a flawed enforcement process and refused to admit that its handling of the 'case against Jerry Tarkanian' is 'infamous.'"[55] But, the NCAA was flawed and the case was infamous.

The NCAA, however, partially reformed its due process standards only after the U.S. House of Representatives held a hearing on "Intercollegiate Sports" in the spring of 1991.[56] In addition, a number of states passed due process laws to bring about greater fairness to NCAA enforcement actions.[57] In response to legislative and government pressure, it was not surprising that the NCAA responded and hired Rex Lee, former U.S. Solicitor General and president of Brigham Young, to head the study of its due process with a Special Committee to Review the NCAA Enforcement and Infractions Process. Lee had represented the NCAA in the Jerry Tarkanian case and had defended successfully the position that the NCAA didn't need to follow due process because it was not a "state actor" in its argument before the U. S. Supreme Court.[58] Obviously, the NCAA hoped to have Lee "in its pocket," and was not anxious to have government intervention and more restrictions on its investigative process.

Nevertheless, the Lee Committee made 11 recommendations to improve the fairness in NCAA procedures, some of which were adopted by the NCAA.[59] The NCAA accepted the Lee recommendations to give an institution notice of an impending investigation and more importantly created an appeals committee for violations assessed by the Committee on Infractions. Yet the NCAA failed to open its infractions committee hearings to the public nor did it establish a group of neutral former judges as hearing officers to resolve factual disputes before the Infractions Committee imposed penalties. This would be expected under genuine American due process.[60] Significantly, two decades later, the Committee on Infractions (COI) did not notify Penn State of an impending investigation of the Sandusky Scandal. Instead, President Emmert would questionably, and probably illegally, ignore and bypass the COI following the Sandusky revelations with his November 17, 2011 condemnation letter to Penn State's president. Real due process was not high on Emmert's agenda.[61]

The NCAA and Violations at the Time of the Sandusky Crisis

In 2012, when the NCAA's administrators rejected bylaw protocol and elected to punish Penn State in its own cynical way, there was good Machiavellian reason to do so. The NCAA and its leadership were under a great deal of public scrutiny and condemnation for high visibility cases of athletic corruption under Emmert's and his predecessor's leadership for the past couple years. These involved such national institutions as Ohio State University, University of Alabama, University of Miami, and University of North Carolina. In addition, the day the Jerry Sandusky Scandal broke, the next Heisman Trophy winner, Auburn's Cam Newton, was found by the NCAA not to be in violation of its rules when his father, a year before, tried to get the junior college athlete to attend Mississippi State University for a payment of between $100,000 and $200,000.[62] The same year, a half-year before the Sandusky Scandal, the penalties that the Committee on Infractions gave to the University of Southern California were upheld by the NCAA Infractions Appeals Committee. Among other penalties, they resulted in a two-year ban on football bowls, a one-year basketball post-season ban, and a reduction in number of football and basketball scholarships. For receiving improper financial benefits, Reggie Bush was asked to relinquish his Heisman Trophy.[63]

At the time the NCAA was pressuring Penn State to sign a Consent Decree or face the threat of a possible death penalty, several high visibility cases were going through the NCAA Committee on Infractions. At Ohio State, the Committee on Infractions charged football players with selling player memorabilia to the owner of a tattoo parlor for cash, and there was a cover-up by the highly successful football coach Jim Tressel.[64] Ohio State received a bowl ban while Tressel was exited as coach by Ohio State.[65] The NCAA administration may well have hurried the Consent Decree "justice" meted out to Penn State in July 2012, just prior to the charges facing Ohio State in its meeting with the Committee on Infractions on August 12, 2012. Taking only a week to penalize Penn State by bypassing the Committee on Infractions made it look like Mark Emmert and the NCAA were quickly taking charge of athletics rather than taking years as in the Ohio State case.

The University of Alabama had several NCAA violations in the first decade of the 2000s, principally for illegal recruiting and payment of players. It was completing its three years of probation when Penn State was sanctioned.[66] Prior to the NCAA probation, there was a fear at Alabama that it could be given the death penalty for major violations, as it had only just completed its probation for a previous penalty before being cited again. Mark Emmert, when he was head of Louisiana State University in 2004, had been the individual who hired Nick Saban, later the Alabama coach. Saban once said of Emmert that he "is absolutely the best boss I've ever had. He is the most significant reason I was interested in the job. Never once," Saban emphasized, "has he disappointed me." The connection between Emmert and Saban may not have influenced the NCAA to give a lesser penalty to Saban and Alabama, but it certainly allowed skeptical individuals to think there may have been an influence in the punishment process.[67]

The results of the University of Miami investigation, going on prior to Penn State's punishment, was more reprehensible than that at Alabama because players were being paid off by a felon in prison, Nevin Shapiro, a Miami booster. Shapiro was guilty of a nearly $1 billion Ponzi scheme, fraudulent investor scam, not associated with the University of Miami. But, at Miami he provided cash payments to athletes and in addition food, housing, clothing, and prostitutes. Even worse, in some people's minds, was the NCAA's $19,000 payment to Shapiro's attorney to gain information of the illegal activities through subpoena powers not available to the NCAA. Though Miami had been on NCAA probation in nearly every decade from the 1950s, it did not receive the death penalty, in part because Miami, unlike Penn State, chose self-imposed penalties including a two-year ban on post-season contests. President Donna Shalala, knowledgeable of how the NCAA operated, unlike Penn State's Rod Erickson, told the NCAA that fairness and due process were lacking and that "we have been wronged in this investigation."[68] It was a truism similar to what Erickson might have used had he been better informed at the time. However, the NCAA never investigated Penn State, it only accepted the highly questionable conclusions of the Louis Freeh Report, a document that Erickson and the Board of Trustees accepted without reading or any critical examination. The NCAA became embarrassed about its role in the Miami investigation. Instead of firing Emmert for his organization's faulty investigation, Emmert fired Julie Roe, Vice-President for Enforcement. More about that later.

Concurrently with the investigations of Alabama, Ohio State, and University of Southern California at the time of the release of the Freeh

Report and the bullying of Penn State by the NCAA to sign the Consent Decree, the case of the University of North Carolina Chapel Hill unfolded. Placing both the University of North Carolina and the NCAA in trying situations, the scandal dealt with the fraudulent course work in the African and Afro-American Studies program. Like Penn State and the Freeh Report, the University of North Carolina conducted an independent investigation, called the Wainstein Report, after Kenneth Wainstein, a former federal prosecutor. The African and Afro-American Studies (AFAM) curriculum began in the 1970s, but after Prof. Julius Nyang'oro, with a law degree, took over as head of AFAM in 1992, the program deteriorated academically when classes and independent study courses were created, intended for keeping eligible poor-performing athletes. Shortly before Penn State's Sandusky Scandal broke, the North Carolina administration became aware of fraudulent grades given to athletes for courses they did not attend. For the most part only one paper was required—one that was not always written by the athlete nor graded by a faculty member; often it was not read and generally was graded with an "A."[69] Prior to the scandal, the North Carolina program was symbolized by one of the great basketball coaches, Dean Smith, considered "Mr. Clean" by most individuals, similar to the way Joe Paterno was thought of at Penn State—both revered as god-like.

In a way, however, not dissimilar to Penn State, when Dean Smith won his first national championship in 1983, just months after Paterno won his first, there was increased pressure to keep winning national basketball titles and to win consistently in football. Thus, North Carolina recruited athletes with minimal academic backgrounds who were admitted into North Carolina as special admits when they could not meet North Carolina standards. There was a need to keep special admits and other players eligible—the AFAM was crucial to North Carolina's success. (According to retired vice chancellor for academic affairs at North Carolina, Samuel Williamson, football got about 15 special admits each year.[70]) In early 2012, before Jerry Sandusky was sentenced to prison for violating young boys and before the release of the Freeh Report and the signing of the Consent Decree, North Carolina was found guilty of academic fraud and failure to monitor the football program. The NCAA issued a bowl ban, reduction of scholarships, and three years of probation.[71] Coach Butch Davis was fired. Yet, the entire case about the African Studies fraudulent course work lingered for the next several years awaiting additional NCAA action that finally happened in 2017. The outcome—there were no NCAA penalties.[72]

Along with these major cases of wrongdoing under consideration by the NCAA to consider at the time of the Penn State Consent Decree, the NCAA was in the process of changing its enforcement policies with tougher penalties. Less than a year after becoming NCAA president, President Mark Emmert called for a meeting, principally of university presidents, to discuss problems within the NCAA and what to do about them. At the August 2011 two-day retreat with over 50 university presidents in attendance, one of the participants who spoke about the need for greater discipline for violators was Penn State president Graham Spanier. In just a few months, Spanier would lose his position for faulty leadership when the Sandusky Scandal erupted. However, prior to that, at the conclusion of the two-day NCAA retreat, Spanier claimed, "Presidents are fed up with the rule breaking that is out there; we are determined to elevate the academic standards. . . . Violators," Spanier said, "should be afraid now. . . . A lot of things have reached the boiling point."

Emmert, who would remove statements by Spanier from the NCAA website soon after the Sandusky Scandal broke, expanded on Spanier's words emphasizing what he wanted relative to punishing wrongdoers. "Those penalties," Emmert emphasized, "need to create a healthy fear of being caught or the implications of being caught." The NCAA, Emmert commented after the presidents' retreat, needs "to make assertive change."[73] Tougher enforcement was a major need, he believed. President Ed Ray of the Oregon State University and head of the NCAA's Executive Committee, was made chairman of a NCAA Working Group on Enforcement coming from the retreat. Ray was emphatic on changing the risk-reward for breaking NCAA rules and to "make people who behaved badly wish they hadn't."[74] Ray's Working Group Enforcement Committee was created to restructure the enforcement arm of the NCAA and to intensify the severity of penalties. Ray's attitude and the discussion of severe punishments would have major implications for the Penn State Consent Decree in 2012 when the Freeh Report was released. At that time, and without reading the Freeh Report,[75] Ray was the major individual on the NCAA Executive Committee who wanted Penn State to be given the death penalty.

The Impact of NCAA TV Money on Enforcement

From the early era of enforcement, penalties for violations of NCAA rules were seldom enforced until the organization had enough money to conduct investigations. The increased financing came with the NCAA-sponsored national basketball tournament and income generated from the NCAA football television contracts following the Second World War. The creation of the NCAA basketball tournament in 1939 came about the month before the first commercial telecast occurred in America. The so-called "March Madness" tourney and television grew up alongside each other, though there was no connection at first and for many years. The NCAA got into post-season basketball play only after a private promoter, sportswriter Ned Irish, helped popularize the sport during the Great Depression by inviting such teams as Adolph Rupp's Kentucky team and the great one-handed shooting Hank Luisetti of Stanford University to play games in New York's Madison Square Garden. Filling the Garden with spectators awoke New York's Metropolitan Basketball Writers Association, with Ned Irish in the lead, to invite teams for a national championship in the same venue. The 1938 National Invitational Tournament was born.[76] With the success of the NIT, the NCAA saw the possibilities of a national championship and the next year brought out its own tournament that was held on the Northwestern University campus in Evanston, Illinois. The event recorded a meager $42.54 profit, a far cry from the $3/4 billion it grossed three-quarters of a century later.[77] Not until 1946, the year after World War II, was the NCAA tourney telecast by WCBS in New York, and on the national level the first telecast took place in 1954 when LaSalle University's Tom Gola helped defeat Bradley University, 92-76. Because the three leading TV networks (ABC, CBS, and NBC) ignored the tourney, the basketball finals produced less than one percent of the riches brought in from the NCAA football television plan into the 1960s.[78] Yet, because of the way the tourney and television revenues were divided, the March Madness revenues meant a great deal to the running of the NCAA and whether it could afford an enforcement staff. The basketball revenues were divided equally between the NCAA office and the teams involved in the tourney, while the NCAA headquarters received only about four percent of the football TV revenues. The basketball tourney would eventually become the dominant financial factor for the NCAA, while the TV revenues to the NCAA would eventually be eliminated by the U. S. Supreme Court's antitrust ruling and the breakup of the NCAA football telecasting in 1984.[79]

It was, then, not surprising that when infraction penalties were first created in the 1950s, the execution of NCAA rule violations lacked a properly financed enforcement arm. Prior to the TV revenues, the entire NCAA enforcement operating budget early on was $5,000, not even enough for supporting one individual. That was about to change once the NCAA decided to control the telecasting of football contests, with a small percentage of the revenue from broadcast rights going to the NCAA headquarters. In the decade and a half following the passage of football TV controls by the NCAA in 1951, the NCAA's income from football telecasts rose from less than $6,000 to over $260,000 annually. In the same time period, revenue from the NCAA basketball tourney (March Madness) rose from $130,000 to nearly $500,000.[80] These two dominant men's sports allowed the NCAA to hire enforcement officers to better police the two sports that presumably had the most violations of recruitment and payment of players. So because there were two sports that were bringing in the vast majority of income to the NCAA, it was logical that the national organization would place most of the emphasis on enforcement on Division I men's basketball and football. That continued well into the next century. If Jerry Sandusky had been a retired assistant coach for the Penn State fencing team, there is little likelihood that the NCAA would have pursued the case as it did after 2011. President Emmert would have almost assuredly stated that the NCAA does not get involved in a criminal case unless it violated the NCAA Constitution and Bylaws. Because it didn't involve NCAA rules, Emmert would have let the hypothetical NCAA case die.

The decade from the mid-1960s into the 1970s found dynamic growth of NCAA wealth from men's basketball. It began with dominating African American players in the 1960s, when Texas Western with five black starters beat all-white Kentucky. Black dominance continued with UCLA and Lew Alcindor (Kareem Abdul-Jabbar), and in the 1970s exploded and was culminated by the most dynamic NCAA finals to that time when Indiana State's Larry Bird played for the championship led by Earvin "Magic" Johnson's Michigan State. By the end of the twentieth and into the twenty-first century, the NCAA was flush with money so that it could pay off its harassment of coach Jerry Tarkanian with $2.5 million as if it were a tip to a doorman, and it could spend far more money on law suits than its total income in the 1950s.

By the time of the Jerry Sandusky Scandal, the NCAA was approaching $1 billion in revenue each year and had exceeded that figure by the time the NCAA was facing millions in legal fees from several lawsuits against it resulting from the Penn State infractions case. Even larger lawsuits were possible from the Ed O'Bannon and Sam Keller cases in which the NCAA was guilty of monopolistic practices involving the illegal use of star basketball and football player likenesses in video games as well as cases resulting from football helmet related concussions. The NCAA, however, with its tens of millions of dollars of legal fees each year could easily afford them as its accumulation of unrestricted net assets that could be used was well over $1/2 billion.[81] Nearly all of the NCAA's wealth was the result of its control of the NCAA Division I basketball tourney in which television ad revenues used to pay the NCAA were larger than those of professional football's Super Bowl.

NCAA enforcement and resulting legal suits, while a large part of NCAA expenses, were easily paid for by annual $60 million to $80 million surpluses available at the time of the Sandusky Scandal. Nevertheless, the NCAA would settle out-of-court when it felt that the possibility of losing was such that it would be much cheaper, and less embarrassing, to settle than to keep the litigation going.[82] This was the situation when the NCAA caved in to the Pennsylvania state senator Jake Corman lawsuit against the NCAA following the Consent Decree. At the time of the Consent Decree, the NCAA illegally bullied Penn State President Rod Erickson into signing the single most damaging sanctions to any institution in the history of the NCAA. How all that came about is the focus of this historical investigation.

Chapter 2

Penn State's Previous Violations, Isolation, and the Sandusky Case

*There is no tyranny more cruel than that which is perpetrated under
the color of the laws and in the name of justice.*

Charles de Montesquieu (1734)

A Few Penn State Athletic Violations

Penn State University appeared to have had the fewest violations of NCAA rules of any big-time institution in the history of the NCAA when the Jerry Sandusky Scandal erupted in November of 2011. The record, however, was not spotless—except to the general public. The "lily-white" national image went back several generations. By the time the NCAA first began investigations of potential wrongdoing in the early 1950s, Penn State had hired Michigan's Ernie McCoy as athletic director and dean of the School of Physical Education and Athletics. He was a stickler for following rules of competition. For example, after McCoy was informed that assistant coach Joe Paterno was putting pressure on a professor to raise an athlete's grade, he called Paterno into his office and forcefully stated that if he ever again put pressure on a professor for an athlete's grades, he would no longer be at Penn State.[83] That incident was not a violation of NCAA rules, but rather Penn State rules under Dean McCoy. He once told the track coach in the 1960s, John Lucas, that the auto ride Lucas gave to a freshman athlete from the airport to campus was illegal, a violation of NCAA rules. Lucas was told in clear language that if this were done in the future, his coaching career would be at an end.[84] The McCoy era at Penn State (1952-1970) with Rip Engle as the head football coach (1950-1966) set the stage for what was probably the cleanest athletic program in America.

The fact that athletics were housed in an academic college at Penn State from 1930 until 1980 may have been a key factor in Penn State's athletics being held accountable to both academic standards and athletic rules.[85] Athletics in other big-time schools from their origins to the 1970s were not in academic units.[86] Most were housed under the university president as in a business office or were independent and generally outside of the administrative and financial control of the university. When Joe Paterno was asked to become athletic director in 1980, he made it clear to president John Oswald that he would not take the position unless athletics were taken out of an academic unit and placed in the financial office of the Vice President for Finance and Business.[87] There, athletics would be placed under a former captain of the football team and friend of Paterno, Steve Garban, an individual who lacked significant academic credentials. It may not be surprising that all football violations came after 1980, when there was no effective academic oversight of football or other men's or women's sports at Penn State.[88]

However, the first Penn State violation at the national level was in the women's program, specifically basketball. It dealt with a violation in recruiting. At the time, 1977, women's sports across the nation were under the control of the Association of Intercollegiate Athletics for Women (AIAW), formed only five years before. Women in leadership positions were divided over the question of recruitment and payment of players, as it did not fit well into the AIAW's emphasis on the educational value of athletics, unlike the commercial-professional model of male athletics that had developed in the nineteenth century and continued under the National Collegiate Athletic Association. Penn State's women basketball coach, Patty Meiser, was making a "talent assessment" (recruiting) of a high school player. On her first recruiting trip, she saw June Olkowski performing in a Philadelphia game. Following the game, Meiser was introduced to Olkowski's parents. They invited her to come to their house for dinner, an act that had recently been made a violation under the changing rules of the AIAW.[89] After the illegal visit, the chair of the AIAW Ethics Committee, Joan Hult, was informed of Meiser's actions after it was reported in a newspaper article. Hult was a professor from neighboring University of Maryland and particularly opposed to recruiting and offering scholarships for women. Because the payment of players through scholarships had been sanctioned by the AIAW a couple years before, she had given up coaching tennis at Maryland. However, as leader of the AIAW Ethics Committee, she was instrumental in handing out a one-year probation to Penn State for Meiser's misstep.[90]

By the 1980s and 1990s, Penn State had several more coaches and teams cited for violations, principally recruiting abuses. By then women's sports were no longer under AIAW auspices as the control of women's sports was taken over by the NCAA.[91] At least four women's sports were cited by the NCAA or Big Ten Conference for illegal recruiting. In field hockey, Penn State's head coach Char Morrett-Newman was reprimanded by the Big Ten for the recruiting of Heather Atkinson in 1991, and an assistant coach made illegal contact with a high school athlete three years later. In lacrosse, a NCAA rule was violated when its game jerseys carried two logos. A volunteer women's volleyball coach was illegally compensated in the mid-1990s. Women's basketball coach Rene Portland was caught illegally recruiting a high school student when she was accompanied by an unauthorized recruiter in 1993, in her 13th year at Penn State. The next year, Sherwin Anderson made an illegal visit and was made ineligible to participate in basketball at Penn State. Two women gymnasts were illegally recruited in 1994 and also became ineligible for the Penn State team.[92]

Penn State Football Violations

The men's sports, including the dominant sport football, were also cited several times for secondary or minor violations. The men's volleyball team was cited for violating off-season conditioning activities in 1995. The assistant wrestling coach violated a recruiting rule the previous year, and the athlete was made ineligible for participation at Penn State.[93] Joe Paterno's football program was not spared being caught for violating NCAA rules. Although Penn State's athletic director in the 1980s and 90s, Jim Tarman, once stated that Penn State's football program had never had a recruiting violation in his 27 years at Penn State, it was not true.[94] Five years before his 1985 comment, Penn State coaches had contacted a high school athlete, Mark LeBlanc, illegally. At about the same time, another football prospect, Jackie Shields, was given an illegal workout at a Penn State facility and was handed a small gift that was not allowed by NCAA rules. Only one month after President John Oswald announced that Joe Paterno would be the next athletic director, the NCAA censured and reprimanded Joe Paterno and the Penn State football program. The violation, however, was kept confidential with only a letter going to

President John Oswald and was kept out of the media. Oswald in turn wrote Paterno to "prevent any future violations of the NCAA rules and regulations."[95]

Another known Paterno violation, which made national news, revolved around a star high school linebacker from Montclair, New Jersey, Quintus McDonald, in 1985. McDonald was making up his mind whether to play football at Penn State or the University of Southern California and did not commit on the first day to sign a letter of intent to attend a certain university. Nine days later, Paterno and his offensive coordinator, Fran Ganter, arrived in Montclair for the signing. By NCAA rules, head coaches were not allowed to be at the signing. Paterno was. A local newspaper reported the signing, and the NCAA was immediately informed that Paterno had broken the rule. The fact that Paterno had been on the NCAA rules committee that had formed the rule was likely noted by David Berst, head of NCAA enforcement, who ruled that Paterno's action was "isolated, minor, or inadvertently violated."[96] There was no penalty for Paterno or Penn State.

While it is clear that the Penn State athletic program had NCAA and AIAW violations prior to the Jerry Sandusky scandal, they were minor and in relation to other big-time schools were only a "blip on the radar screen." While nationally allowing illiterates and academically inept athletes into college was not a NCAA violation, there was the case of a North Carolina State player, Chris Washburn, whose Scholastic Achievement Test score was lower than one would expect of a fifth grader.[97] This was the period of the 1980s when there were almost no NCAA rules for eligibility because of grades or test scores, but hundreds of other rules for recruitment and payment of players existed in an attempt to keep a level playing field. It was also one of the worst periods in the history of intercollegiate sport for violating those same rules.

The most blatant case of recruiting and paying players was that of Southern Methodist University. While Paterno was watching Quintus McDonald sign his letter of intent, SMU coaches, administrators, president, members of the governing board, politicians, and boosters knowingly were paying salaries, buying cars, changing academic grades, and otherwise providing for a nationally ranked football team starring players such as Eric Dickerson and Craig James.[98] SMU, having the most major violations of NCAA rules over a period of years, was levied the popularly known "death penalty" in 1987. The total of Penn State violations for a half-century seemed minor to this one case at Southern Methodist.

The "Lily White" Image and NCAA's Mark Emmert

When the Sandusky Scandal broke, Penn State was one of four Division I institutions in the major football conferences with no major violations in their history; the others were Boston College, Northwestern, and Stanford.[99] It may be significant that three of the four were private institutions, and Penn State acted like one with much less than 10 percent of its budget coming from the state legislature, while its football coach was perceived as following the rules for over four decades. However, it is not surprising that when a scandal arose, it was related to football, since about half of the major NCAA violations were football related.[100]

That Penn State was considered "lily white" by many, may have been a major reason why NCAA president Mark Emmert wanted to nail Penn State to the cross once the scandal broke. Strange how within a year Emmert could do a complete turn-around relative to his belief about Penn State football and Joe Paterno. In January of 2011, Joe Paterno was about to be given the NCAA President's Gerald R. Ford Award for providing significant career-long leadership for intercollegiate athletics. Emmert then stated, "For me, Coach Paterno is the definitive role model of what it means to be a college coach. . . . His 'total-person' approach," Emmert emphasized, "is a terrific example of everything the NCAA stands for."[101]

However, Emmert's need to appear to control an organization seemingly out of control in executing the NCAA Constitution and Bylaws, did an about face the next year when he and NCAA counsel Donald Remy nailed 112 victories, 111 of Joe Paterno's, to wither and die on the cross erected for Penn State. For over two years, Penn State hung by nails on the NCAA cross until, under pressure of a Pennsylvania state law suit, Penn State was taken down from the Consent Decree edifice. Emmert and Remy had exhibited that which Montesquieu, the philosopher and political critic wrote for humanity well over three centuries before. "There is no tyranny more cruel," stated Montesquieu, "than that which is perpetrated under the color of law and in the name of justice."[102] Justice had not been achieved, but Emmert and the NCAA's legal counsel had manipulated the NCAA Constitution and Bylaws to achieve their purpose of appearing to take charge of problems in intercollegiate athletics.

The Sandusky Scandal Unfolds

Nevertheless, President Emmert could not have shown his sinister colors had not Penn State been involved in a former assistant football coach's violations of children on campus at a Penn State football facility. Jerry Sandusky, the honored assistant coach under Paterno for three decades, had founded an organization on June 7, 1977 dedicated to helping at-risk children, The Second Mile. By 1989, at the Inaugural Address of President George H. W. Bush, the new president spoke of "a thousand points of light." In late 1990, President Bush awarded the 194th "Point of Light" to The Second Mile as a shining example of charity work. Joe Paterno had by then written his most complimentary letter of recommendation for any of his assistant coaches when he penned a letter for 44-year old Sandusky to the athletic director at Temple University for its head coaching position. In that 1988 letter, Paterno claimed that Sandusky had "a marvelous character with an impeccable lifestyle." In it, Paterno cited Sandusky as a "wonderful organizer and he has put together a program here called The Second Mile, which started from nothing."[103]

When Sandusky began using boys from The Second Mile for sexual exploitation is not known, but the first authenticated incident occurred in 1998. A decade before, Joe Paterno had written his letter of recommendation, and in January 1998 had told Sandusky that he would not become the next head football coach at Penn State because he was spending too much time with The Second Mile organization. Paterno believed a head coach could not devote considerable time outside of football and his family.[104] This was only a few months before a mother reported to officials of Sandusky's evening showering with her 11-year old son in the Louis and Mildred Lasch Building, the site of the Penn State football locker room and offices. Penn State officials, President Graham Spanier, Vice-President Gary Schultz, Athletic Director Tim Curley, and Paterno were quickly notified of this incident. This was the beginning of three cases, 1998, 2001, and 2008 that became the core of the Sandusky Scandal that broke open in late 2011.

The 1998 occurrence was important to the eventual NCAA Consent Decree because of the way it was interpreted in the months after the Sandusky Scandal leading up to the damning NCAA penalties. On May 3, 1998, Jerry Sandusky and an eleven-year old boy were in the Lasch Football Building, where Sandusky had an office and there was exercise equipment that the young boy was excited to use. While there, Sandusky wrestled with the youth and afterwards took a shower with him. Showering with children was not unusual for Sandusky at Penn State, or for other coaches to observe, though it might not have been common at other university's athletic departments. At that time, Sandusky lifted the boy and gave him a hug before taking him home. When he arrived home, his mother noticed her son's wet hair while the boy was seemingly upset about his on-campus experience. The next morning, the boy's mother called a licensed psychologist, Alycia Chambers, who had previously worked with her son. Chambers, understanding pedophile patterns, suggested that the boy's mother call the Penn State police. By noon, a Penn State detective, Ron Schreffler, interviewed the boy, while Chambers reported to the Pennsylvania child abuse line after consulting with colleagues. The incident was reported to the Centre County Children and Youth Services. A caseworker, who was without psychological license credentials, John Seasock, conducted an evaluation and deemed that Sandusky "didn't fit the profile of a pedophile."[105] Seasock was listened to by authorities— Chambers, while daring to challenge a local heroic coach, was not.

The Pennsylvania Department of Public Welfare became involved in the investigation, as was the Centre County District Attorney's office. The District Attorney was Ray Gricar. He met with those who provided child protection services, and decided not to prosecute Sandusky, probably because, as another DA noted, "You don't want to go after someone high profile unless you have a compelling case."[106] Gricar did not have compelling evidence beyond a man hugging a youngster in a shower. To prosecute a community icon such as Sandusky, who was honored for creating The Second Mile for at risk children and instrumental in helping Penn State win two national championships in football, would take more than the questionable act of showering with one of his Second Mile children. After all, Sandusky had been seen by members of the athletic staff previously showering with other young boys.

The administrators of Penn State athletics, from coach to athletic director to vice-president for business and finance, and finally to the president, must have been relieved that Gricar chose not to pursue the Sandusky incident. All four, Joe Paterno, Tim Curley, Gary Schultz, and Graham Spanier, were informed of the shower incident within a day of the boy's mother calling the psychologist, Alycia Chambers. Vice President Schultz was probably first informed by the chief of Penn State police, Thomas Harmon. The day after Penn State was involved, Schultz held a meeting with unidentified individuals to discuss the situation that occurred in a university building. He kept notes in which he wrote, "Behavior—at best inappropriate @ worst sexual improprieties." He then jotted down a prophetic comment—"Is this opening of pandora's box?"[107] It was, but it was not then revealed to the outside world.

The case remained for about a month. In that time the four concerned administrators kept in touch with each other while police chief Harmon held off making a crime log entry in his official documents. Nor was the situation reported to the Penn State Office of Human Resources, something that was generally done in potentially illegal activities. Early on, athletic director Curley emailed both Schultz and President Spanier under the heading "Joe Paterno," in which Curley wrote, "I touched base with coach. Keep us posted." That day in early May, Paterno was off to Nashville, Tennessee for a business meeting with officials at Burger King, returning to fly to Boston for an alumni relations and fund raising mission. Arriving home, Paterno took off for Atlanta, with the Sandusky matter not far removed from his thoughts. "Coach is anxious to know where it stands," Curley inquired of Gary Schultz. "Anything new in this department?" Curley wondered. By the end of the month, before the case was closed, Curley asked Schultz, the administrator over the police, whether there was "anything new in this department."[108] This situation was not taken lightly by the athletic administration until the investigation officially concluded when the District Attorney, Ray Gricar, declined prosecution, and the incident was concluded with an emphatic "CASE CLOSED."[109]

The relief exhibited by the four administrators was probably not more than that which Jerry Sandusky experienced. It should be noted that apparently not one of the four administrators asked Sandusky not to shower with children in the Penn State locker room or to bring them on campus. Nor is there evidence that any one of the four inquired about the youngster before or after the incident was closed by legal authorities. In addition, no one seemingly discussed with The Second Mile administrators bringing young people from their organization onto the Penn State campus or Jerry Sandusky's role in continuing that activity. That Penn State had a written agreement with Sandusky when he retired to work closely with The Second Mile and continued for the next decade was certainly an obstacle to controlling future conduct of Sandusky on campus. That agreement in 1999 stated that Sandusky and Penn State "agree to work collaboratively with each other in the future in community outreach programs, such as the Second Mile. . . ."[110]

Warning signs, however, from this first Sandusky shower incident should have alerted the Penn State administrators to the possibility of any future incidents. The first investigation was kept out of the media, allowing the Penn State football program and Joe Paterno to continue getting national accolades for the success of the Grand Experiment and the University to use the "pristine" athletic program for all the benefits it could deliver in good publicity, attracting students, and raising funds. After government officials dismissed the investigation, it was rather easy for the few informed Penn State officials to dismiss it with a sigh of relief almost as if it were unthinkable that the community's highly esteemed Sandusky might be a pedophile.

When the 2001 Sandusky incident with a young boy occurred, the situation was quite different. Less than three years before, university officials had been notified, but when the district attorney and others found no pedophile actions, university administrators could quietly go on seemingly unencumbered with a potential problem. However, when Mike McQueary, a member of the coaching staff, observed Sandusky in the same Lasch Football Building questionably showering with another young boy, the first Penn State administrator informed was Joe Paterno, not a government official such as a police officer or the Centre County Children and Youth Services. Now Penn State athletics was directly involved, with the previous incident not easily forgotten. How the same four administrators would react would foretell the fate brought upon Penn State when the Sandusky Scandal eventually broke open a decade later. McQueary, whose accounts of the Sandusky-boy encounter have varied, told the head coach the next morning that Sandusky was seen, according to Paterno, in the shower "fondling" the boy, and it was of "a sexual nature."[111]

How coach Paterno reacted upon hearing McQueary's story has been criticized by many, but legally what he did was right on target. He informed his titular superior, athletic director Tim Curley. Sandusky was no longer an employee of Penn State as he had retired in the spring of 1999 and soon honored with emeritus professor status, seldom, if ever, granted to an assistant professor. The emeritus status may seem inconsequential, but at the time it was granted, the individual who would become president upon the exit of Graham Spanier following the Scandal was Rod Erickson, newly appointed Provost. Erickson examined the emeritus request, showed his "uneasiness" with it but nevertheless agreed to the Sandusky emeritus status.[112] So Paterno, Curley, Schultz, and Spanier (who initiated the emeritus status to a Happy Valley icon) were in a delicate position, caught between doing the right thing legally and acting ethically. Would protection of the image of the athletic program and Penn State hold sway over the ethical treatment of a potentially sexually abused child?

Tim Curley, following a call from Paterno, in turn phoned Gary Schultz, his superior in athletics to arrange a meeting with Paterno and the two of them. The three discussed the situation that same weekend, while Schultz spent time with Penn State Counsel, Wendell Courtney, who billed Penn State for nearly three hours of work. The next day Schultz and Curley met and reviewed the 2001 Sandusky-child incident, trying to determine if the Department of Public Welfare should be informed. President Spanier met with the two administrators and asked the important question if there was evidence that Sandusky was doing anything more than "horsing around." In the meantime, vice-president Schultz asked Penn State police chief, Tom Harmon, if he could see the 1998 police file on Sandusky. All of this was festering among the administrators, but no government authority or officials of The Second Mile were contacted—and it continued for another two weeks.[113]

Finally, 18 days after the shower incident, Spanier, Schultz, and Curley met and tentatively agreed to take three actions, 1) talk with Jerry Sandusky, 2) contact The Second Mile, 3) and inform the Department of Public Welfare. But this changed after Curley spoke with Joe Paterno. "After giving it more thought and talking it over with Joe yesterday," Curley emailed Schultz and Spanier, "I am uncomfortable with what we agreed were the next steps." Curley suggested only first talking with Jerry Sandusky, not informing The Second Mile or the Department of Public Welfare. President Spanier replied that "this approach is acceptable to me," but, he warned, Penn State becomes "vulnerable for not having reported it." Spanier's comments would come back to haunt him during his 2017 trial and finding for child endangerment, something actor Charlie Chaplin might have described as a life's irony "for doing the wrong thing at the right moment."[114] The McQueary-Sandusky encounter was never reported to the Department of Public Welfare, and The Second Mile director, Jack Raykovitz, was informed only a month later.[115] Ironically, Gary Schultz, four months later, agreed to sell Penn State land to Jerry Sandusky's The Second Mile for $168,500, the same price Penn State paid for it several years earlier. One can wonder how all of this was happening without a discussion of the land transfer with either the executive committee or the full board of trustees in the Spring of 2001.

The Problems of Athletic Isolation

The situation with Sandusky was quietly kept in isolation, just as was the athletic department isolating the situation around the women's basketball coach, Rene Portland. Hired by Joe Paterno when he was athletic director, Portland was, for years, violating federal and state laws and Penn State's own policies about the treatment of lesbians on her team. Portland had played college basketball at a small Catholic school near Philadelphia, helping Immaculata College win multiple national championships in the early 1970s before becoming a successful coach at St. Josephs College and the University of Colorado. That both Portland and Paterno were Catholics may have contributed to Portland's belief that homosexuality was a sin, and lesbian women on the Penn State team should be treated with disdain and certainly removed from her program when discovered. That action was a violation of equal protection under the U.S. constitution and Title IX when passed in 1972. Title IX stated "no person in the United States shall, on the basis of sex. . . be subjected to discrimination under any educational program or activities receiving federal financial assistance." Penn State passed a sexual orientation policy in 1991 to, as President Joab Thomas stated, "protect all members of the university community against invidious discrimination including members of the Penn State lesbian and gay community."[116] Portland had dismissed lesbians, or suspected lesbians, from her teams almost from her first year of coaching, but a decade later she was actually breaking Penn State policy.

Nobody in the athletic department or the university did anything about it for her first quarter-century of winning basketball in what was considered the most important women's sport on campus. Portland admitted opposing lesbians on her team in 1986 when she was quoted in a Chicago newspaper, "I will not have it in my program."[117] Yet, it took two decades for Penn State to take any action against her for violating her players' civil rights, and then only after an African American was dismissed for allegedly (but mistakenly) being a lesbian. Jennifer Harris, a starter on the basketball team in 2005, was dismissed by Portland at the end of the season. Harris initiated a federal civil law suit against Portland and athletic director, Tim Curley, just as the Penn State Office of Affirmative Action was completing an investigation of Portland, culminating with a finding against Portland of conducting "hostile, intimidating, and offensive harassment" of members of her team.[118] With the lawsuit in the public's eye, Penn State could no longer ignore Portland's illegal behavior. The case never came to trial and was resolved out of court with Penn State settling with Harris. Portland, who had been given a small fine by President Spanier following the investigation, resigned soon after the settlement. [119]

Isolation of Rene Portland's illegal actions could occur more readily without athletic department involvement in part because of an action taken by new athletic director Joe Paterno before he hired Portland. Prior to Paterno accepting the athletic directorship from President John Oswald, he demanded that athletics be removed from an academic college or he would not accept the position.[120] Oswald succumbed to Paterno's demand, doing an about face from his belief stated earlier that year. "We are proud of the way in which this program [of athletics] is organized as a part of one of the academic colleges," Oswald told his board of trustees, "and not a program that is set aside as a separate part of the university."[121] Oswald soon, without trustee approval, agreed to remove athletics from the control of an academic dean and place it where Paterno directed, under the Vice President for Finance and Business. In that office was a former football captain, Steve Garban, who would then be given the control of the athletic purse strings as well as facilities and the hiring of all athletic personnel, such as Rene Portland. With Paterno's friend, Steve Garban, in the business office, it would practically insure the promotion of football the way Joe Paterno wanted it. Placing athletics in a business office, rather than an academic unit, removed Paterno and athletics from any effective academic eyes, and allowed the program to carry out its activities in relative privacy.

Isolating problems in athletics, whether it was Portland's sexual orientation discrimination or Jerry Sandusky's sexual behavior, was in contrast to a half-century of athletic policy in which athletics were housed in an academic unit. The educational control of athletics originated in 1930, when an academic unit housed both athletics and the physical education program.[122] It began when the Board of Trustees created the School of Physical Education and Athletics. By the time Joe Paterno became athletic director it was called the College of Health, Physical Education, and Recreation (HPER). The Department of Physical Education was the home of all the coaches including full professor Joe Paterno. Because of the perceived ineffectiveness of the athletic director, Ed Czekaj, a decision was made by President John Oswald, to remove Czekaj.[123] By installing Joe Paterno in that position, the new athletic director could control how football income was spent rather than how the Dean of HPER felt it should be expended. That Oswald made his decision without board of trustees' approval should be emphasized, for three decades later another president, Graham Spanier, did not effectively communicate with his board about the Jerry Sandusky events. Thus, when the Sandusky Scandal broke in November 2011, all four members of the Penn State administration dealing with Penn State athletics could be found guilty, either in the courts or in public opinion, of isolating athletics and creating for Penn State the greatest humiliation in its history.[124]

Chapter 3

The Scandal Breaks: Firings, Freeh Hiring,
and a NCAA Letter to President Erickson

*An hypocrite with his mouth destroyeth his neighbor: but through knowledge shall
the just be delivered"* [and] *"A ruler who lacks understanding is a cruel oppressor. . . .*
Proverbs, 3:27; 28:16

On November 4, 2011, the Attorney General's office in Harrisburg
released a damning indictment of Jerry Sandusky's sexual involvement
with eight boys over a period of years. Standing behind a podium the next
day, the state attorney general, Linda Kelly, was accompanied by huge
photo posters of two Penn State officials, along with Jerry Sandusky. That
athletic director, Tim Curley, and vice president, Gary Schultz, had equal
representation with Sandusky in large photos near the podium revealed much
about how Penn State administrators were viewed by the attorney general's
office.[125] It wasn't just an ex-assistant football coach who was indicted, but
Penn State administrators in the visualized form of the two of the four
principal individuals (Schultz, Curley, Joe Paterno, and President Graham
Spanier) involved in the big-time football program. Almost immediately
Gary Schultz retired and Tim Curley was removed from his position, even
though President Graham Spanier praised both administrators. "Tim
Curley and Gary Schultz have my unconditional support," Spanier stated
the day the Sandusky indictment became public. The two "operate at the
highest levels of honesty, integrity and compassion."[126] Acting almost as
quickly, the board of trustees fired (or accepted the resignation) of President
Spanier and ousted the football coach of 61 years, Joe Paterno.

The Central Mountain Molestation Initiates the Grand Jury Probe

The Penn State Board of Trustees was in turmoil. The members had
been kept in the dark about the Sandusky grand jury investigation. It was

due in part to President Graham Spanier's reluctance to bring up details of the investigation and partly to trustee members, even the seven lawyers on the board, who were not curious enough to raise questions though they knew a grand jury was involved with Penn State administrators.[127] The grand jury probe began after the revelation of a third major Sandusky event. This time it was a middle school-high school child, a former Sandusky Second Mile kid, in the Central Mountain School District more than a half-dozen years after the incident reported by Mike McQueary to Paterno in 2001. Jerry Sandusky had volunteered to help coach the Central Mountain High School football team, less than 30 miles from Sandusky's home near State College. In the fall of 2008, a freshman at Central Mountain, Aaron Fisher, broke his silence by informing school officials, accusing Sandusky with sexually abusing him for several years. After some hesitation to report the iconic ex-Penn State assistant coach to legal authorities, officials at Central Mountain described the alleged sexual abuse, eventually reaching the district attorney of Clinton County. The Clinton County D.A. then sent the case to the district attorney of Sandusky's home county, Centre County. There, because of strange circumstances, District Attorney Michael Madeira withdrew from the case because his sister was married to one of Sandusky's adopted sons. The case was then directed to the state attorney general's office, headed by an individual, Tom Corbett, who was about to run for governor. Attorney General Corbett received the case in March of 2009; the election was November 2010.[128]

Within months, Corbett decided to investigate the Central Mountain youth's allegations with a grand jury, but it was a long process. Instead of investigating with a team of agents in what he knew would be a high profile case, Corbett placed one investigator on the case, Anthony Sessano, a narcotics agent of the Attorney General's Bureau of Narcotics Investigation and Drug Control. Assigning only one agent might have been appropriate since there were more than a dozen agents looking into a major Pennsylvania corruptions case of legislators illegally paying bonuses to campaign workers and staffers. It was called Bonusgate.[129] But delaying from 2009 until after the 2010 gubernatorial election, which Corbett won, was criticized as politically motivated. Some individuals involved in Jerry Sandusky's The Second Mile contributed hundreds of thousands to Corbett's political campaign. While that might strongly influence any politician, a later investigation concluded that the grand jury inquiry was not delayed for political purposes.[130]

The investigation of Tom Corbett came from the opposing political party, the Democrats, in the form of the new attorney general, Kathleen Kane. The investigative Moulton Report, however, was not an indictment of Corbett for a slowed investigation of Sandusky. It was delayed, according to Moulton, because of the need to have more than one individual from Central Mountain High School, Aaron Fisher, claiming that Sandusky was abusing him. As the report claimed, there was a problem with "a vulnerable and troubled victim making accusations against a pillar of the community."[131] It took time to find other abused individuals to testify against Sandusky. In addition, both Penn State and The Second Mile were reluctant to turn over records, and The Second Mile required a contempt motion before it cooperated with the Attorney General's office.[132] Not until the summer of 2011 did the Attorney General investigators feel confident that they had enough evidence to bring Sandusky to trial. By this time, they had multiple individuals willing to testify as well as evidence from a search of Sandusky's home and also finally discovering the 1998 Sandusky report held by the Penn State police department. However, *Harrisburg Patriot-News* investigative reporter, Sara Ganim, had already written her front-page story exposing to the public a vast amount of information on Sandusky and the Aaron Fisher allegations she had presumably acquired from a member of the grand jury, the grand jury judge, or from the attorney general's office.[133] Ganim's Pulitzer Prize winning exposé was not at first believed by many, certainly not trusted enough for members of the Penn State Board of Trustees to raise questions of President Spanier at the spring 2011 trustees meeting after Spanier testified before the grand jury.

Only after the 23-page grand jury presentment, based on eight alleged abuses of children by Sandusky, was released on November 4, 2011, was the general public ready to believe that Jerry Sandusky was a pedophile. The damaging presentment was exactly one year to the day that the attorney general's office received a tip that Mike McQueary had knowledge about a Sandusky shower incident with a young boy years before.[134] It was a breakthrough after a long search for boys other than Aaron Fisher who had sexual contact with the former Penn State assistant coach. In about two months, the Grand Jury received the Penn State police report of the 1998 shower room incident. With these three important cases, happening in 1998, 2001, and 2008, the push to indict Sandusky followed in 2011, months after the attorney general,

Tom Corbett, was elected governor.

If the grand jury indictment of Jerry Sandusky was a shock to those associated with Penn State athletics and well beyond, the indictment of the athletic director, Tim Curley, and the vice president in charge of athletics, Gary Schultz, may have been a greater incredulity for many of those who knew them. Both Schultz and Curley were charged with perjury, failure to report child abuse, and child endangerment.[135] The two had been in charge of athletics since the mid-1990s, both being chosen to their important positions after serving Penn State as administrators since the 1970s.

The Firing of Joe Paterno and Exit of President Spanier

While the court cases of Schultz and Curley would drag on for years, the board of trustee sacking of a 16-year president and a 61-year football coach almost immediately followed the grand jury presentment. The trustees were evidently unanimous in ousting the two most visible individuals at Penn State. Spanier was forced out, according to a group of trustees later trying to explain why the firings occurred as they did, because the board was "blindsided" by the president they claimed did not inform the trustees of the Sandusky investigation properly and openly.[136] The *New York Times* interviewed thirteen trustee members shortly before Joe Paterno died in early 2012. One trustee said that Spanier told members of the board a half year before the November 2011 indictment, "We deal with crises every day at this university. We won't have a problem with this."[137] In addition, the president irritated the trustees when he changed the wording of a press release that had been discussed with the trustees soon after the Sandusky Scandal broke. Spanier, in a short period, had lost credibility with the trustees, and few mourned his quick exit.

The trustees' firing of Joe Paterno, the Happy Valley icon, had a devastating effect on the community and among the alumni across the nation. In the several days before the firing, not one of the 32 trustees went to Penn State's Joe and Suzanne Paterno Library and looked up any book on crisis management and relayed findings to the group. The stunned and impassive trustees had various reasons why no one challenged John Surma's call for a "vote" on ousting Paterno, for he was acting for board president, Steve Garban. President Garban, former Vice President for

Finance and Business overlooking athletics and former football captain, had slipped out as board presider shortly before the votes on Spanier and Paterno took place.[138] When Surma surveyed the 32 trustees and asked, "Does anyone have any objections" to firing Paterno, there was silence. Only Mimi Barash Coppersmith, an emeritus member of the board of trustees warned before the question of firing was raised, "Coach Paterno is revered here in State College."[139] The confused trustees, with a kind of consensus agreement to fire the coach, did not know how to inform Paterno of the late evening crisis meeting. If a member of the board went to the Paterno house, when strong supporters of Paterno surrounded the home, there could be a confrontation. If Paterno was called to come to the board meeting at the Nittany Lion Inn on campus, it could lead to students and Paterno supporters to another conflict. If the board waited until the next day to inform Paterno, there undoubtedly would be word that he was fired, and a riot might occur.

What to do? Send a note to the best-known individual at Penn State, who had served for six decades and in many ways helped to create a great university, not just excellent football teams. Fire the coach by having the coach call Surma, who would deliver the "you are fired" message, was the decision by the trustees. The poor board judgment might have been averted had Penn State accepted an offer by a prominent crisis manager, Steven Fink, to be involved in the crisis management of the case. Noted Fink, "Never hold press conferences or issue statements in the middle of the night." To Fink, the trustees had a "knee-jerk decision to fire Paterno with a late-night phone call, . . . a misguided move by a timorous board filled with fear and trepidation."[140] Unfortunately for the future of Penn State, not only did Graham Spanier lack a crisis management plan before he was fired, but the trustees of a four billion dollar enterprise were equally unprepared to manage the emergency.[141]

Later, in an attempt to justify the firing, some of the trustees claimed that Paterno should have done more relative to the child reported to him by Mike McQueary. In addition, some said that Paterno had questioned the authority of the trustees when he said that the trustees should not worry about him, that he would retire at the end of the year.[142] Other trustees said that Joe Paterno leading a "We are...Penn State" cheer, a highly repeated refrain by Penn Staters, at his home when students were surrounding him was insensitive. It was, to a number of trustees an arrogant act by Paterno and a challenge to the Board. Stated

Trustee Kenneth Frazier, who would lead the hiring of Louis Freeh to investigate the scandal, "Every adult has a responsibility for every other child in our community," including the football coach.[143]

The deed of firing had been done, and it was questioned broadly not only in Happy Valley, especially by the alumni, but across the nation, and even internationally. One Penn State alumnus, shortly after the scandal arose, summed up what many felt toward the Paterno firing, and he told the trustees: "What has come out since the scandal broke has been appalling. You have terminated a 61 years employee, who has done more good for the University than anyone else, over the phone." He continued, "You ignored briefings month's ago that there was an investigation. You could not think to even ask a question? You can't get your stories straight today, and you are in hiding."[144] Similar condemnations were repeated well into the future.

What the Penn State trustees had done to the two administrators, especially coach Paterno, was seldom couched in terms of lack of "due process." The concept of "due process" became a bedrock of American justice and dated back four centuries before American colonization to England's Magna Carta or the "Charter of Liberties" of 1215 of the Common Era. In early November 2011, the trustees were not concerned with "due process." This is surprising since seven trustee members with law degrees were trained in due process, yet not one of them spoke out for due process that coincides with what is just or fair. Due process is the right to be treated fairly by people in position of authority. Or as Justice Felix Frankfurter wrote in the Supreme Court case of *Solesbee v. Balkcom* in 1950, "Due process is that which comports with the deepest notions of what is fair and right and just."[145] President Spanier at least had the occasion to present his actions before being dismissed. Joe Paterno was not even given that opportunity. While the U. S. Constitution, in the Fifth and Fourteenth Amendments, demand due process by the federal government and the states to protect life, liberty, or property, Penn State and all institutions of higher education are not bound by the same principle.[146] However, the American sense of fair play demands it, placing an emphasis on a hearing before action. No hearing was held. However, as the condemnation of the trustees remained, the 32 members of the board quickly decided to ease the criticism by ordering an investigation of how and why the Sandusky Scandal came about.

The Louis Freeh Group is Hired to Investigate

The trustees, in part to extricate themselves from their actions or inactions, almost immediately called for an independent investigation, a common reaction to any bad situation. The theme "We will get to the bottom of this," became top priority, just as any corporation might attempt, trying to save itself from immediate condemnation. While it was too late to gain redemption for members of the trustees for the widely condemned method of firing the icon of Happy Valley, the creation of an independent investigative team made it look like the trustees were no longer primarily a rubber stamp for President Spanier. The trustees would do something, even though they had done almost nothing after they learned of the grand jury probe from newspapers and a little from President Spanier much earlier in the year.

The task of choosing a prominent investigative team was given primarily to board member Kenneth Frazier and to some extent the vice-chair Ron Tomalis, who had contacts with the governor's office for possible investigative teams.[147] Frazier, a 1975 Penn State graduate, was not a lightweight as he had graduated from Harvard Law School and practiced law in Philadelphia for over a decade before joining Merck as in-house counsel for the drug firm. Frazier led Merck out of a multi-million dollar Vioxx lawsuit in which the acute pain-relieving drug unfortunately led to heart attacks and strokes. He eventually became president and then CEO of Merck.

Three significant firms from a large list were looked at before the Freeh Group was chosen, but only two were interviewed, the Freeh Group and Michael Chertoff, both recommended by the governor's General Counsel office.[148] Frazier stated in a legal deposition that because Chertoff was a classmate of Frazier at the Harvard Law School and the fact that his Covington law firm also represented his Merck drug company, that it was a negative—probably looked at by some as a conflict of interest.[149] Frazier did not note that the one chosen, Freeh, was associated with Pepper Hamilton, who represented Merck in the same Vioxx case. (Later Pepper Hamilton purchased the Freeh firm two months after the Freeh Report was released.)[150]

Besides Freeh being the former head of the Federal Bureau of Investigation and generally being highly regarded by the public, Frazier believed that the Freeh Group was sensitive to child sexual abuse issues and would be independent and come freely to conclusions he "deemed appropriate."[151]

Yet, what appeared to be most important to Frazier and Tomalis, as Frazier told the trustees, is that Freeh is "more at ease with the media side of things and it is clear that this will be his #1 priority."[152] Thus being sensitive to child sexual abuse issues in the investigation was less important than how the Sandusky Scandal played to the media. Public relations dominated Frazier's thoughts and likely that of the entire board of trustees.

If Penn State's Frazier had looked carefully at the Freeh Group, he would have found several indications that it might not be up to the task of a successful investigation. From a sport standpoint, when Louis Freeh was head of the Federal Bureau of Investigation, several of his agents were punished for tricking Richard Jewell, who was accused wrongfully of the 1996 Atlanta Olympics bombing, into answering questions without legal counsel. In addition, the FBI, under Freeh's leadership, was accused of leaking information about Jewell during the investigation.[153] In another sport-related inquiry, Freeh's group undertook an investigation in 2011 of charges of bribery in the soccer Federation Internationale de Football Association, FIFA. Following a flawed Freeh investigation, that resulted in a lifetime suspension for bribery by Mohammed bin Hammam, of the small country of Qatar in the Persian Gulf, the suspension was challenged and taken to the international Court of Arbitration for Sport in Lausanne, Switzerland. Less than a week after the Freeh Report was released, July 12, 2012, the Court of Arbitration concluded that the report by the Freeh Group relied "entirely on 'circumstantial evidence. . . .'"[154] This was something akin to the Sandusky-Penn State Freeh Report—drawing false conclusions with unclear proof. No officials at Penn State were apparently aware of the findings of the international arbitration court, nor did they question the veracity of the Freeh Report before accepting the findings and allowing, without challenge, the NCAA to use the defective report to punish Penn State and its football program.

There were other questionable actions taken under Freeh's leadership of the FBI from 1993-2001 that made debatable his leadership qualities for investigating the Penn State response to the Sandusky Scandal. These included the FBI actions of the Freeh administration with the burning of the Branch Davidians building killing many women and children in the 1993 Waco, Texas incident; the inept FBI pursuit and wrongful holding of scientist Wen Ho Lee in the 1999 Los Alamo National Laboratory case; and the withholding of documents for the defense in the Oklahoma

City bombing case of 1995.[155] As one Oklahoma City critic noted when the Freeh Group was chosen by Penn State in November 2011, Freeh "screwed up here and he's going to screw up there."[156] Unfortunately for Penn State, after spending over $8 million on the report, the detractor was correct. Later, Ken Frazier probably wished that he had never stated, "Judge Freeh has unimpeachable credentials. . . ."[157]

The NCAA Mark Emmert Letter to Penn State

Four days before the Freeh Group was hired to conduct an investigation, President Mark Emmert of the NCAA wrote an unprecedented, and with no legal authority, letter to Penn State's new president, Rod Erickson, on November 17, 2011.[158] The day prior to Emmert's important letter, David Berst, for four-decades a part of NCAA enforcement and Division I governance, tried to convince Emmert that any Penn State violations should go through the NCAA Committee on Infractions. Berst stated that he had "lost the argument. . . . Mark wants more." Emmert, according to Berst, wanted to "look at the athletic culture" at Penn State.[159] The "more" that Emmert wanted would be Emmert illegally taking the case away from the Committee on Infractions and using principally himself and counsel Donald Remy to eventually draw up unparalleled sanctions against Penn State.[160] The Penn State letter, Berst later stated under oath, was outside of the enforcement context of the NCAA.[161]

Despite questionable authority taken by Emmert, the lengthy letter was to President Rod Erickson less than two weeks following the Sandusky grand jury charged, but then unproven, revelations. The letter was sent even though the NCAA's Julie Roe, Vice President of Enforcement, believed the Sandusky Scandal was "a criminal matter" not one within NCAA jurisdiction.[162] Nevertheless, the letter was accepted by president Erickson as an official request that was not to be questioned by Penn State. It was the first time that athletically-naïve president Erickson needed sound legal advice about the NCAA, but he got none.

The Emmert letter asked four major questions:

-Has Penn State complied with the NCAA constitution and bylaws?

-Has Penn State exercised institutional control?

-Has each alleged person behaved consistent with NCAA principles?

-What Penn State policies are in place relative to Grand Jury Report behaviors?[163]

Attached were five more pages and 28 additional questions calling for lengthy answers by Penn State, such as "What is the difference between the university culture and the athletics department culture?"; "How is the 'power coach' held accountable for upholding the rules and acting ethically?"; and "Do you think that the coaches and administrators effectively avoided improper conduct or questionable acts and exhibited positive and exemplary moral values when learning of allegations against the former assistant football coach?"

In the letter, Emmert stated that the NCAA would "utilize any information gained from the criminal justice process in our review. . . ." There was no mention that the NCAA would employ non-judicial information such as the Freeh Report. In fact, in an interview with ESPN's SportsCenter one week before his letter to Erickson, Emmert stated: "We of course don't get involved in criminal investigations, and we will let the criminal investigation go forward until all the facts are established, and then we'll do an inquiry to see what action should be determined."[164] Showing the hypocrisy of the NCAA president, the NCAA never waited until the facts were established and never used any criminal justice evidence from the anticipated future trials for athletic director Tim Curley or vice president Gary Schultz noted in the grand jury presentment. Emmert's written action (and later fairness) was similar to the verbal tenet of the Bible that states, "An hypocrite with his mouth destroyeth his neighbor: but through knowledge shall the just be delivered."[165] Or, as another proverb in the Bible emphasizes, "a ruler who lack understanding is a cruel oppressor."[166] Nearly all evidence for the Emmert-led NCAA sanctions (lacking due process) came from the problematic and one-sided Freeh Report. Knowledge, and possible justice, would come later, if that time ever came.

It was fairly evident by the NCAA letter of November 17, 2011, that Emmert had made up his mind that lack of institutional control and an institutional culture dominated by football would justify the toughest sanctions that the NCAA had given since Southern Methodist University was penalized with the death penalty in the late 1980s. Strangely, according to David Berst the long-time administrator at the NCAA, there was no requirement in the NCAA Bylaws for Penn State to respond to the NCAA president's letter. Nor was there previously ever a letter from any NCAA president to any institution, according to Berst, "asking questions outside of the enforcement context but where the answers might lead to the enforcement context."[167] Nevertheless, the letter looked to President Erickson as if it was an official demand from the intercollegiate governing agency. Erickson never outwardly questioned the letter— something not to be proud of.

Penn State accepted as fact that it must answer the multitude of questions of the lengthy NCAA letter to Erickson less than a fortnight following the Sandusky presentment. Answering the letter, however, was about to change. Erickson handed what he thought was a demand to respond to the NCAA to Penn State counsel, Cynthia Baldwin. She was a former member of the Pennsylvania State Supreme Court and later president of the Penn State Board of Trustees prior to becoming counsel to the university. She appeared competent. Not completing her task by early December, Baldwin asked Emmert for an extension to respond to his request if it were needed.[168] "According to questions being asked in your letter," Baldwin wrote to Emmert, "it became evident that [they] should be answered in the course of the investigations currently in progress." What Baldwin wanted, was to have the Freeh Group complete its work and then "determine if a further response from the University is necessary."[169] The NCAA agreed.

It was natural for the investigative Freeh Group to ask some questions similar to those in the Emmert letter, for the Freeh Group, the NCAA, and the Big Ten Conference (Penn State was a member since 1990) were in regular contact about the investigation. For instance, the Big Ten's counsel wanted a "similar role that the NCAA is taking in collaborating with the Freeh Group."[170] Penn State was aware of the cooperation with the NCAA, and board of trustee member, Ken Frasier, supported the collaboration. Early on, the NCAA provided the Freeh Group with appropriate questions to ask witnesses; running email and other communications database searches of terms such as "infraction, secondary violations, self-report"; and a list of potential witnesses, including transferred athletes, football camp employees, former coaches and administrators, and the athletic compliance staff.[171] Nevertheless, head of the Freeh investigation, Omar McNeill, considered it an "independent" investigation, while many considered it collaborating with the NCAA.[172]

The Freeh Group Investigation Begins

Louis Freeh's group was given carte blanche to conduct its investigation. One of the first actions was to hold a cooperative 'on the ground" meeting at Penn State in its Nittany Lion Inn. Ironically, this happened on the 70th anniversary of the Japanese attack on Pearl Harbor that began America's entry into World War II. Invited to what turned out to be the Freeh Group's opening attack on Penn State were representatives of the Freeh Group and an associated law firm, the NCAA, and the Big Ten. All, as might be expected, were lawyers. Representing the Freeh Group were Louis Freeh, Judge Eugene Sullivan, who had been on the legal defense team of President Richard Nixon's Watergate investigation; Omar Y. McNeill, lead investigator for the Freeh Group; and Barbara Mather, a partner with the Pepper Hamilton law firm in which Freeh was associated. Two from the NCAA were head counsel, Donald Remy, and head of NCAA enforcement, Julie Roe. The Big Ten was represented by its counsel, Jon Barrett, who was continually concerned that the Big Ten might be left out of the process and the sharing of information.[173]

The NCAA representatives made clear to the Freeh Group that their major issue was whether Penn State had "institutional control" over athletics.[174] During the investigation, the NCAA and Big Ten wanted the Freeh Group and chief investigator Omar McNeill to have revealed information that they might use to impose penalties on Penn State. The NCAA's Donald Remy told the Freeh Group's Omar McNeill that the NCAA was most interested in "issues involving institutional control and ethical conduct" at Penn State, citing specific provisions in the NCAA Constitution.[175] When asked later in his deposition in the Corman v. NCAA case, McNeill said that the kind of information the NCAA and Big Ten desired was not offered to them. Updates of who was being interviewed and how far along the Freeh Group was in its inquiry, not specific information gleaned such as interviews, documents, or potential NCAA violations, was what McNeill said the NCAA and Big Ten received.[176] According to McNeill, the NCAA and Big Ten did not get from the Freeh Group what they wanted. The internal emails and discussions of the Freeh Group were locked up for years. There was no "right to know" legal request recognized, and what was communicated among the Freeh investigators, the NCAA, and the Big Ten throughout the investigation remained unknown.[177]

By the end of December 2011, the NCAA had created a list of questions shaped by counsel Donald Remy that he hoped the Freeh Group would use when it began its major investigative mode in the new year.[178] Whether these questions were used in the over 400 individuals interviewed by the NCAA in the next half year is not known, but Remy would be the NCAA liaison to the Freeh Group and Penn State through that period.[179] So, from early January 2012, when Penn State counsel Cynthia Baldwin was questioned by the Freeh Group until early June when ex-president Graham Spanier was finally interviewed, the Freeh Group gathered the majority of its material with a group of young lawyers spread over the campus and around the community. A "gaggle" of investigators flocked into the Penn State Archives in the Paterno Library to search through thousands of university records as well as examining the records held in Old Main, the administration building. They were given free reign to go through documents including emails of the principal figures involved in the Sandusky Scandal. In the end, the Freeh Group used those documents to produce its over 200-page story that it claimed was a culture problem at Penn State that lacked institutional control over the program of athletics. It also particularly condemned four individuals closely connected to the actions related to Jerry Sandusky—President Graham Spanier, Vice-president Gary Schultz, Athletic Director Tim Curley, and coach Joe Paterno.

Though it is not clear from the Freeh Report the names of the 400-plus individuals who were interviewed, the list likely contained the following people with knowledge of athletics:

- All members of the Penn State Board of Trustees including its President Steve Garban, Staff members of Human Resources and its Vice President Billie Willits;
- Dean Barbara Shannon, involved in Jerry Sandusky gaining emeritus status upon retirement;
- Staff members of the communications office;
- Counselors of The Second Mile;
- Athletic staff members and past coaches including Don Ferrell;
- Former Penn State Faculty Representative to the NCAA, Scott Kretchmar;
- Sports camps counselors and its coordinator, Richard Bartolomea;
- Penn State administrative staff, including Kimberly Belcher,

Gary Schultz's assistant;

- Former Penn State police chief Steven Shelow and Penn State detective, Ron Schreffler;
  - Department of Welfare's Jerry Lauro;
  - Counselor for Youth Services, John Seasock;
  - Joe Paternos assistant Sandy Segursky;
  - Penn State janitor, Ron Petrosky;
  - Former Vice President of Student Affairs, Vicky Triponey;
  - Counsel to Penn State, Cynthia Baldwin;
  - President Rod Erickson;
  - Past-president Graham Spanier; and
  - Anthony Lubrano, who would soon be elected to the Trustees.[180]

Evidently missing from those interviewed were key individuals Jerry Sandusky, Michael McQueary (and his father John and Dr. Jonathan Dranov, to whom McQueary first reported the 2001 shower incident), Joe Paterno, Gary Schultz, Tim Curley, Jack Raykovitz of The Second Mile and his wife Katherine Genovese, a Second Mile official, Victim # 2, seen by McQueary, Wendell Courtney, Counsel to Penn State and The Second Mile, Tom Harmon, Penn State police head, and 15 individuals who were involved in the Sandusky incident first revealed in 1998.[181] The individuals not interviewed by Freeh may be more important than those interviewed in determining the value of the Freeh Report.

What was reported in the Freeh Report, factual and conjectural, was the basis for the NCAA's punishment of Penn State that would rock the entire Penn State institution and those associated with the university. The contents of the Freeh Report were accepted by some, such as the Penn State Board of Trustees, as the truth in the Scandal. The trustees accepted it without qualification, without fully reading it, and without considering the consequences. Others, including a Pennsylvania state senator, Jake Corman, and the Paterno Family, were not willing to accept much in the report, especially its conclusions. Questioning the report led to two major lawsuits by Corman and the Paterno Family. A seemingly large majority of the Penn State alumni also rejected the report including the report's condemnation of iconic Joe Paterno. This all happened shortly after the Jerry Sandusky trial that resulted in a guilty verdict on most counts of molesting boys and the released investigation results of the Freeh Group.

Chapter 4

The Sandusky Trial Ends, the Freeh Report Follows, and the NCAA Pounces

"Nobody has a more sacred obligation to obey the law than those who make the law."

Jean Anouilh (1946)

[Authoritarians] do not defend due process—they defend decisive action.

Edward Snowden (2013)

Penn State President Rod Erickson, Counsel Cynthia Baldwin, and new Athletic Director Dave Joyner, as well as the Board of Trustees, had more than a half-year to study (or reject) the NCAA and Mark Emmert's terse (and questionably legal) letter to Erickson of November 2011 and to understand how the NCAA dealt with errant institutions.[182] From that date, when the Jerry Sandusky Scandal broke and the Freeh Group was hired to investigate, until June and July of the next year, when the Sandusky trial was held and the Freeh Group released its findings, Penn State administrators did little to prepare for the NCAA. Erickson had been thrust into a position he did not covet upon the sudden exodus of President Graham Spanier. The well-liked provost was unprepared to take on an athletic and university crisis that was dropped into his lap by failures of the previous administration. The new president, a spokesperson for the University admitted, "knew little about the athletics side."[183] Erickson, who turned over communicating with the NCAA to counsel Cynthia Baldwin, was more determined to try to mollify the alumni and others who were upset with the firing of Paterno rather than collecting data on the NCAA and its infraction policies that might be used against Penn State. In short, the administrators and the board of trustees lacked due diligence. Thus informed decision-making was deficient relative to dealing with potential infractions resulting from the Sandusky Scandal.

Shortly after Joe Paterno's death in January of 2012, Erickson attempted to regain some lost respect for Joe Paterno by putting together a potential mass email letter praising Paterno. The president praised Paterno's "iconic coaching career," and for the "Grand Experiment," "Success with Honor," and "lifting our academic reputation."[184] The board of trustees, however, rejected the letter. Dutifully, President Erickson surrendered to his board of trustees, which itself had previously questioned little, challenged nothing, and lacked investigating anything prior to the Freeh probe.[185]

In retrospect, it is clear that both Erickson and the trustees took the advice of the public relations firms, La Torre Communications in Harrisburg working with the world's largest PR firm, Edelman. The mantra, even before Edelman and La Torre were hired, was to "move forward" or as Richard Edelman stated, "Go Forward Strategy."[186] The Edelman firm hammered the "forward progress and change" and "continually moving forward" theme to Erickson and the trustees prior to the Sandusky trial and release of the Freeh Report.[187] The $2.5 million hiring of two PR firms just prior to the release of the Freeh Report to not only communicate with the outside world but also internally with the students, faculty, and alumni was criticized. Wrote one individual just after the PR hiring announcement: "Is it necessary for a university administration to hire an outside firm to advise it on the management of its communications with inside stakeholders who share governance responsibilities," such as the faculty?[188] Obviously, the administration felt so as it charged rather aimlessly "moving forward."

Erickson did not appear to prepare Penn State to deal with the crisis to come after the trial and approaching NCAA sanctions. The Penn State leader's response was to just get the turmoil out of the way and "move forward" as quickly as possible. For Erickson, that was logical for he knew almost nothing about athletic operations or crisis management. As Erickson stated in a deposition in the 2015 Corman vs. NCAA lawsuit, "I was always quite distant from the athletic operations. . . . I don't think Coach Paterno knew who I was for many years. . . ."[189] The Penn State individuals who knew the most about how the NCAA operated were gone—exited president Graham Spanier, deposed athletic director Tim Curley, and retired faculty athletics representative Scott Kretchmar and his predecessor John Coyle. They were evidently never contacted for their inside knowledge of NCAA policies and procedures. Penn State administrators, having no crisis management plan, were as unprepared as was Penn State's legal counsel, Cynthia Baldwin. She was probably as uninformed about athletics and the NCAA as was Erickson and who looked forward toward her announced retirement rather than to justice for Penn State.

Sandusky's Trial Sets the Stage

The trial of Jerry Sandusky took place before the release of the Freeh Group findings, but a torrent of confusing activity related to the scandal was taking place shortly before the trial. The Penn State alumni, many of whom were indignant over the firing of Joe Paterno, continued their protest after his January 2012 death. A total of 86 mostly agitated alumni members became candidates for three elected alumni positions on the Board of Trustees, positions won by alumni who strongly opposed the firing of Paterno by the Board of Trustees. There were 7,000 signatures on a petition turned into College Township, but never acted upon, to rename Park Avenue "Paterno Way." Ex-president Graham Spanier was ready to begin a new position in national security with the Federal government when a member of the Board of Trustees informed the Freeh Group, who helped prevent his hiring. New athletic director, Dave Joyner, fired Mark Sherbourne, associate athletic director, presumably because he delayed turning over papers of the deposed athletic director Tim Curley. Mike McQueary, the whistleblower about Sandusky showering with a kid in the football locker room, said that he would sue Penn State on employment issues. Reporter Sara Ganim, who broke the Sandusky story, won the Pulitzer Prize for her investigation. The Second Mile, from which most of Sandusky's victims came, was closing since the wealthy who backed it financially turned their backs on the organization.[190] All of this happened shortly before the Sandusky trial when a jury of seven women and five men were chosen, eight of whom had Penn State connections. Local newspapers could hardly find room for any other news than the Sandusky Scandal.

The trial was completed well before any of the dozen or so legal cases surrounding the Sandusky Scandal were taken up. Although there were attempts to move the trial away from Happy Valley, it took place in the Centre County courthouse in Bellefonte, 10 miles from the university. The scene was of national if not international importance as television trucks and individuals surrounded the building in the warm days of June 2012. The trial began June 11th. On the same day, NBC reproduced leaked emails written among Graham Spanier, Gary Schultz, and Tim Curley. The emails indicated that the three were discussing the Mike McQueary 2001 revelations of the showering incident and whether the allegation should be reported to governmental officials or kept isolated among the administrators.[191]

Email revelations, however, did not take center stage in the county seat as testimony, with vivid descriptions by those who were molested by Sandusky, ensued during the next few days. Yet, the greatest revelation during the trial did not take place in the courthouse. As the trial was about to close, adopted son Matt Sandusky revealed that his father had also abused him over the years. Matt Sandusky's disclosure never became testimony because it was rumored that Jerry Sandusky would testify in his own behalf, but not after Matt indicated that he would take the stand. Neither testimony of Jerry Sandusky nor his adopted son would likely have altered the outcome. After a dozen days, the trial came to an end after Jerry Sandusky was found guilty of 45 of 48 sexual abuse counts. The most noise created during the 12 days surely was the high-pitched screeches of joy heard in the Bellefonte Court Yard at 10:04 p.m. when the verdict was read.[192]

The Freeh Report is Released

Almost immediately after the guilty verdict, Mark Emmert and his staff at the NCAA began preparations for their actions against Penn State—awaiting only the Freeh Report that they knew was nearly completed. Both the NCAA and the Big Ten were aware from regular communications between them and the Freeh group over the past seven months that the Freeh Report was due shortly after the trial. Without doing any investigation of Penn State, the NCAA based its response almost entirely on the Freeh Report. Unfortunately for justice to Penn State and for future respect for NCAA decisions, the NCAA allowed the Freeh Report to stand in the place of a true investigation of any Penn State failure to uphold the NCAA Constitution and Bylaws. The Freeh Report had almost nothing to do with specific violations of NCAA Bylaws and Constitution. President Emmert and his counsel Donald Remy took the Freeh Report and used it without investigating the Penn State situation as was dictated by the NCAA bylaws and constitution. The two, Remy and Emmett, were the architects of the Consent Decree forced on Penn State.[193] The Freeh Report, costing over $8 million, was meant for use by the Penn State Board of Trustees to respond to and move forward from the Sandusky Scandal. It was not intended to be an investigation of whether Penn State broke NCAA rules and thereby gained a competitive athletic advantage over its competitors. According to one close observer, "the NCAA took this report and used Penn State's own resources to do them in."[194]

The Freeh Report was released on July 12, 2012. It stated nothing about specific violations of NCAA policies, though the NCAA Bylaws had a clause about loss of institutional control over athletics that the organization could use to pin down most any questionable activity on a campus. To the benefit of Emmett and the NCAA, even the Freeh Report contained several passages that condemned Penn State and its administrators that could be called lack of institutional control. Exaggerating its conclusions based upon more than 400 interviews and a few email accounts, The Freeh Report stated "the most saddening finding by the Special Investigative Counsel is the total and consistent disregard by the most senior leaders at Penn State for the safety and welfare of Sandusky's child victims." Graham Spanier, Gary Schultz, Tim Curley, and Joe Paterno, according to the Freeh findings, "failed to protect against a child sexual predator harming children for over a decade." The most damning condemnation of Penn State was the statement that read, "a culture of reverence for the football program that is ingrained at all levels of the campus community."[195]

The Freeh Report conclusions overreached the facts. It is a stretch of the imagination to state that there was "total and consistent disregard" for Sandusky's victims when there was only one clear problematic area for a decade after Mike McQueary reported a shower room incident in 2001. The previous 1998 incident was dismissed by legal authorities including the police, department of public welfare, and district attorney when it was determined that there was "lack of clear evidence of a crime."[196] The supposition that four administrators did not protect against a sexual predator for over a decade is not true even though they were aware in 2001 of a reported shower incident, one not reported to governmental officials. The erroneous Freeh Report conclusions were enough for many to reject the entire flawed investigation, despite the report's collection of many facts previously not revealed.[197]

Even more questionable was a Freeh statement based upon no facts that the culture of football dominated and was "ingrained at all levels" of Penn State.[198] Freeh's obvious exaggeration for effect made his report suspect as a propaganda invective. To believe that Penn State's outstanding Department of Meteorology was dominated by football, as in being there principally to predict the weather (which it did) for Penn State football games, was pure insult. To say that the exceptional theatre department at Penn State was dominated by the culture of football was as polemical as Shakespeare in King Lear calling Oswald "the son and heir to a mongrel bitch."[199] To assert that the strong astronomy department was dominated by the culture of football was as foolish as believing, as the Roman Catholic Church officially did until 1992, the sun revolved around the earth.[200] No wonder the Freeh Report was questioned by many, though the board of trustees and President Erickson swallowed it as if no former head of the FBI could be stretching the truth for effect.[201] Unfortunately for Penn State, the members of the board of trustees accepted the Freeh Report the same day it was released—many having done so inexcusably without first reading it.[202] President Erickson and the board of trustees got caught on the wrong side of the Sandusky Scandal: Admitting all and questioning nothing.

The Freeh Report condemned the four Penn State administrators, Spanier, Schultz, Curley, and Paterno, but at the same time condemned the board of trustees for being a rubber-stamp group to the will of the president. Spanier was the only Penn State administrator who, being deeply involved in the Sandusky Scandal, was interviewed by the Freeh Group. While the Freeh investigating group failed to interview many important people for a variety of reasons, it interviewed Graham Spanier only when the report was nearly completed. The report was released on July 12th, but Spanier was interviewed only earlier that week. He admitted to the Freeh Group that he was most interested in the "visibility and the public relations aspect" of the Sandusky revelations though he admitted "protecting children requires the utmost vigilance." Spanier also told the investigators that he did not know of the first, 1998 Sandusky event, though the Freeh Report reprinted the emails among Spanier, Tim Curley, and Gary Schultz shortly after the first shower room event.[203] It was the documenting of a series of emails (noted in Chapter 2) from the three administrators that dominated the 267-page report and evidently greatly influenced the two principal creators of the NCAA Consent Decree, Mark Emmert and counsel Donald Remy.

Emmert, Remy, and the NCAA Snatch the Moment

Mark Emmert and Donald Remy would snatch the moment that had been created by the Sandusky presentment the previous November and his trial a half-year later. One could almost guarantee that the president of the NCAA would never have written the November 17, 2011 letter to President Erickson had there been no highly visible national NCAA violations cases (Ohio State, Miami, Southern California, North Carolina) for which the handling by Emmert and the NCAA were being condemned in the media.[204] Or, as Jonathan Mahler of the *New York Times* penned in an apt analogy, Emmert "was no longer able to ignore the widespread scandals that have been piling up faster than linemen on a fumble."[205]

Emmert must have felt compelled to act outside the legal due process rules of the NCAA Constitution and Bylaws by writing the unique and illegal letter in which he threatened Penn State with "acting starkly contrary to the values of higher education, as well as the NCAA." As a governmental whistleblower has stated, those with an "authoritarian mindset. . . do not defend due process—they defend decisive action."[206] Further, the NCAA would "utilize any information gained from the criminal justice process [which the Freeh investigation was not] in our review."[207] David Berst, one of the NCAA staff with the longest term of duty and involved for decades with enforcement, concluded in testimony under oath that there was no requirement in the bylaws for Penn State to respond to the Emmert letter. He determined that there was no example "where the president of the NCAA wrote to a member institution asking questions outside of the enforcement context but where the answers might lead to the enforcement context."[208] "Mark," Berst emailed the Commissioner of the Big Ten, Jim Delany, "wants more."[209] That "more" was extra-legal. "Mark wants more" appeared to be the mantra of the NCAA until the Consent Decree was foisted on Penn State and its ill-informed president.

 A long-time member of the NCAA Committee on Infractions and then Commissioner of the Colonial Athletic Association agreed with Berst. The NCAA, Tom Yeager stated, is taking action "outside its rules," and the Emmert letter is "unprecedented."[210] In other words, what Emmert did was illegal and outside the NCAA Constitution and Bylaws. Obviously President Erickson would not know the exact rules, but he might have asked knowledgeable individuals associated with the

NCAA to advise him what the NCAA could or could not do. Erickson lacked due diligence, the care that a reasonable person exercises before entering into an agreement, such as signing the Consent Decree in July 2012 with the NCAA. The Consent Decree nullified the need to answer the November 2011 NCAA letter but gave Penn State the worst penalties ever handed out by the NCAA.

The day the Freeh Report was released, it was quite obvious what the leaders of Penn State wanted to do: Leave the Sandusky Scandal as quickly as possible and "MOVE FORWARD." A two-day Board of Trustees meeting was held on the Penn State Worthington Scranton campus during which the three most important individuals responded, President Erickson, Karen Peetz, Board president, and Ken Frazier, leader of the board committee that recommended Louis Freeh to do the study. President Erickson used the term "Move Forward" four times in his presentation, Karen Peetz, three times, and Ken Frazier once.[211] Yet, Frazier's use of "move forward" only once indicated that he had concerns about accepting the Freeh Report too quickly. Only the month before, Frazier stated that once the Freeh Report was received, the board should meet "to digest and discuss the findings and recommendations."[212] The board never did.

The public relations hires, however, had obviously told the Penn State leaders to "move forward" as quickly as possible and get past the Sandusky Scandal. The concept worked, at least with the trustees, who, with a press release accepted the "full responsibility for the failures that occurred" and only wanted "to heal and move forward."[213] As an expert in crisis managements has stated, the board of trustees "rushed to drink the hemlock. . . . [and] deprived Penn State of due process."[214] As the meeting of the trustees came to a conclusion, not surprisingly, there were no questions about the Freeh Report—only a commendation for President Erickson for his 37 years of dedication to Penn State and for leading Penn State through the first three-quarter year of the crisis.[215] Yet, some of the worst impacts on Penn State were about to happen from the corrosive hands of the NCAA's Mark Emmert and counsel Donald Remy.

The mantra to "Move Forward" was etched in the mind of President Erickson as he soon had to deal with Mark Emmert of the NCAA to receive and accept whatever punishment the NCAA was about to deal out to his institution. Too little too late—the day before the Freeh Report was released, Erickson hired an individual who was quite well acquainted with NCAA policy dealing with violations of its bylaws, Gene Marsh. He was an Alabama lawyer who had spent a number of years on the NCAA Committee on Infractions and had represented several universities, including Alabama and Michigan, when charged with wrongdoing. Marsh had also previously been engaged by Penn State in a wrestling violation question.[216] Marsh was on vacation with his wife on an isolated island off the coast of Maine. While he and his wife likely did not want to be bothered, he accepted the well-paid position of counseling Penn State. As it turned out, attorney Marsh was of little help, and he may have even been a hindrance as the penalties to Penn State were expanded over the next week when he became the important liaison between Penn State and the NCAA.

President Emmert was not on vacation, though the chair of the NCAA Executive Committee was. Ed Ray, president of Oregon State University, was also chair of the NCAA "Working Group" attempting to reform NCAA enforcement policies. Ray believed that the "public trust in intercollegiate athletics has been lost and needs to be restored." How? By increasing penalties through a "risk-reward analysis for the intentional violation of national policy that fails to deter scoff-law behavior. . . ." New rules, Ray believed, needed to be written to provide "strong and swift enforcement of those rules. . . ." Why? Because he believed there was a "public distrust of the NCAA's ability to police itself."[217] Ray had led the "Working Group" in the NCAA Presidential Retreat the previous August. It was formed by President Emmert to reform NCAA policies. Ray had previously headed the search committee and "strongly endorsed" the choice of Emmert as president the year before. Ray was committed to bringing about tougher penalties that were to be acted upon shortly after the Freeh Report was released and Penn State was brought to a "court sentencing" by Emmert.[218] That moment in the NCAA's history was the opportunity for Emmert to do what he had wanted to do since the NCAA presidential retreat was held the year before. That is, Emmert said, the "need to act and why we need to act quickly. . . ."[219]

On the day the Freeh Report was released and just before Ed Ray began a vacation in Hawaii, Ray emailed NCAA's Julie Roe, Vice-President of Enforcement. He was concerned that the NCAA appeared to be doing nothing about the Penn State situation that had been before the NCAA since the previous November. His email, with a copy to Emmert, is noteworthy:

I am concerned about the connection I see in comments on the Penn State story and the NCAA. . . . I think it is worth reconnecting with legal authorities to determine if there is enough flexibility and access to information for the NCAA to get on with an assessment of issues at Penn State. The sounds of silence are not good. If Penn State could have Louis Freeh conduct an investigation over the last year, why haven't we done anything?

Some clarity about when Penn State is expected to respond to the four questions asked and the timeline or triggers for the NCAA assessment of matters seems appropriate to me. Announcing in three weeks the sweeping changes in enforcement, culture and penalties we intend to implement over the next two years while remaining silent on the Penn State matter could easily invite cynicism even from those who are rooting for us to get this right.[220]

Thus the actively-reforming university president called upon the NCAA to do something drastic. Penn State was in a nearly perfect position to carry out what he and Emmert thought would be a lesson for all big-time institutions. Ray was one of only two on the 19-member NCAA Executive Counsel, formed of university presidents, who initially voted to give Penn State the death penalty within days and was crusading for the toughest penalties ever issued by the NCAA. The Oregon State president was knowledgeable about the NCAA Committee on Infractions, which by NCAA regulations should have dealt with the Penn State situation. The day following the Freeh Report, he again emailed Roe and Emmert calling for immediate "NCAA sanctions." He cited an ESPN article by Rick Reilly, the well-known sportswriter. Reilly had come to loathe college football and also Joe Paterno. Reilly wrote that he hoped "the NCAA gives Penn State the death penalty it most richly deserves." He believed that Penn State "deserves the worst penalty the NCAA can give."[221] For Ray, void of other information, to accept Reilly's version as the truth is reprehensible. Even worse is Ray's admission that he did not read the Freeh Report until after he, as head of the NCAA Executive Committee, voted to accept the Consent Decree.[222] The Ray episode tells us a great deal about the entire NCAA process and how unfair it was to Penn State.

Ray gave Mark Emmert an OK to recommend whatever he wanted for punishing Penn State including the "Death Penalty." It reaffirmed what Emmert had already planned—nail Penn State to the cross. But, how could Penn State be given the death penalty when the NCAA's own website, and indeed its bylaws, clearly stated that the death penalty could only be given for "repeat" major violations? The previous head of the Committee on Infractions knew this when he defined the death penalty. "If an institution is a repeat offender within a five-year period" Paul Dee wrote in 2010, it is "eligible for consideration for the imposition of the death penalty."[223] Penn State had never had a major violation—ever. Removing that visible definition found on the website was the decision of Emmert's NCAA.[224] Emmert, however, could not remove the death penalty definition from the NCAA Bylaws, documents available to be read by Penn State officials. Erickson's mind was elsewhere, and his lawyer advisors were of little help. They never read the NCAA Bylaws to see the definition of the "Death Penalty."

Onward to the Consent Decree

President Emmert first contacted President Erickson on Friday the 13th of July, the day after the Freeh Report was released. He called Erickson asking him to produce answers to the November 17, 2011 letter by the first of August, in a little more than two weeks. Following the call, Emmert discussed the situation with Julie Roe, NCAA Vice-President of Enforcement. It was at this early discussion following the Freeh Report that the two NCAA administrators discussed whether the Penn State situation was really within the jurisdiction of the NCAA or if it was only an issue for the state and federal judicial courts to decide as a criminal matter. After the Emmert-Roe discussion, Roe stated in an email to the NCAA's Vice-President of Academic and Membership Affairs, Kevin Lennon, for the NCAA to "assert jurisdiction on this issue" would "be a stretch." Nevertheless, Emmert wanted to make it an enforcement issue, to which Roe told Lennon, "I characterized our approach to PSU as a bluff, . . . [and Emmert] basically agreed."[225] Emmert did not want to take the Penn State situation to the NCAA Committee on Infractions, because he thought the committee, for which Roe was directly involved, would not be tough enough on Penn State. To Emmert, "we may win the immediate battle but lose the war when the COI [Committee on Infractions] has to rule."[226] The comment that "Emmert wants more," obviously came into play.

Following the weekend, the situation had changed. On Monday, Emmert contacted President Erickson again, this time after the NCAA president conducted conference calls with both the NCAA Division I Board of Directors and the NCAA Executive Committee. The two NCAA groups dominated by college presidents were shocked by news of the Freeh Report both by comments from Emmert and the national media frenzy. Emmert told Erickson with Machiavellian effect, "that an overwhelming majority of the boards wanted blood to shut down Penn State's football program for multiple years."[227] Erickson did not know that a number of the key administrators of the NCAA were questioning the process that Emmert was following to punish Penn State. Unfortunately for his understanding, Erickson was communicating solely with Emmert within the NCAA and knew nothing about the bluffing.

On the local level, Erickson was receiving relevant information from Penn States' liaison attorney to the NCAA, Gene Marsh, who came into the controversy much too late for effectiveness. In addition, Penn State's own General Counsel, Stephen Dunham, only arrived on the campus, replacing the ineffective Cynthia Baldwin, the same day Erickson had his second conversation with Emmert. Dunham didn't even have a telephone or computer in his office and knew little about the Penn State situation, though he had previously been general counsel at the University of Minnesota and Johns Hopkins University and had fine academic credentials.[228] The president believed he could "move forward" away from the scandal with Dunham as his chief counsel and Marsh as liaison.[229]

However, before the NCAA's Mark Emmert and Donald Remy could exact their "pound of flesh" through threatening Penn State into signing the Consent Decree, Penn State had the opportunity to take the usual route of the Committee on Infractions. That is, if the enforcement wing of the NCAA could even determine if any NCAA Bylaws had been violated. It will likely never be known if any specific NCAA rules were infringed because no charges were ever brought against Penn State by the enforcement arm of the organization.

The weeklong "trial" by coercion by Emmert and Remy produced almost exactly what they wanted—a national poster to be displayed for the supposed scurrilous actions of a rogue institution. In an athletic way, what Emmert had won looked similar to the political actions of a president of the United States when he reacted to some successful military operations in Saddem Hussein's Iraq a few years before. Though the Iraq War would go on for another decade, President George W. Bush stood on the USS Abraham Lincoln aircraft carrier under the banner "mission accomplished." Years later, Bush would state that the "photo op" was a major mistake in his presidency.[230] For Emmett, what would occur in the next week was a major mistake of his tenure as President of the NCAA, for less than three years after Emmett and Donald Remy's Consent Decree, Emmett surrendered to the lawsuit of a Pennsylvania state senator and erased the Consent Decree. The NCAA president might have done well to have read Aristotle and considered what he stated: "For man, when perfected, is the best of animals, but when separated from law and justice, he is worst of all."[231] Emmett, lacking in law and justice, appeared too arrogant to apologize and admit that it was one of his major mistakes as head of the NCAA.

How did the Consent Decree come about in one short week? What started out with Emmert's illegal November 2011 letter asking four major questions to be answered, quickly moved in the direction of President Erickson wanting to get the ordeal over with as soon as possible to "move forward." Erickson's eagerness to conclude any negotiations quickly played right into the hands of Emmett. The NCAA president also did not want the Penn State crisis to linger, as were the pending NCAA cases against Ohio State University, the University of Miami, and University of North Carolina for real violations of NCAA policy, unlike that of Penn State. In Erickson's Monday talks with Emmert, he was told that the NCAA presidents viewed Penn State as "the worst scandal ever in sports," and that the "presidents want blood." The presidents, Emmert asserted, "would like to shut your program down for multiple years."[232] Not wanting a 107,000-seat stadium sitting idle, Erickson was swayed rather quickly, but painfully, to come to terms without a death penalty, as Emmett suggested would happen if Penn State did not agree to NCAA terms for a secret and hurried settlement.

Erickson was on the true horns of a dilemma as he sought advice from a small group of ill-informed administrators and outsider Gene Marsh. Michael DiRaimo, Penn State lobbyist and Special Assistant to the President, was concerned that state Senator Jake Corman might intervene with the NCAA while the negotiations were going on. Corman was getting pressure from his constituents complaining that Erickson was not working hard enough to prevent the death penalty. DiRaimo, who would eventually become Penn State's Vice President of Government and Community Relations, told Corman in midweek that Penn State needed to "own up to our shortcomings. . . and appeal for a measured response that doesn't do more damage than what is already done."[233] In other words, appeal to the goodness of Machiavellian NCAA leadership in the form of Emmert—not a good idea.

Pressure, such as the possibility of Corman's involvement, was coming from other areas—particularly those who felt Penn State would deserve whatever it received from the NCAA. Some, according to DiRaimo, were "afraid that the trustees and administration might be supportive of that [death] penalty."[234] A significant event that stirred those in Happy Valley and beyond had just occurred. A plane, towing a banner stating, "Take the Statue Down or We Will" was flown for several hours around State College. While Erickson was talking with Emmert, pressure to dispatch the Joe Paterno statue at Beaver Stadium was growing, at the same time that people were placing flowers and other mementos at its base to honor the iconic coach. A former football captain and then a member of the board of trustees, local surgeon Dr. Paul Suhey, strongly advised Erickson: "Do whatever you need to do to keep the NCAA from giving us the 'Death Penalty.'" With emphasis on the statue, he told Erickson "I don't care [if] you have to bring your own bulldozer over and drag it to your farm, do it!" To Suhey, any decision avoiding the Death Penalty "far outweighs any other issues facing the University from our students, alumni, press, public or Paterno supporters."[235] Probably in an attempt to appease Emmert and the NCAA, Erickson ordered the Paterno statue to be put in storage. But it was too late to gain any concessions from Emmert and Remy. The statue dismantling took place early on Sunday, and later that day Erickson signed the Consent Decree.

Why Erickson Signed the Consent Decree

Before signing the questionable and illegal document, Erickson and his few badly informed advisors went through several agonizing days of one-sided negotiations with the NCAA. Erickson signed the document on Sunday night, but by at least the Wednesday before, the president decided that he would likely succumb to the Consent Decree rather than prolong the agony of a probable two-year investigation by NCAA operatives and having the Committee on Infractions make its decision. By Friday of that week, Erickson emailed three of his closest attorneys working on the case,

Gene Marsh, Penn State counsel Stephen Dunham, and William King, III, an outsider who had worked on a number of NCAA investigations. Erickson wrote:

> The PSU Board has already publicly embraced the findings of the Freeh Report. There's no going back on that. I think it's better to play football this fall—for the sake of our entire athletic program and the University—than it is to keep fighting; we only make ourselves look worse and unrepentant in the eyes of the nation. As you say, we are caught in the 'perfect storm.'[236]

Other than not wanting to appear unrepentant and desiring to continue playing football, how did Erickson come to his decision? In the first place, no advisor, including Gene Marsh, made a cogent argument to take the case to the Committee on Infractions, the logical and legal place to settle violations of NCAA policies. Most of his advisors, with the exception of the outsider Gene Marsh and William King, knew little about the NCAA, and apparently not one had educated himself since the Sandusky Scandal broke. None evidently, including March, knew that it was illegal for the NCAA to give Penn State the death penalty, as there is no evidence that any advisor of Erickson had ever read or knew what was in the NCAA Bylaws. If one were to criticize attorney Marsh, it was that the "expert" lawyer was ignorant about the NCAA Constitution and Bylaws, and he succumbed to the belief that the NCAA could legally give the death penalty to Penn State. No advisors were knowledgeable nor stood out positively in Erickson's dilemma.

That Rod Erickson did not want to have additional investigations at Penn State may well have strongly influenced why he decided to sign the Consent Decree. By going the route of the Committee on Infractions, an investigation of a year or two would have added to other Penn State investigations already in progress. One was by the U. S. Department of Education for violation of the Clery Act passed in 1990 to require the reporting of campus crimes, something that Penn State had not done.[237] In addition, the Pennsylvania State Attorney General's Office was continuing its investigation of crime on the Penn State campus. Then, too, there was the question of how the Middle States Association accreditation agency would look at the Penn State situation. If there was an additional investigation by the

NCAA, Erickson wrote two days before signing the Consent Decree, "there are many more possibilities [of wrongdoing] the more you dig. . . . The addition of the idea of the NCAA picking through all of the football disciplinary player cases," Erickson pointed out, "could yield much more in the way of problems. . . ."[238]

Erickson was referring to the 2003-2007 saga at Penn State when Joe Paterno essentially forced the resignation of the Vice President for Student Affairs, Vicky Triponey.[239] She wanted her office to punish wayward football players for transgressions, such as charges of aggravated assault and rape, rather than have Paterno take care of those illegalities and other indiscretions as he had done for most of his lengthy coaching career.[240] Gene Marsh warned Erickson, "They would interview folks in student affairs to see if there was special treatment. . . ."[241] (Mark Emmert was made aware of the special treatment and the Triponey situation the day after his November 17th letter.)[242] Marsh advised Erickson on the day the Consent Decree was signed: "Don't say this anywhere, but part of the calculation is that they probably would have found some additional NCAA violations. . . . There are others."[243] Limiting the discovery of additional wrongdoing was on the mind of Erickson, who certainly knew the power of coach Paterno and his intrusions into Student Affairs with his aberrant football players a few years before.[244] It was an important consideration—little known and seldom reported by the media. The Paterno situation reminds us of Montesquieu, the French philosopher and political critic of the eighteenth century, who claimed, "constant experience shows us that every man invested with power is apt to abuse it, and to carry his authority as far as it will go."[245] Concerns around Paterno's intrusion into punishment by the Office of Student Affairs cannot be dismissed as a major factor in signing the Consent Decree.

Because the Sandusky Scandal was injurious to the image of Penn State University, Erickson said that he wanted to act quickly rather than spend several years with an investigation. Advisor Gene Marsh, the day the Consent Decree was signed, tried to put the justification for signing the decree in perspective for Erickson. He informed Erickson, if Penn State went through the traditional infraction process, there "would have been this cloud hanging over the campus due to an ongoing NCAA inquiry." It would end up "more expensive and disruptive" to Penn State in the long run. The image of Penn State would be hurt further, and besides, Marsh reasoned, "Emmert would have been furious that PSU walked away from his 'deal.'"[246] Yet, Marsh never once quoted the NCAA Bylaws that clearly dictated the "death penalty" only could be given to repeat major violations.

The NCAA Bylaws were clear that what the NCAA was about to do to Penn State was illegal, but no one at Penn State read the rules. The bylaws stated clearly that the Committee on Infractions "shall be responsible for the administration of the NCAA enforcement program." The "vice president for enforcement," not the NCAA President or the Board of Directors, "shall identify the charges as involving alleged major or secondary violations. . . ." Furthermore the "enforcement staff," not President Emmert as stated in his November 17, 2011 letter to Erickson, "shall provide a notice of inquiry in writing to the chancellor or president." Just as important, "prohibition against specified competition in the sport," the so-called "death penalty," can only be given if "the institution is a repeat violator," and only "if the Committee on Infractions finds that a major violation has occurred within five years of the starting date of a major penalty."[247] None of these statements fit the Penn State case. The NCAA, under Mark Emmert's leadership, might better have followed the ancient advice, "Nobody has a more sacred obligation to obey the law than those who make the law."[248]

As President Emmert violated nearly all of these NCAA written protections of due process, it is clear that any consent decree forced on Penn State was illegal. Or, as an outspoken Penn State alumnus claimed following the NCAA's later capitulating on its Nittany Lion sanctions— "How can you run an honest game when the referee makes up the rules as he goes along. . . ?"[249] Justice to Penn State would be trampled just as the NCAA due process would be trodden. If there was a NCAA rule that institutional presidents could by-pass the Committee on Infractions by signing a "summary disposition" with Penn State, it could only take the action following a "thorough investigation" by the NCAA enforcement staff. Emmert, who certainly knew of the "Death Penalty," rejected an issue that had perplexed the NCAA for decades—the need for due process. Passed at the 1985 special NCAA convention,[250] a meeting incidentally attended by Joe Paterno, the "Death Penalty" came into being, but delegates were warned that the NCAA "must be even more concerned with due process. . . ."[251]

Emmert discarded the tenets of due process, and he did this when he brought up his list of punishments of Penn State to be voted on by both the ruling NCAA Executive Committee and the Division I Board of Directors. According to the Executive Committee report the day before the Consent Decree was signed, only 10 of the 23 members voted to approve the terms of the Consent Decree, while 13 members did not vote for it by being absent or abstaining. One member, President David Leebron of Rice University and former dean of an Ivy League law school, indicated that the rush to vote didn't allow for a "thoughtful consideration."[252] The lawless President Emmert in his rush to ill-judgment and lack of due process could well have been fired for violations of the NCAA Constitution and Bylaws. Some might consider that covering up of vengeful Emmert's blatant violations of the NCAA Bylaws by the NCAA Board of Directors surpassed the charges of a cover-up by Penn State administrators.

Without knowledge of the illegality of sentencing Penn State with a "death penalty," Rod Erickson soon publicly left out many reasons for his action on the night of July 22, 2012 when the Consent Decree was signed, emphasizing the death penalty threat as the primary reason for his doing so. He explained his decision to the full Board of Trustees a few weeks after capitulating to Emmert, Remy, and the NCAA. Speaking to a group that had nearly unanimously backed Erickson through the entire process, he told them what he believed the trustees wanted to hear, the threat of the death penalty convinced him do it for the sake of the university.[253] Otherwise, Erickson said, it would lead to the loss of all men's and women's sports for lack of football revenue, and an empty stadium would have a drastic economic impact on the region. In addition the Big Ten might vote Penn State out of the conference. Penn State challenging the Consent Decree would mean, according to the president, years of litigation and Penn State would probably lose a lawsuit to the NCAA. Besides, Erickson reasoned, the Consent Decree would allow its terms to be modified as conditions changed, and as it turned out he was right on that score. With all these reasons, he added that new coach Bill O'Brien wanted to play games on TV under the Consent Decree. It was a request not taken lightly, for as O'Brien said to Erickson, "the most important thing in any sanction is that we be allowed to play and that we be allowed to play on television."[254] After all, the new multi-millionaire football coach was thought important enough to be brought into the Consent Decree discussion, though ironically it turns out that the entire board of trustees was eliminated from discussions before the Consent Decree was signed.[255]

Above all, Erickson told the mostly supportive board of trustees, the Consent Decree was the best way to move forward. The board would march in step with Erickson until he gladly retired two years later, as he returned to his farm, reflecting his Wisconsin upbringing, outside State College.[256] The board even gave him a hefty bonus and named a building after him, a structure containing the creamery and gallons of Peachy Paterno ice cream. The impact of the Consent Decree would be felt for years, even after the NCAA capitulated on most of its penalties three years later. Dennis Dodd, a writer for CBS Sports, summed up the situation—"It's hard to tell what was more outrageous: The Penn State penalties or the fact that the NCAA rescinded many of them two years later." It was, Dodd stated, "hubris, misjudgment and misguided power" by the NCAA and its president.[257] In short, when Rod Erickson opened himself and Penn State up to Mark Emmert in the Consent Decree, he showed the NCAA president where to insert the knife.

At the point of the signing of the Consent Decree by President Erickson, Mark Emmert had exacted Shakespeare's "pound of flesh," his spiteful penalty, from the Sandusky Scandal.[258] One could compare what Emmert had done to Penn State with the action of the British and American air forces at the end of World War II when they bombed Nazi Germany's Dresden into oblivion because the allies could do it, not for the reason that it was just.[259] Emmert, allowed to shell Penn State through Erickson's fear of the NCAA, "bombed" Happy Valley's Penn State with the strongest fusillade ever brought on a member of the NCAA—not because it was just, but because he and the NCAA could do it.[260]

Chapter 5

How the Board of Trustees' Crisis Management Failed Penn State

Withhold not good from them to whom it is due,
when it is in the power of thine hand to do it.

Proverbs (900s B.C.E.)

No matter how ineffectually President Graham Spanier dealt with the Sandusky situation before and after the scandal broke, the major crisis was exacerbated by the ineptness of the Penn State Board of Trustees. What the trustees did or didn't do impacted the ill-fated Consent Decree that greatly damaged Penn State financially and in many other ways. It also damaged the National Collegiate Athletic Association in the long run by creating the climate for President Mark Emmert to carry out dishonest, illegal, and bullying tactics without restraint. The board of trustees made plenty of mistakes, but the two major ones were the middle-of-the-night firing of a 61-year employee, coach Joe Paterno, without due process and allowing new president Rod Erickson and president of the board of trustees, Karen Peetz, to accept, "**unconditionally**," the investigative Freeh Report upon its release.[261]

The Original 1970 Board of Trustee Blunder

The board of trustees made major blunders in 2011 and 2012, but the original gaffe of the trustees, relative to their ineffectiveness and rubber-stamping of actions of the president, came from their action four decades before, in 1970. The granting of unregulated power to the president by the trustees was understandable at that time because of campus rioting. That occurred during the national crisis in the late 1960s and early 1970s, resulting from the Vietnam War and exacerbated by Civil Rights movement in America at the same time. The conservative leadership of the board of trustees looked negatively at the Civil Rights agitators and those protesting the Vietnam War across the nation and at Penn State. Protests began at Penn State under the administration of President Eric Walker with sporadic demonstrations against the growing American involvement in Vietnam including opposition to the military draft, military research at Penn State, and the Reserve Officer Training Corp on campus. During the fall of 1969, thousands of Penn State students protested the Vietnam War as they jammed the student Hetzel Union Building while the Penn State football team was in its second undefeated season in Joe Paterno's fourth season at the helm. At almost the same time, the small aggregate of Penn State African Americans students protested their numbers on campus and the few black faculty and administrators in the institution. The black students had formed a strident Douglas Association (soon to be known as the Black Student Union) and then, in 1969, the African American students joined with the more radical Students for a Democratic Society (SDS) during 1969 to protest and occupy the office of President Walker. While the Walker administration made an effort to accommodate some of the black students' demands, it was not enough as Vietnam protests consumed Penn State and campuses across America.[262]

By the spring of 1970, student protests had reached a new height at Penn State with demonstrations in the Old Main administration building. President Walker called in a phalanx of state police to disburse the protesters. A number of protesters were charged, but protests continued, including stones being thrown through windows in Walker's on-campus house on April 21st. The board of trustees called an emergency meeting on April 28, 1970 to discuss student disturbances over the past few weeks that caused, in trustees' words, "grave concern and even outrage." The board authorized President Walker to "summarily suspend" any student who was disruptive, and amnesty would not be granted to anyone who violated University rules.[263] Within a week of the trustee action, President Richard Nixon expanded the Vietnam War into Cambodia and all hell broke loose on university campuses, including the Ohio National Guard members shooting of protesters at Kent State in Ohio and a few days later at Jackson State in Mississippi.[264] American campuses were in turmoil; Walker felt under siege.

One supposed solution, that came to haunt Penn State when the Sandusky Scandal broke, was to place near dictatorial power in one person—the president. Shortly after an attack on Eric Walker's campus residence and following the shootings and killings on the Kent State campus, the board of trustees changed the rules of governance stating that "The President. . . shall have final authority. . . to establish policy" at Penn State.[265] Thus, the president would not only administer general policy set by the board of trustees, but would establish the policy under which Penn State operated. The result at Penn State of heightened presidential power is what President Stephen Trachtenberg of George Washington University later called the last of the imperial presidencies in American institutions of higher learning.[266]

The increased presidential power was eventually used to make athletic policy by future presidents. John Oswald (1970-1983), who succeeded Eric Walker the summer when the new trustee power was granted to presidents, used the new authority. It took awhile, but Oswald in time bypassed the Board of Trustees over the administrative location of the athletic department. Beginning in 1930, the trustees had placed athletics within an academic unit. It remained there for a half-century when Oswald removed athletics from the College of Health, Physical Education, and Recreation and placed it in a financial unit of the university. He did this only after Joe Paterno, before accepting the position of athletic director in 1980, demanded that athletics be placed in the university business office (under a former football captain, Steve Garban).[267] It could be argued that the isolation of athletics from academic oversight in a business office was a contributing factor in the Sandusky Scandal.

A decade later, President Bryce Jordan (1983-1990) used his presidential policy-making power to circumvent his board of trustees when he brought Penn State into the prestigious Big Ten Conference.[268] Jordan's action could be justified to some extent because none of the presidents of Big Ten institutions discussed bringing Penn State into the Big Ten with their governing boards before an offer was made. At Penn State, seemingly only one board of trustees member, Joel Myers (President of AccuWeather), protested the solitary action of Jordan without a discussion with the board of trustees. "We need to support debate," Myers complained, "rather than dictates. We need to support discussion and debate."[269] Deliberation was not what the Penn State Board of Trustees or presidents were used to. The tradition of the trustees was to listen each meeting to a lengthy report by the president on the positive progress Penn State was making from board meeting to board meeting. Negatives and debate were almost always absent.[270] Nevertheless, Board President Lloyd Huck brought up the question of the authority of the president to make this important policy change and was told that the trustees had given power to the president in 1970 to make policy, not just to administer it.[271]

Two decades later, President Graham Spanier avoided the trustees once again by not bringing pertinent information about the Sandusky Grand Jury investigation to the board's attention, contributing to the Sandusky Scandal. That it would have been prudent of Spanier to more fully inform his board begs the point, but he did not need to do so. It might have been a good idea for President Spanier to embrace the Biblical Old Testament in the Hebraic "Proverbs" and its truism not to withhold "from them to whom it is due, when it is in the power of thine hand to do it."[272] However, the 1970 board policy of allowing the president to set policy was rather clearly stated four decades before Spanier skirted the trustees. The first policy of the trustees stated:

> The authority for day-to-day management and control of the University, and the *establishment of policies* and procedures for the educational program and other operations of the University, shall be delegated to the *president*. . . .[273]

No wonder, the president of George Washington University called Penn State the institution with the imperial presidency.

Trustees' Inaction in the 1980 Paterno-Garban-Oswald Athletic Coup

President John Oswald removing academic control over athletics could be considered a major victory for Joe Paterno. It probably helped him to win his first national championship. Joe Paterno said that because of Oswald's help, Penn State was able to beat Georgia in the 1983 Sugar Bowl. He could have been referring to removing athletics from an academic unit and placing it in a business unit. Paterno could also have been recognizing Oswald for admitting nine football players into Penn State in 1980, athletes who had been turned down for academic reasons by the Penn State office of admissions, many of whom contributed to the national championship.[274] Removing athletics from an academic unit probably dominated Paterno's reasoning. Though the board of trustees had created an academic unit into which to place athletics a half-century before, the trustees did not question the solitary action of President Oswald in removing athletics from that academic unit. Prior to his singular action, Oswald wanted to know how athletics came to be in an academic unit and searched the late 1920s and early 1930s archival records for trustee actions. He then had the records duplicated.[275] Even after finding out that the trustees created the athletic program within an academic unit, he did not consult the trustees about removing athletics. More importantly, the 1980 trustees did not question Oswald's authority to make a major change in Penn State policy. Trustees remaining silent can have drastic results as occurred three decades later when the board raised no questions about the grand jury investigation in which four key administrators testified, and a half-year later a major scandal arose.

In 1980, when the Paterno-Garban-Oswald coup occurred, Penn State was the only major athletic program in America in which athletics were part of an academic unit.[276] Many believed that administering athletics within an academic unit was a major reason why athletics at Penn State appeared to be lily-white, above reproach, when many institutions were penalized repeatedly for violations of NCAA rules. The cleanliness of Penn State athletics went back to the Ernie McCoy and Rip Engle era as athletic director McCoy ran a tight ship and threatened any athletic employee with unemployment if rules were broken. Rip Engle who was the football coach during most of the years of McCoy, with Joe Paterno as his assistant, followed suit with his football team. When Joe Paterno became head coach in 1966, the unnamed "Grand Experiment" of winning football, following the rules, and graduating players, was already in existence.[277] Paterno's record and his early undefeated seasons made the "Grand Experiment" his own.[278]

By 1978, Paterno had three undefeated teams and was undefeated and ranked number one until disaster hit in the January 1, 1979 Sugar Bowl when some questionable goal-line plays called from the bench and a 12-man on the field penalty helped Alabama win the national championship. The national championship was needed, according to Paterno, for the "Grand Experiment" to truly be successful.[279] At the time, the athletic department was in its last year of being in an academic unit. Paterno, with unequaled power from winning over the years, wanted greater control of how "his" athletic money, mostly from football gate receipts, was being spent. For the previous half-century and more, excess money from athletics (principally football) was often spent on recreational facilities for the entire student body. Facilities constructed from athletic money included such items as the building of Recreation Building, a golf course, tennis courts, racquetball

courts, bowling alleys, ice skating facility, and a swimming pool. The head
of the academic unit (first the School of Physical Education and Athletics
and later the College of Health, Physical Education, and Recreation) would
often make decisions on how excess money would be spent, not the
football coach. Joe Paterno had other priorities.

The same year that Paterno lost to Alabama, the university administration decided to have an administrative review of the dean of Health, Physical
Education and Recreation, Robert Scannell, who was also in charge of the
athletic program. The committee charge was to determine if Bob Scannell
was spending too much time on athletics relative to the academic program,
despite the dominant Department of Physical Education being ranked number one in the nation.[280] There were those in the Penn State administration
hoping that the answer would be yes, that he was devoting far more time
to athletics than to the undergraduate and graduate program of the College.
Thus they would have reason to separate athletics from the College, even
though the physical education department was ranked number one in the
nation. A committee of six was chosen to review the office held by Bob Scannell. It met for an entire year, interviewing key individuals, conducting a uni-
versity-wide survey, and coming up with recommendations. The committee
seemed well balanced with an outsider as chair who was an administrator in
the College of Agriculture. There were three individuals from the college and
two outsiders.[281] The most significant individual, as it turned out, was Steve
Garban, an official in the university office of finance and business. He was a
former captain of the football team in the 1950s when Paterno was assistant
coach. Garban had first worked in the athletic department as ticket manager
and was called to the university administration to work in the business office,
with expertise in athletics. He had his own agenda as a friend of Paterno and
an interest in administering the athletic program.

If the committee had found that athletics should be withdrawn from
the academic unit to strengthen academics, then the logical place to harbor
athletics would be in the business arm of the university. Indeed, the
business office is where athletics were often housed in other universities.
If the committee had recommended this, it would have been logical for
the athletic director to report to Steve Garban. The committee concluded
that Dean Bob Scannell did, indeed, spend a majority of his time looking
after the athletic department and that a change in athletic administration
was needed to take some of the pressure off the Dean to deal with athletic
problems. However, to the great disappointment of Steve Garban, all

members of the committee except for Garban, voted to keep athletics as an integral part of the college. Because athletics at Penn State had worked so effectively under a deanship for decades, the business-financial model favored by Steve Garban was rejected for the academic-athletic model in existence since 1930. The report made it clear:

> The Committee, after many hours of discussion, recommends that the *integration of Intercollegiate Athletics and Academics be retained.* Penn State has a *unique marriage* that works, and the union provides a great deal of prestige to the faculty, coaches, and athletes as well as to the research and instructional components where many of the same personnel function.[282]

Only Garban had argued against the important provision of the report. The report was received by President John Oswald, but the academic-athletic provision was turned on its head in about a half-year when Joe Paterno and Steve Garban got what they wanted—isolation of athletics within a business operation and an opportunity to run athletics the way they felt was best for Penn State and for Joe Paterno and Steve Garban.

From May 1979 when the report was submitted until December of that year, President Oswald came up with a plan to reorganize the athletic department. He deposed the ineffective athletic director, Ed Czekaj, brought in Joe Paterno, and took athletics out of an academic unit and placed it under Steve Garban in the university business office.[283] Paying no attention to his knowledge that the board of trustees united athletics as part of an academic unit, Oswald completely circumvented the trustees when he announced the new arrangement with Joe Paterno as athletic director. Unknown to the outside world, Paterno had sent a strong memo to Oswald that he would not accept the athletic director's position unless athletics were taken away from the dean of the College of Health, Physical Education, and Recreation where it had resided for the past half-century.[284] Being a hypocrite or untruthful, Oswald bent to the will of powerful Joe Paterno, even after earlier that year telling the board of trustees:

> We are proud of the way in which this program [athletics] is organized as *part of one of the academic colleges* and not a program that is set aside as a separate part of the university.[285]

On the same day that Oswald appointed Paterno as athletic director, he announced a cunning policy statement, justifying his action of bypassing the trustees. "On any issues that might require Trustee consideration," Oswald deviously stated, "the President shall inform the Trustees."[286] He obviously had no intention of asking the trustees to withdraw athletics from an academic unit that the trustees had previously created. As would eventually turn out, it was not a wise decision to isolate athletics from the watchful eyes of academics, who often have more than victories as their mission in higher education. It is difficult to calculate the effect the coup may have had in contributing to the Sandusky Scandal. Isolating athletics under Steve Garban in a business office surely was part of the equation. Steve Garban eventually became president of the board of trustees and raised no questions about the involvement of administrators in the scandal, including the participation of his successor in the business office, Gary Schultz. This did not speak well for Garban, the former football captain.

The Trustees Fail to Uphold Board Policy in the Rene Portland Case

While President Oswald was deliberately avoiding involvement of the board of trustees in the Paterno-Garban-Oswald coup, the trustees were essentially veiled, as in the later Sandusky Scandal, from a lower level abuse under the women's basketball coach. Within weeks of Joe Paterno becoming athletic director in 1980, he made the most important hire of his two years as AD when he appointed Rene Portland. The appointment appeared to be of good quality as Portland had participated on three national championships in women's basketball as a member of the Immaculata College team, near Philadelphia, in the early 1970s. She had a good coaching record at both St. Josephs College and the University of Colorado prior to coming to Penn State. As a coach of basketball, she soon became the most important Penn State coach of women's sport as basketball was pushed by the athletic department as the dominant women's sport—something that was true at most colleges in America.[287]

Rene Portland arrived in Happy Valley as a youthful, statuesque, personable, and articulate leader of what administrators hoped would be a leading woman's sport at an institution that had already national leaders in gymnastics, field hockey, and lacrosse. Women's gymnastics, for example, had a national championship squad that filled the Penn State arena of Recreation Hall to over capacity, with the largest crowd ever seen in the facility the same year Portland was hired.[288] The importance of Portland and women's basketball was clear as Portland was the first woman coach hired at Penn State solely to coach, not being involved in any teaching responsibilities as were all of the other Penn State women's coaches and most of the men's coaches. The passage of the Federal Title IX of the Education Act of 1972 would dictate that the women's basketball coach and team would be treated equally with men's basketball, the second most important sport at Penn State.

Title IX had provided great support for coaches such as Rene Portland by promoting greater equality in terms of coaching, facilities, athletic scholarships, and equipment. Yet, Title IX contained wording that would in the end doom the coaching career of Portland, though it would take a quarter-century to come to fruition. Title IX's 37-words would be used to support Portland and women's sports, but in Portland's case eventually used against her. The amendment to the Education Act of 1972 read:

> No person in the United States shall, on the basis of sex, be excluded from participation in, be denied the benefits of, or be subjected to discrimination under any educational program or activities receiving federal financial assistance.[289]

Penn State came under the arm of Title IX as it received federal aid in its operations. Portland also came under the law because the act would prohibit sexual "discrimination," including being denied participation because of being a lesbian or being associated with lesbians. Portland's religion may have complemented her personal bias against lesbians. She was a Roman Catholic (strongly opposed to homosexuality), went to a Catholic college, and early in her career coached at a Catholic university. However, she was then joined by a majority of Americans, religious or not, who condemned homosexuality, and the American Psychiatric Association called homosexuality a mental illness until after Title IX was passed in the 1970s.[290]

Rene Portland was determined that there would be no lesbians on her teams or in any way associated with her teams, such as managers. In the 1980s, Portland was asked about lesbians on her team, and she responded, "I will not have it in my program."[291] Actions against lesbians began almost as soon as she arrived. Early on she had three clearly stated team rules—"No drinking, no drugs, no lesbians."[292] Yet, almost as soon as she arrived, two players, twins Corinne and Chris Gulas, recruited by the previous coach, Patty Meiser, were forced off the team for being lesbians, as well as one of her own recruits, Cindy Davies. They left quietly and did not charge malfeasance on the part of coach Portland. While Portland's discriminatory action continued from the early 1980s until the twenty-first century, no one in the athletic administration challenged her actions.[293] Nor were her actions taken before the board of trustees, who spent considerable time discussing and adding a "sexual orientation" clause to Penn State policies in 1991. The trustees, adopted the sexual orientation policy, advocated by President Joab Thomas, after hours of discussion before a reluctant board. It was intended to help "protect all members of the University community against invidious discrimination, including members of the Penn State lesbian and gay community."[294] That part of the trustee policy, despite Rene Portland's actions, lay dormant for a decade and a half.

Coach Portland ignored the anti-discriminatory policy into the twenty-first century when she dismissed Jennifer Harris, an African American player with star credentials. A federal case against Portland, with the financial support from the National Center for Lesbian Rights, was brought in 2005. The case charged Portland and Penn State for not only violating Title IX but also racial and sexual civil-rights violations under the Equal Protection clause of the Pennsylvania Constitution and the Fourteenth Amendment of the U. S. Constitution, and the Civil Rights Act of 1964.[295] President Spanier never brought this important pending federal case to the board of trustees at a time when, unusual for Spanier, he noted several other problems at Penn State. They included violation of trademark apparel, difficulties from greenhouse gas emission, and what some believed were pornographic paintings from the School of Visual Arts.[296] Despite the trustees earlier having adopted the policy to ban sexual discrimination, only one trustee raised a question about the "on-going investigation involving allegations made against Rene Portland."[297] It was one of the rare cases in which a trustee brought something negative about Penn State up for discussion. Spanier's response to the Harris-Portland situation that had potential major consequences for Penn State and its athletic program was not recorded. Nevertheless, he and his administration wanted the Harris case dismissed.[298] That was understandable to protect Penn State, but to protecting a violator of Penn State policy and national and state law was less justified.

President Spanier was reluctant to treat such a cancerous problem, because he understood Joe Paterno's position at Penn State as the individual with the most influence. Portland had coached for a quarter century without a losing season and had the strong backing of Joe Paterno who honored Portland more than once, stating, "I think Rene has done a great job."[299] She was also honored at the same time by receiving the 2005 "Renaissance Person of the Year" award in Happy Valley for "being a wonderful role model for young women."[300] She was in a similar position as Jerry Sandusky as an icon of the community to many, a beloved coach of a successful basketball program. The trustees remained silent even after President Spanier fined her and put her on probation for her discriminatory actions based on an internal investigation.[301] The board could have brought up its 1991 policy on sexual discrimination, but the members sat and watched the action unfold. Fortunately for Penn State, no major crisis occurred from Portland's actions as arose from the Sandusky Scandal. Within two years, the two sides of the case settled out-of-court, Rene Portland resigned, and a new coach was hired.[302] However, the isolation of the board of trustees and the president continued through the Sandusky Scandal.

Insularity and the Rubber-Stamping Board of Trustees

As with the Portland situation, it was not unusual for the Penn State Board of Trustees to be in the dark when important issues faced the university. One could blame that on the 1970 trustee policy that allowed the president to make policy, including athletic policy. Thus, President Oswald could withdraw athletics out of a trustee-created academic unit without a whimper from the board; President Jordan could join the Big Ten without the knowledge of the trustees; and the trustees would not discuss the case of a basketball coach dismissing a basketball player from the university for the player's supposed sexual orientation, violating university policy and state and federal statutes.

From that standpoint, it was not surprising that the child assault charges against Jerry Sandusky might have been kept in house by the Penn State administration or that the members of the impotent board of trustees would defer to the president as they had been doing for decades, even when they knew damage to the university could result from their silence. Five years after the Sandusky Scandal broke, the U.S. Department of Education reported on the failure of Penn State administrators and trustees upholding the federal Clery Act requiring campus crime reporting. "Senior management failed to inform the BOT of events that threatened to destabilize the University," the report stated, "and the BOT failed to adequately inquire about these same events, even as credible information began to emerge in the press and from law enforcement officials."[303] The Department of Education had exposed, after the fact, a rubber-stamping board and an insular president leading to the worst scandal in Penn State history.

The failure of the board in the Sandusky Scandal began before the scandal broke in November of 2011. A half year before, apparently only one board members reacted to the front page headlines in the *Harrisburg Patriot-News*, "SANDUSKY FACES GRAND JURY PROBE," indicating that a state attorney general's grand jury was investigating child abuse allegations against Sandusky.[304] Although one board member raised a question of President Spanier about the grand jury proceedings prior to a board meeting, the board did not make inquiries of President Spanier when he told the trustees that it was not a big deal.[305] It is curious that not one of the seven lawyers on the board and Penn State Counsel and former state Supreme Court judge, Cynthia Baldwin, raised a question. They should have known that a grand jury investigation might impact Penn State. Here was the board's number one failure in the Sandusky case, to be added to the failures of inquiry in previous athletic cases, such as that of Rene Portland.

Other failures followed. A second major failure of the board was to have no crisis management plan, as any major corporation should have in place. Because of this, the trustees failed a third time when it did not think through the firing of the only national icon at Penn State, probably the best known individual in the school's history, Joe Paterno—and doing it at night, a major faux pas of a panicking board. The fourth failure of the board members was placing their faith in Trustee Ken Frazier, with some help from Trustee Ron Tamalis, to head a Special Investigation Task Force to choose a competent individual to carry out, without adequate vetting, an independent investigation of the Scandal.[306] The board's action was made worse by a fifth decision of the trustees to have the report released to the public before any one of the trustees could look at it to see if there were factual mistakes and questionable conclusions drawn by the Louis Freeh investigators.[307]

Board failures continued. A sixth significant failure of the board, through Trustee President Karen Peetz, was to accept the Freeh Report, facts, conclusions, and recommendations, without reading the document, the day that it was released. This "rush to injustice," Trustee Al Clemens later stated, "I will always regret."[308] A press release on the day the Report became public stated that the trustees accepted the Freeh Report.[309] The seventh failure of the trustees was to allow new President Rod Erickson, unbelievably naïve about the National Collegiate Athletic Association and its enforcement program, to carry out the negotiations with the NCAA without any discussion with the 32-member board of trustees. An eighth failure of the board was to accept the Penn State-NCAA Consent Decree without the entire board of trustees having read or approved it.[310] A ninth fault of the board was to never look into the NCAA Constitution and Bylaws and its Consent Decree to see if it had been negotiated legally and with due process. A tenth mistake was for a majority on the board voting to prevent all board members from reading the documents dealing with how the Consent Decree was negotiated.[311] Failures abounded.

While each one of the noted board failures can be questioned and challenged, the trustee actions only reflected a weak and previous rubber-stamping group of individuals who failed in fiduciary responsibility. For decades they relied on the president to make policy that could have damaging effects upon Penn State, including its athletic program. The tradition of both the board and the president in making decisions in an insular environment was not commendable. The president had the power since 1970 to make policy. As evidenced by reading the minutes of meetings, members of the trustees generally sat through lengthy periods while the president told them of the great strides Penn State was making. This was true educationally and in research. However, he was mum about problems that faced the institution. Rubber-stamping the president's actions while enjoying the social perquisites of being a trustee gave the impression that the prestige gained for being on the board overrode the need for the oversight of the health of the entire university. That appeared true whether it was going along with an ill-informed presidential decision, costing $100 million, to join to two culturally different medical organizations (Geisinger and Hershey), into one or not questioning why there was a grand jury investigation of an iconic assistant football coach.[312]

There were many problems never discussed by the board of trustees, but the impact of the Consent Decree was the most damaging. The trustees accepted the NCAA Socrates-like hemlock dished out to Penn State for what a majority of the trustees believed was closure of the sad episode in Penn State history. What the Penn State president did with the backing of a small group of the trustees was to sign an unconditional acceptance of a lengthy list of punitive and corrective penalties. Closure was not achieved. The management of Penn State may never have been performed more poorly.

Chapter 6

The Impact of the Consent Decree

Do not turn one blunder into two.
                                     Baltasar Gracian (1647)

With little negotiation and a great deal of coercion on the part of Mark Emmert and the NCAA, Penn State's President Rod Erickson signed the Consent Decree on a Sunday night, July 22, 2012, after having Joe Paterno's statue removed from its stadium location earlier that day. If the Penn State president had a desire to irritate the Penn State alumni, it would be difficult to find two more significant events. Not only had Erickson hidden away the bronze symbol close to many hearts, but he agreed to have all of Penn State's football victories under Paterno, from the time of the first known Sandusky incident on the Penn State campus to his last win against the University of Illinois, taken away—all 111 of them. It is ironic that the last recorded victory for Paterno under the Consent Decree was the 1997 victory over Wisconsin, with 2001 Sandusky whistleblower, Mike McQueary, as Paterno's quarterback. A decade and a half later, the list of penalties meted out by the NCAA was far greater than any other ever issued to a member institution. For some, unlike many alumni, no punishment would have been enough. One was the sportswriter Rick Reilly, who felt that all penalties against Penn State would be justified. He wrote an article at the time of the release of the Freeh Report that influenced the head of the NCAA's Executive Committee, Ed Ray, to call for the "death penalty" even before Ray read the Freeh Report.[313] It was Ed Ray who signaled to a receptive Mark Emmert that the more punishing penalties served on Penn State the better, particularly the "death penalty."

The Punitive and Corrective Penalties

The NCAA decided to give Penn State two types of penalties, PUNITIVE and CORRECTIVE, one to punish and one to promote reform. For Emmert and a number of others, Penn State's reaction to Sandusky's actions created the worst scandal in college sport history, even before any civil or criminal charges were brought to court. The **punitive punishments** of the Consent Decree included:[314]

- $60 million fine to create an endowment to prevent child abuse (raised from $30 million during the so-called "negotiations");
- Vacate 112 victories, 111 for Paterno, from the first 1998 Sandusky incident to the end of the 2011 season in which Paterno's replacement, Tom Bradley, won one game;
- Four-year reduction of athletic scholarships in football to 65 from the 85 NCAA limit;
- Four-year postseason football ban with no playoff games or bowl competition;
- Waiver of transfer rules, allowing all Penn State football players and recruits to transfer and immediately play at another school, and to allow any Penn State player to continue at Penn State, drop football, and keep his athletic scholarship;
- Five-year probation for Penn State athletics for all men's and women's teams;
- Appoint an "integrity monitor" to overlook the entire athletic program, and
- The possibility of a future formal NCAA investigation and imposition of sanctions on individuals after criminal proceedings were completed.

The list of **corrective components** of the Consent Decree was even longer:

- Adopt all recommendations of the Freeh Report. Of the over 100 recommended practices accepted by Penn State, one was to "emphasize and practice openness and transparency at all levels and within all areas of the university." This one action would have prevented the Penn State scandal arising out of the Sandusky transgressions;
- Implement an Athletics Integrity Agreement;
- Create the position of Compliance Officer (Athletics Integrity Officer) for athletics;
- Establish a Compliance Council of faculty, administrators, and compliance officer;
- Create a program so that anyone can disclose compliance problems, anonymous or named;
- Appoint a monitor for each sport who will certify compliance;
- Certify by the athletic director an annual compliance certification;
- Produce an athletics code of conduct;

- Provide a yearly training course in the athletic department addressing ethics, integrity, civility, and standards of conduct;
- Warned that if the Athletics Integrity Agreement is breached, additional sanctions including fines and the "death penalty" may result; and
- Appoint an independent Athletics Integrity Monitor (Senator George Mitchell) for five years who will report to the NCAA, the Big Ten Conference, and the Penn State Board of Trustees.

The Damaging Monetary Costs

The monetary cost to Penn State was enormous, approaching a billion dollars as the years passed, including but not limited to the following:[315]

- Millions of dollars needed to implement the Consent Decree punishments and corrective components added to the millions spent on the Freeh Report;
- Legal costs associated with the Consent Decree and the added cost of hiring many more lawyers for Penn State and additional administrators;
- Over $100,000,000 handed out to victims and to be determined future victims of Sandusky;
- Millions spent on hiring administrators such as Clery compliance officer, Title IX coordinator, Ethics and Compliance officer, Human Resources consultants, Strategic Communications officer, child abuse professors, athletic department compliance officers, president, athletic director and associate athletic director, football coaches, police training coordinator, and the firing of an associate athletic director;
- Millions of additional public relations payments;
- Millions spent of additional supervision of minors, building access controls such as cameras and chip readers, new Human Resources information system, new ethics and compliance officer, public access website, Records Management expenses, increase sports camps child costs, compliance training costs, new crisis management plan, and increased insurance costs;
- Costly free counseling services for abused children offered by Penn State;
- Accumulated and potential millions of dollars to defend Graham Spanier, Gary Schultz, and Tim Curley criminal cases;
- Millions spent on defending cases brought against Penn State, such as the Paterno Family lawsuit; Mike McQueary and other coaches lawsuits, and the Emmanuil Kaidanov lawsuit;
- Millions lost because of the NCAA ban on bowl and playoff revenues and the millions of revenue sharing taken away by the Big Ten

for its Penn State sanctions;
   •   Millions of lost revenue from the thousands who decided not to attend future Penn State football games;
   •   Millions lost to corporate sponsorship pullouts;
   •   Costs of stopping athletic building projects such as the natatorium and tennis facilities;
   •   Millions that would be lost because some decided never to again contribute to Penn State in general; and
   •   Millions associated with the cost of Grand Jury investigations, additional trustees expenses and new members, materials required by the U. S. Department of Education, Middle States Commission for Higher Education, removal of the Joe Paterno statue and holding the Paterno memorial services, depositions for numerous law suits, additional police protection, and the costs associated with the Moody's Investors Service downgrade.

In all, the Sandusky Scandal would likely eventually cost in the neighborhood of a billion dollars for a scandal that could have been prevented with more openness and a wiser Penn State administration. That is far more than the $100 million or so that it cost Penn State with the ill-fated decision of Penn State's Graham Spanier to merge Penn State Hershey Medical School with the Geisinger Medical Center in 1997. Almost from the signing of the agreement, attempting to join the two different medical cultures to work together was a disaster.[316] The medical fiasco was soon forgotten by most, but not the Sandusky debacle, whose impact would likely last for decades. Or as Baltasar Gracian warned nearly a half-millennia ago: "Do not turn one blunder into two."[317]

From an immediate impact, the NCAA's taking away Paterno's 111 victories caused the most negative reactions from those interested in the iconic Joe Paterno and Penn State rather than the impact upon innocent children. As Paterno did what was legally demanded of him by reporting a suspected child abuse issue up the administrative chain, no charges were brought against him in the Sandusky presentment of November 2011. There is no evidence presented that Paterno violated any NCAA Bylaw. Whether Paterno should have done more, rather than later belatedly admitting "I backed away," was not an issue the NCAA should have used to condemn his record breaking 409 football victories. The issue became inflamed, and individuals protested by plastering "409" stickers on numerous autos, with at least one Pennsylvania license plate beaming pride in iconic coach—"JVP-409." The statement remained on vehicles longer than the couple years it took to eliminate the NCAA's bullied mistake, the Consent Decree.

How the Coach Kaidanov Firing Was Part of the Consent Decree Fiasco

A damaging Penn State event and another cost, seldom associated with the Sandusky Scandal and the Consent Decree, was the removal of a Penn State coach. It was another blunder, this time by the athletic department and the short-termed athletic director, Dave Joyner, M.D., an all-American offensive lineman in Joe Paterno's 1960s-70's heyday. Coach Emmanuil Kaidanov, of the hidden-away Penn State's men's and women's fencing team, was cast out of his position by Joyner, but more importantly it involved the newly NCAA-mandated Athletic Integrity Officer, Julie Del Giorno. She had been hired following the board of trustees blindly accepting the Freeh Report and its over 100 recommendations for reform. One recommendation agreed to by Penn State in the soon to be signed Consent Decree was to hire an Athletics Integrity Officer to oversee the entire athletic program, ensure compliance, and report any misconduct within the program.

When Del Giorno was hired a half-year after the NCAA and Big Ten Athletics Integrity Agreement was signed by Penn State, her sound background probably made Mark Emmert feel that any future miscreant institution must also have an Athletics Integrity Officer. She was a 1986 graduate of the U.S. Military Academy at West Point with all-American acclaim as a basketball player. She served in both the Persian Gulf War and in Somalia with the military and had administrative positions at West Point, the University of Central Arkansas, East Stroudsburg University, and was chief of staff at Moravian College before taking the Athletics Integrity Officer position at Penn State. It did not take long for her decision-making to be challenged relative to Penn State athletics. The month after Del Giorno signed her Penn State contract, but before she arrived in Happy Valley, the incident took place that caused the firing of Kaidanov.

Emmanuil Kaidanov was a former world-class fencer and late 1970's immigrant from the Soviet Union who achieved 795 victories and 12 national championships in 31 years as Penn State coach. He was not present when one of his women fencers, Kane Gladnick, removed a piece of tape from her knee, rolled it up, and discarded it. However Kaidanov's administrative assistant was there. The scrap tape did look a little like a marijuana cigarette, obviously something that a young fencing administrative assistant felt the need to report to the authorities as an illegal activity when she saw Gladnick drop it. After all, Penn State only a few months before had signed the Consent Decree and the related "Athletics Integrity Agreement" stating that Penn State could be given the "death penalty" for further violations of NCAA rules.[318] The unnamed assistant may have done the correct thing by going over the head of the coach and reporting the supposed incident by anonymously calling a hotline created for that purpose by the "Athletics Integrity Agreement."[319] She bypassed Kaidanov, a Russian with what has been described as a gruff disposition. When Kaidanov was informed, he let his female assistant know that she needed to tell him, not someone else, about the incident. Penn State administrators eventually considered the Kaidanov encounter with the administrative assistant as "retaliation" and "harassment," the basis given for Kaidanov's firing.

The unseasoned athletic director, Dave Joyner, with no athletic administrative experience until Tim Curley was removed from the AD position following the Sandusky revelations, did little relative to punishing Kaidanov when he was informed until Del Giorno arrived on campus. Joyner did not bring together Kaidanov, the administrative assistant, Del Giorno, and Gladnick to discuss the situation. The mistake by the administrative assistant was soon uncovered when Gladnick denied having a marijuana joint and was tested negatively for drug usage, but Kaidanov's discussion with the administrative assistant was not dropped. After Del Giorno arrived, the allegation went through her office. Unfortunately, the later statement by Del Giorno, that she needed to review cases in a judicious manner, was not done in the Kaidanov case. Del Giorno was quoted as saying that she "can be viewed as an honest broker who can conduct reviews, or look into various matters and provide facts that can be used by the Athletic Department and other university leaders in their decision making."[320] She did not do this in the Kaidanov circumstance according to the judge in the case.

Athletic Director David Joyner fired Emmanuel Kaidanov in the summer of 2013, just before the fencing team was about to begin its 2013-14 season. Because of it, Kaidanov sued Dave Joyner, Julie Del Giorno, and Penn State University. "What Penn State wants to do," claimed Kaidanov's lawyer, Alvin de Levie, "is to hide the truth."[321] The suit, which was settled out of court two years later, was based principally on two counts—lack of due process and breach of contract. These two significant counts were not dismissed by Judge Gene Pratter in the Pennsylvania Eastern District Court and awaited a trial against Joyner, Del Giorno, and the university. Judge Pratter stated that Kaidanov had not been granted due process by being allowed to present statements relative to his good name, character, integrity, and reputation before being fired. The judge also refused to dismiss a Penn State charge that Kaidanov never had a contract and could therefore be fired at will. By being at Penn State for 31 years, he held that Kaidanov "successfully pleaded a contract."[322] When the trial was nearing, as in many cases where one side feels it is likely to lose (as with the NCAA in the Senator Jake Corman lawsuit), Penn State decided to settle out of court prior to a possible loss. Kaidanov was, in his own words, "totally vindicated," while the statement from the two sides just indicated that it was "amicably resolved."[323] If money was involved going to Kaidanov, which was most likely, he might have agreed it was amicable. Del Giorno was not fired for her judicious mistake, and Joyner had already resigned before the settlement was announced.[324]

Penn State, however, was the loser for firing Kaidanov with essentially no evidence and without due process. A Penn State athletic administrator's statement early in the Kaidanov case was very revealing. When asked for someone in the administration to have the "guts to stand up" for Kaidanov, the response was "we live in a new world since the Sandusky Scandal."[325] The influence of the Sandusky Scandal and the Consent Decree were so dominating that the Kaidanov situation of a wrongful accusation from a mis-identified marijuana joint could bring about the firing of Penn State's most successful coach in terms of victories and national championships in the previous three decades. One could draw the comparison to a quarter-century of violations of federal, state, and Penn State policy in the women's basketball programs of anti-lesbianism, where the administration would not fire a coach for violations it knew were unlawful. Like signing the illegal Consent Decree, the firing of coach Kaidanov found Penn State running scared, including Athletic Director Dave Joyner and President Rod Erickson, with the help of its new NCAA-mandated Athletics Integrity Officer, Julie Del Giorno.[326]

The Penn State rush to judgment of Kaidanov may have reminded some of the more visible historical rush-to-judgments. One might note the Salem Witch Trials in 1692 in which innocent citizens were falsely accused of witchcraft; the Dreyfus Case in which the French army tried to cover up a wrongful conviction in 1894; the Joe McCarthy witch-hunts of the Cold War 1950s lacking due process; and the early twenty-first century Duke University administrator's unjustified penalties against its lacrosse coach and team members without evidence for sexual crimes.[327] When Joe Paterno's firing was done with no due process, it raised legitimate howls of protest, however when Kaidanov was fired in the mistaken marijuana joint incident, few seemed to care. It says something about how human beings treat iconic figures on the one hand and on the other hand those whose success is more hidden away and forgotten.

The Impact on the Nittany Lion Football Team

The Kaidanov firing was only a small blip on the television screen relative to what many people were interested in—What impact would the Consent Decree have on the prospect for the dominant football team? Other than having Paterno's 111 wins taken away by Emmert and the Consent Decree, the question of the impact of President Erickson's signing to allow all football players, present and incoming, to transfer and begin playing immediately for another school was a dominant concern for many Penn State fans. Once announced in the Consent Decree, Penn State football players were besieged by football programs across the nation to get them to transfer to their schools. Probably the University of Illinois program was the most egregious by sending a posse of coaches to the Penn State campus to scavenge for potential transfers including freshmen just entering Penn State. The lone Penn State player to transfer to a Big Ten institution, offensive tackle Ryan Nowicki, went to Illinois with its newcomer coach Tim Beckman's team. Nowicki was symbolic of the lack of success of most transfers, for he lacked playing time with the Illini and transferred again to Northern Arizona at the season's end. Furthermore, Nowicki's Illinois was soundly beaten by the Nittany Lions, 35-7, when the two teams met two months after his transfer. There was a revenge factor inflicted on the poachers from Illinois.

The Nowicki transfer to a Big Ten school was not a major concern of the football program—that of Silas Redd, however, was. There was a strong belief that if the sophomore star running back the previous year might transfer, it would have a cascading effect upon others who might abandon a sinking ship. If that real possibility happened, the football program could be ruined for years, certainly for the 2012 season opening in just over a month. Two seniors, Mike Mauti and Mike Zordich, have been credited with preventing the mass exodus that NCAA's Mark Emmert promoted. Both Mauti and Zordich talked with new coach, Bill O'Brien, to encourage him to not set a deadline for when Penn State players must decide to transfer or not; rather, the two leaders convinced O'Brien to wait while Mauti and Zordich, with the help of others, talked to each player, convincing most to remain with the team.

Within two days, former members of the team including Todd Blackledge, Jack Ham, Franco Harris, and Matt Millen came back to talk to the team members. Millen, who once had his captaincy taken away by Joe Paterno for not completing a pre-season run but later earned four National Football League Super Bowl rings, got a standing ovation from team members for his rousing talk to convince players to remain at his alma mater. With the leadership from the team and new coach Bill O'Brien and the support of former players, the effect of the NCAA's damning rule was minimized, but not eliminated. Twenty players transferred, de-committed to Penn State, or remained at Penn State while dropping off of the football team but keeping their athletic scholarships.[328] At least four with previous playing time could be considered major losses to the NCAA transfer punishment. More than 60 players remained, thanks in large part to the early action of the two committed Michaels—Mauti and Zordich.

The four transfers who were then considered most damaging to Penn State's football success were Justin Brown, Anthony Fera, Khairi Fortt, and Silas Redd. Brown was considered the most talented receiver and kick returner on the team; Anthony Fera was a starting place-kicker and punter from the 2011 team; and Khairi Fortt was one of the young talented linebackers. However, Silas Redd's departure was discussed as the major loss for the 2012 Nittany Lions. He became the starter for Southern Cal after gaining 1,241 yards as a sophomore at Penn State. Redd was recruited by a stable of USC coaches, flown to Los Angeles, and brought to the Southern Cal campus in a limo by the rapper and movie star, Calvin Cardozar Broadus, Jr., aka "Snoop Dog"—quite an arrival for a young football star.[329] However, in two years at USC, he gained fewer yards rushing than he did in one full year at Penn State. Following college, he was not drafted by any team in the National Football League but played one year for the Washington Redskins before being injured. Anthony Fera did well at the University of Texas as a punter and place kicker, making all-American his senior year, but was not drafted by the NFL. Justin Brown went to the University of Oklahoma and had a good year with 73 receptions and 879 total yards. He was drafted in the sixth round by the Pittsburgh Steelers but did not impress them and was waived. Khairi Fortt starred at the University of California, Berkeley and was a semifinalist for the 2013 Butkus Award as a linebacker, was drafted in the fourth round by New Orleans, but he was waived after an injury.

The departed players almost surely had a negative impact upon Penn State under its new coach Bill O'Brien. Even though coach O'Brien had a remarkable first year with 20 players missing and becoming national Coach of the Year, the lack of depth for the next four years led to mediocre records for the usual expectations of Penn State fans. Winning 8 games and losing 4 in his first year and 7-5 the next was astonishing as the number of scholarship players dropped significantly toward the 65 limit forced on Penn State by the NCAA.

Impact on Football Attendance and Fund Raising

Yet, the departure of players may not have been any more significant than the rather sharp drop-off in spectators attending Penn State football following the Paterno years. That resulted in the loss of several millions of dollars—money that not only supported football but all of the many sports sponsored by Penn State. The historical high points in football attendance were 2008 and 2009 when the average attendance was over 108,000. In Paterno's last full year (2010), the gate averaged over 104,000. Following the scandal, the number of fans in 2012 averaged below 97,000 and almost the same in 2013, rising to over 101,000 in 2014 with a new coach, James Franklin. It fell again below 100,000 in 2015, just above 100,000 in 2016, and rose the next year to over 106,000 following a Big Ten championship season.[330] The actual attendance numbers were far below those figures with 21,000 student seats sold but often about half full. Many of the expensive choice seats at mid-field remained empty for several seasons. The fear of football not being able to support all of the sports activities and future projects was immediate after the $60 million fine from the Consent Decree.

As soon as the Consent Decree was agreed to, it became obvious that the $25 million to come from athletics to help build a new natatorium and lesser millions to construct a new indoor tennis facility would be put on hold as the $60 million fine and other millions needed to comply with the Consent Decree demands would weaken the athletic program. The question of whether Penn State athletics violated the Consent Decree by stopping scheduled projects for any minor sports was never answered. Nevertheless, the signed decree stated, "No current sponsored athletic team may be reduced or eliminated in order to fund the fine."[331] Was the swimming program, with the worst facility in the Big Ten, "reduced" when a $30 million project was stopped? When John Hargis, the successful head swimming coach, resigned in early 2013 to become an associate head coach at Auburn, it suggests that stopping the swimming facility may have impacted the swimming program. There was no question that the over $30 million profit by the athletic department in the two years before the Sandusky Scandal became a several million dollar deficit in the two years following the revelations.[332] It would obviously impact the sports, such as swimming, always dependent upon football money, as were all sports at Penn State except for men's basketball, which received a majority of its money from dividing up Big Ten profits.

Angering the world largest active alumni by the Board of Trustees' firing of Joe Paterno, accepting the Freeh Report without reading it or discussing it, and President Erickson signing the Consent Decree without understanding the NCAA Constitution and Bylaws was enough to influence the financial support given to the alma mater. The year after the Sandusky Scandal broke, alumni and other giving to Penn State dropped considerably, but not for long. Rod Kirsch, Penn State's vice-president for Development and Alumni Relations, reacted almost immediately. "Donors are sad, shocked. . . . they're angry. Some feel betrayed." Terry Pergula, a Penn State alumnus with considerable money from the burgeoning natural gas industry, agreed, saying "Penn State's reputation has been severely tarnished."[333] He did not withdraw his millions for the ice arena, but rather gave additional millions to the project after his original $88 million, the largest individual gift to the university.

As it turned out, while fund raising was a major Penn State problem for a short time, funds continued to come in as Penn Staters and others appeared to contribute in about the same numbers as before to show their support for an embattled university. One gift was from the Penn

State class of 2013 and destined to become iconic similar to the class of 1940 Heinz Warneke-sculpted Nittany Lion shrine. The "We Are" figure was a sculpture by class of 1984 Penn State alumnus Jonathan Cramer. Instead of the 13-ton Nittany Lion sculpture carved out of limestone, Cramer's was constructed of mirror polished stainless steel, 12-feet tall and weighing four tons. It was placed on the east side of campus as one approaches Beaver Stadium from central campus, just as the Heinz Warneke sculpture was sited in 1942 on the west side near "New Beaver Field." This was the location of Penn State football prior to 1960, when the steel stands were dismantled and reassembled into a 46,000 seat stadium on the east side of campus.[334] The "We Are" sculpture was based on the handwriting style of Fred Lewis Pattee, the literature professor who wrote the words to the Alma Mater in 1901, and represented the spirit and pride Penn Staters have in their institution.[335]

The "We Are —Penn State" chant soon began to drown out the "I backed away" statement of Joe Paterno about the Sandusky Scandal, even in fund raising. While the contributions to Penn State dropped from a high of $275 million in 2011, of which a sizable chunk came from the Pergulas for the ice hockey facility. A total of $209 million was raised the following fiscal year in which the scandal erupted. One might have expected the figure to keep dropping, however those contributing for the next three years exceeded that figure by as much as $60 million. The number of annual contributors remained near 190,000, many of whom were alumni. Even more striking was the major two billion dollar "For the Future" capital campaign begun in 2010, a year and a half before the scandal, and came to a highly successful end in 2014 by exceeding its goal with a total of about $2.2 billion.[336] Though the supporters of Penn State were unhappy with how individuals within the institution dealt with the Sandusky Scandal or how Penn State was unjustly treated by the Freeh Report and the Consent Decree, their love of Penn State was not lost in their financial contributions for the life of the university.

Finding an Athletic Director

While Penn State was attempting to live athletically and as a university under the Consent Decree, it soon had to choose an athletic director to replace Dave Joyner, a crisis-chosen member of the Board of Trustees and former football player. Penn State had never had a woman athletic director, and the four ADs dating back to 1970 had come directly from the football program.[337] When new president Eric Barron appointed the committee, it was quite evident that he wanted a change from past athletic leaders. Barron, soon after becoming president in 2014, appointed to the committee only women who were involved in athletics—Julie del Giorno, new Consent Decree-commanded Athletic Integrity Officer; Charmelle Green, Senior Female Athletic Director; Linda Caldwell, Faculty Athletic Representative to the NCAA; and Coquese Washington, women's basketball coach. He could not have filled the committee of seven with only women from among vice provosts and vice presidents had he wished as only one of Penn State's 11 vice provosts and vice presidents was a woman. To complete the AD selection committee, he logically chose Tom Poole, Vice President for Administration, Rob Pangborn, Vice President and Dean for Undergraduate Education, and David Gray (chair), Senior Vice President for Finance and Business, the administrative position to whom athletics had reported since 1980. If the committee was stacked to produce a desired change, it succeeded.

Chosen as the new athletic director was an individual with solid credentials who had been a former athlete at Wake Forest University and administrator in five institutions of higher education for over three decades, Sandy Barbour. Her stays at the University of Massachusetts, Northwestern, Tulane, and Notre Dame came before her being chosen one of the few Division I women athletic directors at the University of California, Berkeley, a position she held for a decade. There she had both athletic successes and failures. University of California teams were in the top ten in the Learfield Sports Directors' Cup six out of her 10 years at Berkeley. Thus the program with a number of winning varsity sports was among the best in the country, like Penn State traditionally.

However, in Berkeley's two most prominent sports, football and men's basketball, were neither championship quality nor were the athletes meeting requirements for graduation. The program under the leadership of Barbour was among the worst in the country for graduating football players, and the basketball team had the lowest graduation rate in the PAC-10 Conference—an embarrassment to those associated with a traditionally top-rated university in America. In addition, more than half of all special admits into Berkeley were athletes. They were allowed to enter Berkeley even when their academic records were so low that they couldn't get admitted into the university without special exceptions (called "presidential admits" at Penn State). Most of the athletes were football and basketball players.[338] The yearly 20 special admits, called "Blue Chip Admits" by Berkeley, were a major reason for California's low graduation rate for its football and basketball teams and a humiliation for Barbour and the university.[339]

Then, too, when she was dismissed as athletic director in 2014, the athletic program was approaching a half-billion dollars in debt as a result of building a new athletic training facility and renovating a historic 93-year old football stadium. No one knew at the time it was constructed in 1923, in a competition with Stanford to see which university could first construct the largest stadium, it was built directly over the San Andreas Fault System's Hayward Fault.[340] A large part of the $321,000,000 stadium renovation was due to the mitigation of potential earthquakes. A failure in an attempt to manage the payment for the structure was a major reason for moving Barbour out of her AD position to an academic position in sport management, as ironic as that might seem. The athletic department projected millions of dollars accruing from the sale of 40-year and 50-year seat rights in the stadium, but the plan fell $120 million short. "Clearly, initial seat sales goals," Barbour conceded, "were overly optimistic." Roger Noll, a Stanford economist with expertise in sports, exclaimed, "I fear a disaster."[341] Because of the delayed debt funding, the disaster might not occur until the twenty-second century of the Common Era.

Barbour felt some of the same impending catastrophe, and she proposed dropping five sports, baseball, rugby, women's lacrosse, and men and women's gymnastics. With pressure and financial help, especially from alumni, no sport was dropped. Barbour's desire to drop sports was similar to the financial crunch when Joe Paterno became athletic director at Penn State in 1980. At that time, he proposed eliminating bowling, fencing, rifle, track, and volleyball and reduced budgets for baseball, basketball, golf, softball, and tennis. Only bowling and rifle were eliminated. Wrote Vice President for Finance and Business, Robert Patterson in 1981, "the 'handwriting is on the wall' for most spring sports."[342] That did not happen either. The financial crisis three decades later at Berkeley was delayed or possibly averted because paying the principal of the enormous debt was put off until 2032 as the university only paid the interest of over $15 million a year, raised to about $30 million a year two decades later when the principal of the loan would be added to the interest.[343]

So the well-travelled, articulate, and energetic Sandy Barbour became athletic director at Penn State, under a good deal of criticism, and was paid handsomely. It was far more than her previous pay by raising her Berkeley salary of $417,000 to $700,000 with bonus possibilities above that.[344] Relative to outgoing Penn State AD, Joyner, it was nearly double his $396,000 salary. In her initial years at Penn State, there were no noticeable faux pas, with one exception. She may not have realized how much supporters of Penn State athletics, especially football, could take an affront to anything dealing with departed Joe Paterno. When the new varsity men's ice hockey team took to the ice against Michigan State in early 2015, they placed the number "409" on their helmets to honor Paterno's football wins, and they did it just after the NCAA capitulated on its ill-devised Consent Decree and gave back the deserved victories under threat of losing the Senator Corman lawsuit. When informed of the hockey stickers, Barbour twittered that they were "inappropriate and insensitive." She may have been politically correct relative to a concern for the Sandusky victims, but was politically thoughtless relative to how important the 409 victories were to Penn State athletic boosters. A twitter reaction to something that should have been thought out brought about a hurried apology: "It was inappropriate," Barbour pronounced, "and insensitive of me. . . ."[345]

The next time a sensitive issue came up, the question of possibly constructing a new football stadium, Barbour was more thoughtful. The issue was what to do with needed major renovation at Penn State's most important venue, the nearly 107,000-seat Beaver Stadium. For years, there had been questions of crammed seating on the dominant metal bleachers, the deteriorating plumbing system, accommodating older spectators, especially getting to their seats, and modern concession facilities.[346] Barbour decided on a master plan conducted by an outside firm for all facilities, knowing that the stadium was the dominating facility in most people's minds. She announced that renovating Beaver Stadium or building a new stadium was on the discussion agenda. It drew major attention even before she opened up public discussions about facilities beginning in the fall of 2015. A variety of opinions were expressed, but there was overwhelming sentiment to retain the history and tradition of the present stadium. "Renovate and move on," one wrote. "Play football while 107,000 fans contentedly crow 'we are,'" stated another. "Beaver Stadium is HISTORIC!" one commented. And a few said they wanted to "change the name to Paterno Stadium."[347]

While the renaming of Beaver Stadium was ripe for discussion emanating from the Sandusky Scandal and the Consent Decree, it would not dominate other considerations. The financing of any major facilities renovations or new constructions dominated. It had to be considered in the context of the athletic and university costs of half-billion dollars and more arising out of the Sandusky Scandal. Penn State athletics could not be put in the position of Sandy Barbour's last institution, Cal-Berkeley, where the problematical payment of a stadium rehabilitation debt caused a crisis for the entire university only a few years before. At Penn State, Barbour was aware that athletics had generally paid its own way without other university funds (unlike Berkeley with constant financial athletic losses). However, because the Penn State president and board of trustees had accepted the Consent Decree and accepted the failures of the Sandusky Scandal, the financial constraints would dominate the future of the institution and its athletic program. That was true even after Pennsylvania state senator Jake Corman's lawsuit against the NCAA was settled out of court resulting in the nullification of a good portion of the Consent Decree. Supporters of Penn State generally praised the agreement. Whether that was just a sound decision for Jake Corman and his political career principally, or a sound decision for the welfare of Penn State, was uncertain.

Chapter 7

Corman's Lawsuit, Leverage, NCAA's "Surrender," and the Paterno Critique

We cannot miss the opportunity to leverage the moment.
Mark Emmert (2011)

I came to bury Caesar, not to praise him.
Shakespeare (ca. 1599)

On January 16, 2015, the NCAA surrendered to a Pennsylvania lawsuit, led by state senator Jake Corman. Almost assuredly, the NCAA would not have settled out-of-court had their leaders believed they would win the case against Corman. The original dispute over the geographical distribution of the $60 million fine had turned into a frontal attack on the legality of the entire 2012 Consent Decree foisted on Penn State. That the NCAA agreed to settle the litigation a month before the case was going to come to trial was a smart move on the part of the NCAA for at least two reasons. First, it was highly likely that the NCAA would be found guilty of a lack of due process and of breaching its own constitution and bylaws. Second, the case would have been tried with a jury from Pennsylvania, giving Pennsylvania's Jake Corman a "home court advantage." Nevertheless, it did help save face for the NCAA. While it was a basic loss to the NCAA, it was a political win for Corman who could exclaim upon the settlement—"The NCAA has surrendered."[348] He was right personally, but not entirely for the sake of Penn State or for justice. Had the case gone to trial, the probability of the NCAA losing and completely eradicating the Consent Decree would have been a total defeat of the NCAA and would have absolved Penn State from the unjust decision for the original coerced signing of the NCAA-Penn State agreement.

The Expansion of the Original Senator Corman Lawsuit and Settlement

The original January 2013 lawsuit by Senator Corman against the NCAA was solely to challenge the NCAA's ruling that the $60 million fine levied on Penn State would be spent across the nation, not kept in state and expended on fighting child abuse only in Pennsylvania. Once the lawsuit was entered into the Commonwealth Court of Pennsylvania, Corman engineered a bill through the state legislature requiring monetary penalties of $10 million or more on institutions of higher education (meaning Penn State) must be held in a trust fund controlled by the state treasury and spent only in Pennsylvania. The bill, known as the Endowment Act, passed with the unusual, nearly unanimous vote of 192-2 in the House and 50-0 in the Senate, quickly becoming law about a month after it was introduced.[349]

The NCAA immediately challenged the act as unconstitutional, but over the next months Commonwealth Court Judge Anne Covey questioned the NCAA's attempt to kill Corman's Endowment Act and other aspects of the senator's case. Judge Covey eventually came to believe that "an organization outside of Pennsylvania can't come in and start dictating to Pennsylvania that they want the money to go outside just because they say so."[350] Her decision to rule the Endowment Act as constitutional was the beginning of the weakening of the NCAA's position in the Corman lawsuit.

Unlike the success of Mark Emmert and Donald Remy in frightening Penn State into accepting the Consent Decree a year before, Judge Covey refused to be bullied by the NCAA in either the Endowment Act or the Corman lawsuit. The NCAA argued that there were no state funds going into the $60 million fine. It reasoned that Pennsylvania could legally spend money outside of Pennsylvania, that Penn State failed to join Corman in the suit against the NCAA, and that Penn State willingly signed the Consent Decree. However, Judge Covey rejected the NCAA's arguments against the Corman lawsuit.[351] Within a year of the Corman lawsuit, Covey became exasperated with all of the NCAA maneuvers to defeat the lawsuit before it could come to trial.

The NCAA's argument that the Consent Decree had been a "good-faith, bargained contract with Penn State to correct violations of the governing body's constitution and bylaws" was a strategic mistake by the NCAA. It was the opening that Corman's lawyer, Matthew Haverstick of Philadelphia, used to expand the challenge to the $60 million fine distribution to question the legality of the entire Consent Decree. Haverstick decided to question the bylaws of the NCAA to see if it even had the legal right to punish Penn State with the Consent Decree. Haverstick believed that the NCAA made a tactical error by bringing up the NCAA constitution and bylaws into the discussion of the Endowment Act and the Corman lawsuit. By April of 2014, Covey's Commonwealth Court began to question the legitimacy of the consent decree as the judge noted the "discrepancies between the consent decree and the N.C.A.A. bylaws."[352] By October of that year, Judge Covey ruled "the NCAA could not avoid the forthcoming trial on the validity of the Consent Decree merely by agreeing to comply with the Endowment Act." She reasoned, "This Court has *three times* declared that the Endowment Act withstands each of the constitutional challenges lodged by the NCAA." Thus, she stated, "only the validity of the Consent Decree remains an open question" as she castigated the attempted "NCAA's end run around this court."[353] The NCAA was certainly in defensive mode from this point onward knowing that Commonwealth Court Judge Covey and likely the future jury chosen from among Pennsylvanians would not be on the side of an out-of-state organization from Indiana.

The depositions for the coming Corman v. NCAA trial further decimated what remained of the NCAA defense of the ill-fated Consent Decree. When Mark Emmert gave his sworn pre-trial deposition testimony in late 2014, he was questioned about a response he gave to an email from Kathy Redmond, a training specialist in campus sexual abuse. Emmert had received Redmond's message the day after his threatening letter to Penn State's president Rod Erickson on November 17, 1011. Emmert's letter to Erickson contained potentially ominous penalties Penn State might receive from what Emmert claimed were administrative abuses. The abuses, Emmert noted in his letter to Erickson, appeared "to have been actions starkly contrary to the value of higher education as well as the NCAA" and showed "deceitful and dishonest behavior."[354] Emmert responded to Redmond, who had suggested to Emmert that he should contact a former Emmert colleague who had ammunition about Penn State's role in the Sandusky Scandal. That individual was Vicky Triponey, the person who was earlier forced out as Penn State Vice President for Student Affairs by Joe Paterno and President Spanier. Emmert thanked Kathy Redmond for the information. Then, he told her that in the Penn State situation "we cannot miss the opportunity "*to leverage the moment.*"[355]

To Corman's lawyer, Matthew Haverstick, the statement "to leverage the moment" would allow him to hammer into the heads of the forthcoming jury that Emmert and the NCAA had "subverted the normal infractions process, coercing Penn State into accepting the consent decree under threat of the so-call death penalty" through its leverage.[356] Since Corman's original bill to keep $60 million within Pennsylvania passed with a 99% majority, there was the likelihood that other Pennsylvania citizens chosen as jurors would vent the same negative feelings about the NCAA and the Consent Decree's punishments handed out to Penn State.

Both Senator Corman and Mark Emmert's NCAA could gain by settling out of court after Judge Covey finally set the trial date for February 17, 2015. If Corman, through attorney Haverstick, could get the NCAA to abrogate most of the provisions of the Consent Decree, he would not only satisfy many Pennsylvanians, who had been condemning the NCAA for its actions, but he would gain political points for doing so. Senator Corman had just won a disputed election for Majority Leader of the Senate following the November 2014 election in which conservative Republicans gained additional control of both state houses. A victory over the NCAA would better entrench him in the Senate and in his electoral district. For Mark Emmert, giving up the Consent Decree after about two years could be rationalized because Penn State had met all of the Freeh Report recommendations for changes at Penn State and the $60 million could finally be used for the reducing child abuse.

More important, however, to the strength of the NCAA, the new agreement between the NCAA and Penn State stated, "Penn State acknowledges the NCAA's legitimate and good faith interest and concern regarding the Jerry Sandusky matter." "Good faith interest," could have and probably should have been challenged by Senator Corman, but was not. In other words, according to the NCAA reasoning, "Today's agreement with Penn State reaffirms our authority to act," stated a member of the NCAA Board of Governors.[357] The real losers of the case, the NCAA and Emmert, could and did "spin" their own positive outcome.

Revelations of Depositions and Exhibits

The revelations from the Corman lawsuit spread to the general populace when the senator released the entire, nearly 5,000-pages of case documents. There were 16 day-long depositions from individuals, nine from the NCAA, six from Penn State, and Jake Corman's.[358] Depositions are examinations under sworn testimony of key individuals before trial. The depositions and the massive number of emails and documents on both sides of the controversy gave a much different story than that which the NCAA was weaving almost as soon as the Sandusky revelations became public over three years before. From several thousand pages of depositions and 229 exhibits containing far more emails and documents, the Corman team of lawyers disputed the Penn State culture problem found in the Freeh Report and repeated by the NCAA. Corman and his lawyers emphasized that there was a greater culture problem within the NCAA than at Penn State, and President Mark Emmert led it. "The NCAA," Corman stated, "was looking to improve its own image at the expense of Penn State."[359] Matt Haverstick, Corman's attorney, reflected on the NCAA: There was a "new sheriff in town; this was going to show the N.C.A.A. as a tough, effective enforcer. Penn State just happened at the right time for them."[360]

The legal documents from the Corman v. NCAA depositions and exhibits told a much different story than was found in the Consent Decree and that the wrong party may have been nailed to the crossbar erected for the Nittany Lions. For instance, when the Corman lawyer was attempting to find out from Mark Emmert in his deposition how he dealt with illegal activities at two of Mark Emmert's former institutions, Emmert "conveniently" forgot much of his leadership history at the University of Connecticut and Louisiana State University. Of the NCAA investigation of illegal help for athletes from athletic counseling at LSU and being put on probation, Emmert said, "I don't remember the details of it. . . ." "Were there sanctions?" he was asked, and he responded, "I don't remember the details of them." Again, Emmert stated, "I don't recall that," when he was asked if there was a separate civil whistleblower suit" in the LSU case. How could he not remember? In his testimony, he evaded well over a hundred times by saying "I don't remember," "I don't recall," or "I don't know" to questions that a person so closely tied to the Consent Decree sanctions would likely have remembered.[361] Emmert might have quoted Shakespeare's *Julius Caesar*, "I came to bury Caesar, not to praise him," when he tried to wipe out both his previous commendations of Joe Paterno and Penn State.[362] The other individual so closely tied to the writing of the Consent Decree, Donald Remy, had an easier time when deposed because he could remain silent and conveniently claim the often-used attorney-client privilege for being NCAA Counsel.

The Corman Case "Statement of Findings"

In the planned lawsuit that was never consummated, the "Statement of Findings" by the Corman team read like the opening statement in a courtroom. Why the NCAA caved into Corman can be found in four concise and well-documented pages released by Corman a few weeks following the dismantling of the Consent Decree. The "Findings" began by stating that the NCAA rescinded Emmert's request of November 17, 2011 for Penn State to answer four basic questions, deciding to rely "solely on the findings of the Freeh Report" to justify the Consent Decree.[363] Only four months before, the NCAA held a presidential retreat in which NCAA leaders sought to "make a bold stroke for reform of college athletics." Once the supposedly independent Freeh investigation began, the NCAA and Big Ten "injected themselves" with regular calls on the status of the "independent" Freeh investigation. They gave the Freeh Group a formal power point presentation and proposed questions to ask potential interviewees, suggested individuals to interview, and provided search terms for document collection and review by the Freeh investigators.[364]

The Corman team "Findings" showed that the "extremely image conscious" Emmert and the NCAA wanted to "leverage the moment" in history, banking on the fact that Penn State was "so embarrassed they will do anything" including the acceptance of the unprecedented sanctions leveled on the Nittany Lions.[365] Convincing President Erickson that the NCAA Executive Committee "wanted blood" and at first was overwhelmingly in favor of the "Death Penalty," Mark Emmert used the death penalty threat that was "unequivocally on the table," to "deceive and manipulate both the NCAA Executive Committee and Penn State to achieve his 'plan' on how to respond to the Penn State matter." From the July 12, 2012 Freeh Report release and 11 days later the signing of the Consent Decree was a "rush to judgment" with a pre-printed execution date for the Consent Decree three days before it was signed. In that period of time, "the NCAA progressively increased the penalties set forth in the Decree," with the example of increasing the fine from $30 million to $60 million. The NCAA demanded, Corman stated, that the findings of the Freeh Report be accepted as part of the Consent Decree "cram down" proposition.[366]

In short, the Corman team believed the NCAA "lacked legal authority to impose the Consent Decree," relying on the NCAA Constitution, Article

4.1.2(e) that does not give it that power but only permits "adopting and implementing policies to resolve core issues." There was no provision in the NCAA Constitution or Bylaws for the NCAA Executive Committee to impose a Consent Decree as admitted by the NCAA administrator, David Berst, with four decades tenure at the NCAA.[367] Thus the Corman team felt confident that any jury trial with the NCAA led by Mark Emmert, who Corman felt was not credible, would likely end up in a victory for Corman over the NCAA. The situation before the trial in early 2015 looked dire for the NCAA.

Nevertheless, the NCAA with a half-billion dollars in reserve could easily have afforded the legal battle, if it thought it had some reasonable chance of winning. If it settled out of court, it would cost the NCAA much less, even if it paid the legal expenses of Corman and the state of Pennsylvania as part of the out-of-court settlement. It could also justify eliminating the Consent Decree by saying that now there would be $60 million available that could be used to help prevent child abuse. In addition, Emmert could brag that Senator Mitchell's reports, as Athletics Integrity Monitor, had given Penn State a clean bill of health and thus the football team could return to competition on a level playing field, something that had been missing for the past three seasons. The NCAA could return to other business without the potential loss of an important lawsuit and concentrate on operating another successful March Madness basketball tournament that would bring a significant portion of a billion dollars into its treasury. That money could be used, when, as the NCAA stated in its official spin on the Corman case, "the NCAA will aggressively defend the Paterno estate's challenge to the validity of the now-replaced consent decree."[368] The NCAA may have believed that by settling the Corman Case, it would be easier to win the Paterno Family challenge. That may have been true.

The Paterno Family Critique Reflects the Corman Suit

Or perhaps the NCAA felt that the pending Paterno Family lawsuit would be settled in a similar manner to the Corman case. That proposition was not likely, because the Paterno situation was an attempt to save the reputation of Joe Paterno from further deterioration and raise his status to its once loftier iconic state. Achieving justice for Penn State and saving face for the Paterno family appeared to be a greater motivator than keeping Pennsylvania money in Pennsylvania and restoring 212 football victories to the Penn State football team or even restoring all the football scholarships the NCAA had removed. The Corman case, for all it had done, had not achieved justice solely by eliminating most of the NCAA judgments against Penn State. The NCAA had gotten off easily and was not punished for violating its own constitution and bylaws.

In many ways, the Paterno Family Critique and eventual lawsuit were similar to the Corman case. Both were aimed at the illegal Consent Decree in which the Paterno family and Penn State suffered "extensive, substantial harm" as NCAA leaders continued "their unlawful conduct by threatening to impose 'harsher sanctions' and even the 'death penalty'" if Penn State did not cooperate. As in the Corman suit, Mark Emmert and NCAA Executive Committee Chair Ed Ray "ignored their own rules and denied plaintiffs any of the rights and process to which plaintiffs were entitled." Further, the Paterno group claimed the NCAA ignored its own rules including that it had "no authority to interfere in a criminal investigation to address a matter that has nothing to do with athletic competition."[369] That the Corman case and the Paterno Family eventually joined forces when they conducted a joint deposition from Oregon State president Ed Ray in late 2014, was a further indication that the two cases were similar in nature.[370]

Unlike state Senator Jake Corman, the Paterno Family challenged the Consent Decree within days, not months, of the illegal NCAA Consent Decree action foisted on Penn State. Lead lawyer for the Paterno Family, Wick Sollers, sent a letter to Mark Emmert and the NCAA less than a fortnight following the signing of the July 23, 2012 Consent Decree. The letter gave notice of the intent to appeal the Consent Decree based on the NCAA acting "hastily and without any regard for due process" built on the "deeply flawed" conclusion that was "incomplete, rife with unsupported opinions and unquestionably one-sided." The strongly worded notice to the NCAA concluded, "to severely punish a University and its community and to condemn a great educator, philanthropist and coach without any public review or hearing is unfair on its face and a violation of NCAA guidelines."[371] Nevertheless, it would be almost 10 months before the Paterno Family lawsuit would be brought against Emmert and the NCAA.

Originally, the Paterno Family lawsuit encompassed far more individuals than those just in the Paterno family. It was reinforced with the names of members of the board of trustees, Penn State faculty, former football coaches, and former football players. These included trustees, Al Clemons, Peter Khoury, Anthony Lubrano, Ryan McCombie, and Adam Taliaferro; faculty, Peter Bordi, Terry Engelder, Spencer Niles, and John O'Donnell; former coaches, William Kenney and Jay Paterno (Joe Paterno's son); and former players, Anthony Adams, Gerald Cadogan, Shamar Finnay, Josh Gaines, Richard Gardner, Justin Kurpeikis, Patrick Mauti, Anwar Phillips, and Michael Robinson.[372]

Prior to the May 2013 lawsuit, the Paterno Family decided to fully dissect, and if possible destroy, the Freeh Report. The day the Freeh Report-based Consent Decree was released, the Paterno Family announced "the sanctions announced by the N.C.A.A today defame the legacy and contributions of a great coach and educator without any input from our family or those who knew him best."[373] The immediate reaction resulted in a document released a half-year later in the Paterno Family rebuttal to the Freeh Report, what it called *Critique of the Freeh Report: The Rush to Injustice Regarding Joe Paterno.*" The *Critique* was well over 200 pages in length, nearly as long as the Freeh Report, and included lengthy criticism of the Freeh Report by three legal, medical, and psychological experts, giving a lie to both facts and conclusions found in the Freeh Report. One of the three hired by the Paterno Family was the highly visible former U.S. attorney general, governor of Pennsylvania, and federal prosecutor, Dick Thornburgh. His 40-page rebuttal to the Freeh Report claimed that the Freeh Report was "seriously flawed, both with respect to the process of the SIC's [Freeh] investigation and its findings related to Mr. Paterno." He specified the Freeh Report findings were "not accurate, supportable or fair."[374]

Agreeing that the Freeh Report was fatally flawed was a medical doctor psychiatrist from Johns Hopkins Hospital and expert in child abuse, Fred Berlin. He concluded his report claiming "the lack of factual support for the [Freeh Report's] inaccurate and unfounded findings . . . and its numerous process-oriented deficiencies was a rush to injustice and calls into question the credibility of the entire Report." In addition, Berlin called the Freeh Report "irresponsible and self-serving."[375]

A much more nuanced report was that of Jim Clemente, a former Federal Bureau of Investigation profiler, prosecutor, and child abuse expert. With well-documented reasoning, Clemente stated that the Freeh Report investigators "failed to properly factor in the dynamics of acquaintance child sexual victimization into their investigation. Consequently," Clemente reasoned, the Freeh Report "misinterpreted evidence and behavior and reached erroneous conclusions." Clemente, a victim of childhood abuse himself, offered a lengthy analysis of the 1998 and 2001 Sandusky-child incidents, the only two in which the four Penn State administrators were involved. He concluded that "nice-guy" acquaintance offenders, such as Sandusky, conduct their criminal activities right under the noses of society and shouldn't be blamed as a result of the "culture of college football." He charged that the Freeh investigators "did not find any actual evidence of an agreement to conceal between Curley, Schultz, Spanier, and Paterno."[376] Thus, the NCAA erroneously using the Freeh Report as fact condemned Penn State and resulted in Penn State being penalized unjustly for unproven evidences in the forced Consent Decree.

Reaction to "The Paterno Report"

The Paterno Report condemning the Freeh Report drew quick reactions but hardly any quicker than that of Louis Freeh. Within a day of the *Critique* release, Louis Freeh had a response to the Paterno Report calling it a "self-serving report," which, of course, it was. Freeh gratuitously stated, "I respect the right of the Paterno family to hire private lawyers and former government officials to conduct public media campaigns in an effort to shape the legacy of Joe Paterno," but he emphasized this "does not change the facts established in the Freeh Report. . . ." He then quoted from the 1998 and 2001 emails among Graham Spanier, Gary Schultz, and Tim Curley that were used as the basis of the Freeh Report condemnation of the Penn State leaders. He used these to bolster his argument that those three plus Joe Paterno "failed to protect against a child sexual predator harming children for over a decade." Freeh then exaggerated with his condemnation of Paterno when he wrote that "Paterno was on notice for at least 13 years that Sandusky. . . was a probable serial pedophile."[377] One may recall that child welfare workers, police, and the district attorney dismissed the 1998 incident. So the 2001 child-shower incident reported to Joe Paterno by Mike McQueary was the single "notice for at least 13 years" for condemnation of Paterno.

For those, other than Louis Freeh, who wanted to condemn the Paterno Family and Joe Paterno's involvement in the Sandusky Scandal, it was rather easy to call the Paterno *Critique* a weak attempt at trying to dismiss Joe Paterno's involvement. One could point out the damning emails revealed in the Freeh Report from those saved by Gary Schultz. One in particular was the use of the term "coach" in which it is quite clear that it referred to Paterno, but the Paterno Critique indicated that it may well have been referring to Jerry Sandusky.[378] It may be that the Critique came well after most people had made up their minds about Paterno and his involvement in the Sandusky Scandal.

With the out-of-court settlement of the Corman-NCAA lawsuit in 2015 and the highly visible Paterno Family *Critique of the Freeh Report,* actions against the illegal sanctions by the NCAA and impugning of Joe Paterno were left principally to a Paterno Family lawsuit. The Paterno Family, right after the Corman suit conclusion, stated it intended "to continue the job of uncovering the full truth in this case."[379] For the next few years, the lawsuit would linger in court. Both sides apparently had plenty of money needed to carry out the litigation. With the pending trial, the trustworthiness of the NCAA was to be tested. More importantly to the Paterno Family and many others, Joe Paterno's legacy was at stake.

Chapter 8

The Joe Paterno Legacy and the Consent Decree

If thou wouldest win Immortality of Name,
either do Things worth the Writing or write Things worth the Reading.
Thomas Fuller, ca. 1660

"If we're so able to vividly remember the worst a man did,
can't we also remember the best?"
Adam Taliaferro, 2012

To many people, the most damning action taken by NCAA President Emmert and Counsel Donald Remy in the Consent Decree was taking 111 victories away from coach Joe Paterno for the years 1998 through 2011. This action dropped him from number one historically, with 409 victories, to fifth place all-time. The dates reflected the time from the first report of a boy sexually violated by Jerry Sandusky to the end of Paterno's career. Taking victories away from a coach who never had a major violation of NCAA rules in his 61 years of coaching at Penn State, 46 as head coach, brought an outpouring of anger to many who had followed Paterno's career. In addition, it should be noted that Paterno was never accused of any criminal actions in the Sandusky Scandal. Of all the myriad penalties foisted on Penn State, this was the one intended to destroy the legacy of Joe Paterno. Being the coach with the most victories in major college football, 409, was the single achievement in his illustrious career that stood out to many people since he took over as head coach in 1966. The Consent Decree stated emphatically, "Head Football Coach Joseph V. Paterno failed to protect against a child sexual predator harming children for over a decade" and "repeatedly concealed critical facts relating to Sandusky's child abuse from the authorities. . . ."[380] The legacy of Paterno was besmirched by this action as much as any that the NCAA could have taken. Could a lawsuit by the Paterno Family following Joe Paterno's death do two things—determine the illegality of the Consent Decree and help restore the legacy of Joe Paterno?

The Legacy Began with Wins

When counsel for the Paterno Family responded to the Consent Decree and the Freeh Report supporting it, lead attorney Wick Sollers was in effect making a major attempt to restore the legacy of Joe Paterno by challenging the illegal document forced upon Penn State. With hardly an exception, college coaching legacies begin exclusively with winning records. This was true in football with Knute Rockne at Notre Dame; General Robert Neyland at Tennessee; Bud Wilkinson at Oklahoma; and Bear Bryant at Alabama, Texas A&M, and Kentucky. In men's and women's basketball it was similar with Adolph Rupp at Kentucky; John Wooden at UCLA; Dean Smith at North Carolina; Pat Head Summit at Tennessee; Geno Auriemma at Connecticut, and Mike Krzyzewski at Duke. At Penn State, the now-lost legacy of Hugo Bezdek from the 1920s began with a 30-game streak without a loss.[381] About a half-century later, the legacy for Joe Paterno began, not with something known as the "Grand Experiment," but with a 31-game unbeaten streak starting in his second season as head coach. Thus the 31-game streak without a loss near the beginning and the 409 victories at the end were the crown jewels. In between, the "Grand Experiment," the "success with honor," the national championships, five undefeated seasons, and the extraordinary fund raising and academic support by Paterno for Penn State University came as a result of a record of success on the field of play. It was how Paterno expanded upon his athletic success that brought him the accolades, iconic image, and his eventual legacy.

Beginning his career as head coach in 1966, Paterno had a cumulative losing record when Penn State lost its first game to underdog Navy in his second season. Thus he was five wins and six losses in his first 11 games. The sports editor for the Penn State *Daily Collegian* wrote that Paterno "didn't quite have what it takes to be a head coach at a big university."[382] Yet, with only one more loss early in the season, Penn State went on to be undefeated the rest of that year, the next season, and the one following. Paterno's star had risen abruptly. This bright and articulate coach would continue to be idolized despite how his assistant coaching elder, Jim O'Hara, described him after Paterno lived with O'Hara's family for a decade. Paterno, O'Hara said, had a "fiery temper, a 'short fuse,'" while being "impetuous, impatient, and critical of those who did not agree with him."[383] Or as Paterno put it himself, "I was a know-it-all, we'd get into meetings and I'd be screaming and shouting."[384] To the author, Bernie Asbell, who helped write his autobiography, Paterno said he was "a damn loudmouth, unable to keep quiet. . . . I was too sure of myself to listen to others. . . ."[385] These qualities on the inside of the football operation may have combined effectively with his external personality of being witty while articulating his Grand Experiment program to the larger public. Paterno was on his way to becoming a legend in his own time.

Celebrity Status Following the New England Patriot's Offer

Wins continued as his celebrity status grew. Paterno was offered the University of Michigan position after his first undefeated season in 1968, but the more than a million dollars proposal from the New England Patriots after the 1972 season to coach in the National Football League gave him an almost mystical quality to a number of people. Why would a coach turn down a million dollars to coach and have part ownership of a professional team, and live in New England where he graduated from an Ivy League institution? (In 1973, Paterno's salary was $33,192 a year for the next three years.[386]) After verbally agreeing with Patriot owner, Billy Sullivan, to come to Massachusetts, he changed his mind by the next morning. In his public relations statement, Paterno noted that he "had a dream that Penn State could be the greatest in everything, whether it was a library, whether it was the soccer team. . . I feel that I can still make some sort of contribution to some of those goals. The challenge of that is what kept me." It may also have been that Sue Paterno loved bringing up their growing family in Happy Valley in her home state of Pennsylvania. Agreeing with Paterno's decision, President John Oswald, a former football captain at DePauw University in Indiana, stated, "Coach Paterno's value to the University goes far beyond his work with the football team. His quest for excellence in all things, his keen intelligence, his style and his sense of humor add distinction to the entire University community."[387]

After Paterno turned down the lucrative New England Patriot offer following a strong "Joe Don't Go Pro" campaign by Mimi Barash Coppersmith, a local entrepreneur, Pennsylvania's governor, Milton

Shapp, proclaimed a Joe Paterno Day at the end of March of 1973. To celebrate the event, a Lutheran minister and backer of Paterno, Elton Richards, arranged a testimonial dinner before more than 700 fans near Harrisburg at an expensive $25 a plate dinner. There, the coach was given a new auto and a vacation trip to Italy to include a private audience with Pope Paul VI—where, someone quipped, Paterno would be canonized. Mentioned as the "Man from Nazareth," an alumnus of Brown University, Paterno's alma mater, referred to the new Paterno book, *Football My Way*, as the "First Book of Paterno."[388] If he was not canonized, he certainly was crowned that night in the Commonwealth of Pennsylvania.

The Commencement Address

There was enough adulation for Penn State to invite the celebrated coach to deliver the commencement address for the 1973 graduation ceremony in Beaver Stadium. For a football coach to deliver the commencement address at any institution was an unusual event. It had never been done at Penn State, even when Hugo Bezdek was winning an unprecedented number of victories in the 1920s, and he was making more money coaching than the Penn State president was paid.[389] No one as well known as Paterno had been invited to give a Penn State commencement address since Dwight Eisenhower and Nelson Rockefeller in the mid-1950s. No one would again do so until Bill Clinton in the mid-1990s. Because of the legacy Paterno eventually achieved, no commencement address has been quoted like that of the eventual Hall of Fame coach. While few commencement addresses are remembered, Paterno endeared himself with his polished and quotable talk from the most recognized individual in Penn State's history.

Paterno began by saying he accepted the invitation by President Oswald "because I realize that in a day when materialism is rampant, many of you felt that my interest in doing other things beside making money has in some way helped you to reaffirm your deal of a life of service, of dignity, and of a life of meaning which goes beyond financial success."[390] His recent turning down a million dollar deal with the New England Patriots, and staying at Penn State with a $33,000 salary, came to endear him among Penn Staters. Endearment continued as Paterno gave his best-known line after he noted that other commencement speakers would give an "opinion on Watergate," the President Richard Nixon scandal, but

Paterno wouldn't. Then he said with emphasis, "I'd like to know, how could the president know so little about Watergate in 1973 and so much about college football in 1969?"[391] A roar came from the 18,000 seated in the about-to-rain, then 57,530-seat, Beaver Stadium. The cover-up by President Richard Nixon in the Watergate break-in was certainly on the minds of Americans that year, and Penn State fans didn't forget Nixon proclaiming the winner of the 1969 Texas-Arkansas game the national champion while snubbing Penn State, undefeated for the past two years.

More important to the historical Jerry Sandusky Scandal were several comments Paterno made in his commencement address. Surely Joe Paterno could not have known in 1973 what would come to light in 1998, 2001, and again with the Pennsylvania Grand Jury presentment in November of 2011, when he uttered, "Don't underestimate the world—it can corrupt quickly and completely." Neither was he thinking of high-ranking Penn State administrators when he told the new graduates, "We shall act, and we shall act with good intentions. Hopefully, we will often be right, but at times, we will be wrong. When we are, let us admit it and immediately try to right the situation." Paterno was referring to losing the Vietnam War not to the Sandusky Scandal when he said, when individuals are wrong "let us admit it and immediately try to right the situation. . . ," for "we stand bigger for admitting it."[392] The coach never publicly admitted that any of the Penn State administrators were wrong in how they dealt with the Sandusky Scandal, although he admitted he, personally, should have done more—that he "backed away."[393] "Success without honor," Paterno emphasized in 1973, "is an unseasoned dish, it will satisfy your hunger, but it won't taste good."[394] The wisdom Paterno uttered in his commencement address was touted as coming from an individual with integrity and far more than just a successful coach at a big-time university. The talk before about 4,600 graduates has been quoted with regularity over the decades—a salute to "canonization" of iconic Paterno.

Only a few months after his Commencement Address, Paterno's third undefeated football team was led by Penn State's only Heisman Trophy winner, John Cappelletti. What the star running back did that season on the field was capped off at the Heisman Trophy Award ceremony. Cappelletti's acceptance speech, with Joe Paterno at his side, could not have been more symbolic of the quality Paterno sought for players in his Grand Experiment. Cappelletti showed that he was well educated, articulate, and compassionate when he praised his younger brother, Joey, who had fought a much harder battle struggling with leukemia as an eleven-year old than Cappelletti experienced in his football uniform. "You get the bumps and bruises. . . on the field," Cappelletti said as his eyes began to well-up, but for Joey, who takes shots every other day and very painful bone marrow tests, "he never complains, he never asks why; he accepts it but refuses to give up." Joey was the inspiration for Cappelletti who stated, "this trophy is more his than mine."[395] Cappelletti's talk from the heart appeared to be a true measure of the success of Joe Paterno's Grand Experiment in turning out players such as John Cappelletti. Only days after the Heisman Award, Paterno was honored in the "Saints & Sinners Roast" of the coach, after which Paterno donated his $1,000 fee to the Children's Hospital in Philadelphia in the name of Joey Cappelletti.[396]

The Championship is Finally Gained

Even with three undefeated teams and a winning record unsurpassed by other coaches, Paterno lacked having a national championship in his ledger. If Paterno's brother George was correct when he said, "Joe's the most intensively competitive person I've ever known," not winning a national championship must have gnawed at him continuously as he compiled undefeated or nearly undefeated teams year after year.[397] After the 1969 season, following two undefeated seasons, the Penn State coach popped off about President Nixon knowing about football by awarding Texas the national championship, while not knowing about the Watergate break-in. Several years later following the undefeated season paced by Heisman Trophy winner, John Cappelletti, he procured championship rings for the team, though the team never reached that distinction in the polls.[398] After losing the 1978 national championship in a Sugar Bowl game against Alabama in which questionable play calls came from the bench followed by a 12-men on the field penalty proved costly, Paterno nearly resigned as coach, believing that Bear Bryant outcoached him. He told a *Sports Illustrated* reporter, "In the eyes of a lot of people, we have to win a national championship or else Joe Paterno and the Grand Experiment are both failures."[399]

It was likely his belief, for he began asking Penn State presidents to allow more "presidential admits" and bringing in academically deficient but star athletes to better compete for national championships.[400]

Presidential admits were not condoned at Penn State dating back to the coach Rip Engle and athletic director Ernie McCoy era of the 1950s and 1960s. Nevertheless, the strategy of allowing academically inferior athletes into Penn State worked. In 1982, with the efforts of a number of those admits, Penn State defeated Georgia for its first national championship. While previously Paterno had been crowned with undefeated seasons, had rejected a million dollar offer by professional football, and given a graduation address, he was now idolized, often worshiped, by admirers of the coach as a national champion.

Paterno and the Gift of Giving

Charitable giving, such as the Children's Hospital donation, began early in Paterno's head coaching tenure, and it continued throughout his career and even after his firing and subsequent death. Though Paterno may have given his legacy much less thought than winning a national championship, the maxim of the seventeenth century Englishman, Thomas Fuller, seems appropriate. "If thou Wouldest win Immortality of Name," the clergyman wrote, "either do Things worth the Writing or write Things worth the Reading."[401] Paterno did little writing, but he did many things worth writing about. Much was about giving. It began in the 1970s when he and Sue had five children to raise in their modest home. Nevertheless, he had a significant income in addition to his more than adequate salary of $33,000 in 1973 and $55,000 five years later. He had additionally thousands of dollars coming from summer football camps, radio and television shows, bowl game bonuses, product endorsements, and cash bonuses awarded by the Penn State president.[402] In the 1980s, after winning his first national championship, Joe and Sue Paterno began to make significant financial gifts, especially to Penn State. In 1986, the year the Penn State football team would win its second national championship, the Paternos gave $100,000 to the Penn State library and $50,000 for scholarships to minority students.[403] This was part of the first successful major capital campaign in Penn State's history, "The Campaign for Penn State." Paterno started it all. The Paterno campaign for money for Penn State came after the 1982 national championship victory over Georgia, when Paterno was asked to speak before the board of trustees. In that talk, rather than wax eloquently over the triumph for him and his team, he berated the trustees. "Basically, the Board is in a lot of ways reactionary. . . .," Paterno told the board, for the board needed to get out front and "raise money so we can endow chairs for star professors." He told the trustees that it needed a three-year fund-raising campaign so that not only the football team could be number one, but also that the academic departments could be rated in a similar manner.[404] Paterno's desire to seize the moment and quickly raise $10 million, turned into a $352 million capital "Campaign for Penn State," of which Paterno was co-chair.

In Paterno's trustee talk after his first national championship, he told the 32 trustees "without a great library, you can't have a great university."[405] It took a decade, but Stuart Forth, Dean of Penn State Libraries, eventually went directly to Paterno to ask for his support for a large library addition. Even though Forth's action bypassed and offended the Penn State Office of Gifts and Endowments, Paterno by this time had so much influence that Penn State president Joab Thomas initiated a specific "Campaign for the Library.[406] Joe and Sue Paterno gave a quarter million dollar gift and combined with other contributions, many by Joe Paterno's own solicitations, nearly $14 million was raised. It added to the state's contribution for the $34 million structure, named the Joe and Sue Paterno Library. As much as Paterno enjoyed having the library named after the two of them, he had tried to get William Schreyer, president of the board of trustees and head of the financial services firm of Merrill Lynch, to give $7 million to have Schreyer's name attached to the library.[407] Schreyer declined, but he soon contributed over $50 million to endow the Schreyer Honors College. After the Sandusky Scandal broke and the Consent Decree was about to be signed, the Joe Paterno bronze statue was purged from its stadium setting, but the Paterno name remained on the library.

Acts of giving continued on an accelerated basis during the last three decades of Paterno's life as he and Sue Paterno contributed significantly to the liberal arts field, including the library. In 1984, they endowed the library with a $120,000 gift, and also directed royalties from the sale of Penn State Paterno memorabilia into the fund.[408] Then in 1995, Paterno directed a $100,000 gift from the Union Pacific Corporation as a contribution to the University Library.[409] Paterno and his wife also endowed a professorship in University Libraries, and even after he was fired, the Paternos gave the library a $50,000 gift.[410]

Contributions to the Penn State libraries were only a small part of the Paternos' gifts to the University and thus contributing greatly to his (and

Sue's) legacy. Shortly after chiding the board of trustees into a major fund raising effort after his first national championship, the Paternos created endowed scholarships for minority students. In addition, a scholarship in the classics in the College of Liberal Arts was created under the name of his high school teacher, Rev. Thomas Bermingham, SJ. The Catholic priest had convinced Paterno to read and translate from Latin the *Aeneid* by the ancient Roman writer, Virgil. A graduate fellowship in Liberal Arts was created honoring Paterno's parents. Graduate and undergraduate scholarships were created in the School of Architecture and Landscape Architecture honoring Sue Paterno's mother and father. A Paterno Fellows program for undergraduates was begun in partnership with the Schreyer Honors College.[411]

The Paternos also contributed to teaching and research, especially in the liberal arts, of which both Paternos were literature majors. Joe graduated from Brown University in 1950 and Sue from Penn State a dozen years later. In 2001, a newly funded position, the Paterno Family Professor in Literature, attracted a leader, a prominent cultural critic and professor of literature, Michael Bérubé.[412] As an individual who appreciated ancient literature, Joe Paterno was instrumental in saving the study of classics at Penn State in the 1990s. Susan Welch, the Dean of the College of Liberals Arts, planned to drop classics for lack of enrollment, but the powerful Paterno, suggested it would be a bad decision. He convinced the Dean that if classics were retained, he would help to financially fund it. As a result of Paterno's persuasion, a new Department of Classics and Mediterranean Studies was created.[413] The Paternos' substantial endowment of the new department was an indication of the power one individual, a football coach, might have over the educational development of a university. As part of the Grand Destiny capital campaign at Penn State from 1996-2003, over $50 million was raised for the liberal arts in the $1.3 billion effort. Both Sue and Joe Paterno served on the Liberal Arts Development Council for the successful campaign. While the Grand Destiny campaign was going on, the Paternos created the Paterno Family Fund in the Richards Civil War Era Centre, for better understanding the implications of a central event in American history. No one at Penn State had a greater impact on the visibility of the liberal arts than either Joe or Sue Paterno.

Although suggestions to rename Beaver Stadium for Joe Paterno came as early as 1991, there were other ways for which Joe Paterno's achievements were recognized.[414] One was the creation of an All-Sports Museum at Penn State. With a push by Paterno, the museum was constructed as part of the 2001 stadium expansion to 107,000 seats. When the museum opened the next year, it was much more than a testament to football success at Penn State. The gallery featured all sports dating back (almost) to the first baseball game played in Lock Haven in 1866, a year after the Civil War ended, and the first football game, rugby style, played in 1881 in Lewisburg.[415] The museum might have been the site for the Joe Paterno bronze statue. The iconic representation was dedicated at the time of the stadium expansion the week after Joe Paterno's 324th victory, surpassing Alabama's Bear Bryant. Rather than being placed within the museum, the statue was placed outside the stadium. There it remained until hours before President Rod Erickson signed the NCAA Consent Decree. It was then hidden away, but there were those who believed a good venue for the statue to be out of danger would be in the All-Sports Museum. This facility was another of Paterno's dreams, for which he contributed a quarter-million dollars. It came true well before the Sandusky Scandal exploded.[416]

The Legacy Damaged and the Underside Revealed

A year after Joe Paterno's death, the individual most responsible for putting the All-Sports Museum together, Lou Prato, stated that "Maybe by the 25th anniversary of his death, the statue will be back up, raised back up from this disgrace." To Prato, "Joe's legacy is still to be determined."[417] Less than one year following his death, the statue was hidden away in storage, while Paterno's life-sized image painted conspicuously on a State College wall had had its halo removed. Meanwhile his name had been removed from a Nike child day-care center in Oregon by co-founder, Phil Knight. Further, "Paternoville," the student encampment at the stadium prior to football games, had been renamed "Nittanyville." The Big Ten removed Paterno's name from the Stagg-Paterno Big Ten Championship Trophy, and the NCAA had eliminated 111 of his victories. The NCAA also vacated his 2011 honor of winning the NCAA Gerald R. Ford Award for his career leadership in intercollegiate athletics. In other efforts damaging his legacy, the sale of Paterno memorabilia was discontinued by Penn State, and even a sandwich named the "Joegies," was eliminated at a campus eatery. These were only the most visible attempts to distance the Paterno image from the American conscience. As Jim Meister, a past president of the Penn State Quarterback Club, stated, Paterno "doesn't exist anymore in the lore of Penn State."[418]

Paterno's underside was beginning to be revealed more than it had ever been before. The negative aspects of Paterno's personality and deeds became magnified as people piled on the coach, for they believed and as Paterno stated, "I backed away" from the child molestation. This, despite the fact that he reported what he knew of the 2001 incident up the chain of command. If Paterno lacked visible empathy for victims of Jerry Sandusky, there were others who brought up incidents in Paterno's life that placed him in a darkened light. One of those dark spots came with his changed attitude toward sports reporters. Where once, early in his career, Paterno went out of his way to inform and entertain reporters, in later years it appeared to be more of a jousting match with sports journalists. Paterno complained that many attempted to "miseducate their readers, corrupt the meaning of athletics, and inflict unjustified pain on players." Sports writers, he once stated, are often "young, inexperienced, artless, and not very good."[419] A number of reporters believed that Paterno began to bully more than to inform them.

Paterno's penchant for bullying reporters came from those who raised questions that he did not want to answer or undercut the values of his Grand Experiment. Possibly the most egregious involved a young Penn State *Daily Collegian* reporter, Denise Bachman. She asked the coach if hypocrisy existed in his Grand Experiment when so many of his players were being cited for criminal violations or infringements of Penn State policy. Rather than deal with the difficult question, Paterno reacted to Bachman with "You're a smart ass and you can quote me on that." Using the power of the pen, the sports editor of the *Collegian* reacted to Paterno's outburst and soon reported, "Paterno is heading more in the direction of becoming the jackass he thought his [wayward] players were."[420] John Harvey, who was news adviser to the *Daily Collegian* for a dozen years mentoring student reporters and editors of the *Collegian,* agreed with Bachman. Following the NCAA Consent Decree, that highly criticized Paterno for allowing Jerry Sandusky to continue to exploit young boys, Harvey was not complimentary about Paterno's role with the press. "Paterno would belittle" student reporters, Harvey commented, "and the other reporters would chuckle along with him."[421] A number of biographers of Paterno have commented on his latter years of bullying, often from reporters, including Joe Posnanski,

Gene Wojciechowski, Pete Thamel, Bill Lyon, Frank Fitzpatrick, Jonathan Mahler, Michael O'Brien, and long-time local writer Ron Bracken.[422] In forty years of reporting local sports, Bracken pointed out the "intimidation bully factor" of Paterno, who, at times "put his foot right on your throat" if he disagreed with the reporting.[423]

Probably more important to the criticism of Paterno and his image was how he dealt with the criminal and illegal activity of football players. The criminal activity and violations of university policy of scholarship athletes at Penn State, like those in so many college football programs in America, far exceeded non-football players.[424] Violations included such actions as illegal drinking on campus, drunk driving, aggravated assault, burglary, and rape.[425] For many years of Paterno's tenure as head coach, he had an unwritten policy with the local police that, with most violations, the police should call him quickly if a football player were arrested. The coach would then dish out any punishment that he thought was appropriate. This would not be reported locally and thus no damage to the pristine image of Penn State football would occur. According to reporter Ron Bracken, the relationship with the police "created somewhat of a monster" because legally the athletes "weren't held accountable" for their actions. After observing Penn State football for most of Paterno's career, Bracken believed that this gave the football players "a feeling of diplomatic immunity."[426]

If there was a kind of diplomatic immunity for Paterno's players, there was no clearer example of it than in the middle of the first decade of the twenty-first century. As Paterno was closing his eighth decade of life and fourth decade of head coaching, he ran directly into conflict with the authorized university disciplinarian, the Vice President for Student Affairs, Vicky Triponey. The young administrator had ideas quite different from Paterno on how athletes should be treated for violations of Penn State policy. She wanted equal treatment with other students, not special treatment by the coach. She arrived on campus in 2003 just after a football player, Anwar Phillips, had been expelled from Penn State. He had been charged with a felony sexual assault, but Paterno allowed him to play in the Citrus Bowl in Orlando, Florida just days before the Spring term expulsion notice would take effect. To Paterno the playing of Phillips was "no business but mine," and he wanted to continue that policy.[427] Triponey would have to deal with similar cases in the months ahead, and she wanted to use her authority. Whose business was it to discipline wayward athletes, the coach or the mandated vice president for student affairs?

After several athlete assault cases in 2004 and 2005, in which Triponey tried to work with Paterno and the Athletic Department, she found Paterno impossible to work with as he wanted full control over his offending athletes. In the next two years, there was a power struggle of unequal entities, something similar on a more global stage a century before in which Teddy Roosevelt, the "bully pulpit" president of the United States, used his power to obtain the Panama Canal Zone in an effort to build a canal.[428] On an international scale in the early twentieth century, the U. S. won with a show of force—on the local level in the early twenty-first century, Joe Paterno was triumphant. Soon, Vicky Triponey was forced out of her position, just as a century before Colombia was forced out of the control of Panama. Joe Paterno won when he received the authority to discipline his players from President Graham Spanier.[429] The football program was protected by a newly modified justice system for athletes. While this series of incidents was kept quiet at the time, when it was revealed following the Jerry Sandusky Scandal, it only led to another blemish to the Paterno legacy.[430]

There were other cases of questionable behavior to decry the status that Joe Paterno had achieved over more than six decades of service to the university, but none was brought to national attention as were actions or inactions in the Jerry Sandusky case. Paterno had acted legally by reporting an alleged sexual misconduct up the chain of command. But to many, that was not enough. One important judgment was that of the judge, John Boccabella, who sentenced Graham Spanier, Gary Schultz, and Tim Curley to jail sentences for their actions in the Sandusky Scandal. Boccabella, in early 2017, opined that Paterno, "the legendary football coach, could have made that phone call [to police] without so much as getting his hands dirty" when Paterno was informed of Sandusky's actions by Michael McQueary in 2001.[431] The opinion that a person in his position could have and should have done more was often expressed. His ethics were questioned. Paterno's admitted that he "backed away," and that his statement "with the benefit of hindsight, I wish I had done more," were not principled responses.[432] Asked one critic, "Would he have done something more or differently if it were his son that was abused?"[433] Another responded that "the supposedly moral coach, the legendary molder of young men, when confronted with a choice between doing more to protect alleged child abuse and doing less to protect it chose to do the least required by law." The detractor wanted to know why a coach who wanted total control, didn't take total control over this incident.[434] A writer for *Christianity Today* concluded, "The one grand experiment that mattered most—his own ability to live up to success with honor—has failed."[435] An individual who had just read the Paterno Family "*Critique of the Freeh Report*," responded with what appeared to be an accurate summary of the feeling about Joe Paterno's role in the Sandusky Scandal. "Those who back Paterno will never change their opinions," commented an individual to an *NBC Sports* article, "and those who want the guy hung in effigy will certainly not be swayed either to minimize the significance of his perceived role in the cover-up."[436]

More than a half-dozen years after the Sandusky Scandal broke, there was little consensus on the legacy of Joe Paterno. No one was more active in defending his legacy than his wife, Sue. For four years, she stood fully behind the Paterno Family lawsuit against the NCAA to prove the Consent Decree illegal and to restore the legacy of Joe Paterno. She had once written to all former Penn State football players defending Paterno's legacy stating that he was a "moral, disciplined man who never twisted the truth to avoid bad publicity."[437] Yet, Paterno had at one time asked the president to admit nine players, who were academically non-admissible to Penn State, while at the same time telling a major academic journal, the *Phi Delta Kappan*, that he seldom asked for special, presidential, admits.[438] However, Sue may not have known about presidential admits, for Paterno once advised a group of coaches telling them, "Your wife doesn't have to know anything" about what goes on in the program.[439] A cynic of Joe Paterno's statements and opposite actions might have quoted the words in Tina Turner's hit song at about the time Paterno took over Penn State football—"I can't believe what you say, because I see what you do."[440] Not everything Joe Patero did was positive toward an affirming legacy.

The Penn State alumni, however, have been highly supportive of restoring the legacy of Paterno. One group, formed by alumni right after the Sandusky Scandal broke, the PS4RS (Penn Staters for Responsible Stewardship), loudly condemned Penn State's administration for its handling of the Sandusky Scandal, and especially in the firing of Joe Paterno. In an attempt to gain leverage for influencing university policy, the PS4RS, in the next three years, endorsed nine members of the Board of Trustees, all of whom were elected to the 32-member governing body.[441] Focusing on preserving the stature of Penn State and the reputation of Joe Paterno, PS4RS opposed the Freeh Report and Penn State's signing of the Consent Decree. Moreover, those trustees who PS4RS helped elect, opposed the majority of the Board members on a number of other issues. While the PS4RS is not officially recognized by any power group at Penn State, if it could control university policy, it almost assuredly would review and reject the Freeh Report, condemn the now dismantled Consent Decree and the NCAA, and restore the hidden-away Joe Paterno statue. Nevertheless, even with the overwhelming election to the trustees of Joe Paterno's son, Jay in 2017, its efforts were unsuccessful.

It is difficult to determine anyone's legacy in the decade of the death of that individual. Legacies often change over time as it has, and likely will, with Joe Paterno. An example of a legacy change of a powerful individual on the national scene was that of J. Edgar Hoover, the former FBI director. Hoover was head of the FBI for 48 years, and beginning in the 1920s he became the icon of justice in America. When he died, President Nixon honored him, and congress ordered his body to lie in state in the U. S. Capitol, the first time a civil servant had ever been so honored.[442] After his death, like that of Paterno, many negatives came to light. Those included Hoover's abuse of power and his war on homosexuals, communists, and blacks—specifically Martin Luther King. Yet, soon after his death, the new FBI building on Pennsylvania Avenue was named for J. Edgar Hoover. However, Hoover quickly came under attack, something similar to what Sue Paterno said of her husband—"an endless process of character assassination."[443] While Hoover was praised for his 48 years as FBI head, and Paterno was honored for his 46 years as head coach, the longevity of service gave critics ample opportunity to uncover and point out character flaws.

Could one major incident or character flaw ruin the legacy of an individual who was known as Saint Joe? Paterno was a multiple coach-of-the year recipient; holder of the coaching record of most big-time college football wins; the only winner of all of the traditional four featured bowl games, Cotton, Orange, Rose, and Sugar; honored as *Sports Illustrated* "Sportsman of the Year"; winner of the National Collegiate Athletic Association Gerald R. Ford Award for lifetime achievement; an individual who may have helped raise more than a billion dollars for Penn State; and probably the only coach to have a university library named after him. Could the "I backed away" admittance and condemnation for doing so in a child molestation case place a black mark on his legacy? It is possible that the legacy of Paterno may lie on this one moral lapse. As someone pointed out shortly before the NCAA Consent Decree was issued, Paterno was "a Great Man who was a Great Coach who made a Great Mistake."[444] Possibly, one close to Paterno may have summed up Paterno's legacy better than some others. Adam Taliaferro was a Penn State defensive back, paralyzed from making a tackle in the 2000 Ohio State game, shortly after Joe Paterno was informed of Jerry Sandusky's first revealed episode with a young boy. Taliaferro, who became a corporate lawyer and New Jersey state legislator, stated in early 2012, the day after Joe Paterno died: "If we're so able to vividly remember the worst a man did, can't we also remember the best?"[445]

It seemed possible that both the Senator Corman and the Paterno Family claims against the NCAA would not only show the illegality of the Consent Decree but would strongly influence how Joe Paterno's legacy might rise in the future. Yet, if it rises, it is not a guarantee that it will remain high. Any highly visible figure's image may rise or fall depending on historical circumstances—just as happened for over two centuries in the legacy of Thomas Jefferson. The writer of the Declaration of Independence could be described, as was Paterno—"an icon, but not a saint, really just a man."[446] Jefferson has been cited as the Renaissance Man of America for being an agronomist, archeologist, architect, astronomer, diplomat, inventor, lawyer, librarian, linguist, musician, philosopher, and politician—an all around scholar and doer. Yet, his racial legacy has been condemned as the owner of hundreds of slaves while having a sexual liaison and six children with Sally Hemings, one of his slaves.[447] If Jefferson was not perfect for writing the principled "all men are created equal" and then not acting on it, the future picture of Joe Paterno may prove to be something less than the idealistic "success with honor" when not all of his actions relative to children at risk were honorable.

The Senator Corman and Paterno Family lawsuits were terminated without jury trials, and that left open questions, possibly negative, about Joe Paterno's legacy. Yet, one could conclude that what the NCAA did to Joe Paterno and Penn State in the Consent Decree was far worse than the many faults of Penn State and its administrators, including Paterno, in dealing with the Sandusky Scandal. How the NCAA used the faulty Freeh Report to draw up the Consent Decree and its lack of due process involved in its construction was a black mark on the national organization and specifically its president Mark Emmert. If each of the two lawsuits had been carried to a culminating trial, a jury of Joe Paterno's peers would have had an important impact on Paterno's legacy.

Chapter 9

The Paterno Family Lawsuit Attack on the NCAA

Thy speech was light as in the wind, and rashly made.

Homer, ca. 762 B.C.E.

*"We possess a once in a lifetime legacy that demands complete restoration—
Coach Paterno's legacy."*

Bill Oldsey, 2016

The Paterno Family Lawsuit Begins

No sooner had the Corman lawsuit against the NCAA been settled out-of-court in 2015 than the Paterno Family lawsuit became front and center. The Paternos, however, were previously far ahead of Corman in determining to fight the Freeh Report, Mark Emmert, and the NCAA Consent Decree. If they could help it, Sue Paterno and her children would not have Joe Paterno nailed to the football crossbar, erected by the leaders of the NCAA. They believed the NCAA should be permanently affixed, not the icon of Happy Valley. The Paternos had hired a prominent lawyer, Joseph Sedwick (Wick) Sollers, III, and a public relations specialist, Dan McGinn, almost immediately after Paterno's firing in early November 2011.[448] Both had served prominent individuals in the nation's capital. While McGinn addressed issues in the court of public opinion for the image of Joe Paterno, Sollers addressed legal issues. Upon release of the Freeh Report in July of 2012, Wick Sollers was almost immediately asked to put the lie to it and how it was used illegally in helping to create the NCAA Consent Decree and damaging Joe Paterno's legacy. It was not likely that the Paternos would be bought off by settling out-of-court with the NCAA, because Sollers would not likely have been hired, as he had been a Washington, D.C. defense lawyer and former counsel to President George H. W. Bush.[449] But, what if the Paterno Family won the NCAA lawsuit but lost the legacy battle at the same time? It was certainly possible that the NCAA could be proven guilty of breaking its own bylaws, while at the same time new material in court depositions could be damaging to Paterno's legacy.

Sue Paterno was flush with cash in 2013 and was able to back a lengthy lawsuit. Prior to the Sandusky Scandal breaking, the Paternos had millions of dollars stashed away, even after donating $4 million or so to the University. The largess came from income worth several millions each year from Joe Paterno's salary, summer football camp revenue, contract presidential bonuses, bowl game bonuses, Nike shoe endorsements, television and radio contracts, public speaking engagements, royalties from television and other product endorsements, and wise investments. While there were a number of estimates of an estate worth about $10 million, it was almost certainly far more than that.[450] The Paternos might have easily been worth that before Joe was fired, but at the conclusions of his career, Penn State paid Paterno an additional $5.5 million reflecting what he would have received by contract had he retired at the end of 2011.[451] In addition, as a member of the Pennsylvania State Employees' Retirement System for 61 years, his pension reached $13.4 million with an initial pension payout of $10.1 million to Sue Paterno.[452] Three months after Paterno's death, a Centre County judge permanently sealed testament in order to keep the public from knowing about his effects.[453] Despite the NCAA having upward of a billion dollars stockpiled for use in its many lawsuits, the Paterno Family could well afford a lengthy lawsuit in an attempt to salvage the coach's legacy.

The Paterno Family lawsuit would differ little from Senator Corman's suit against the NCAA. Both condemned the NCAA for the punitive and corrective components of the Consent Decree inflicted on Penn State. Within days of the July 23, 2012 Consent Decree being deviously imposed upon Penn State, Sollers sent an email to Mark Emmert in which he stated that the Paterno Family wanted justice under due process. To Sollers, "due process will not hide the truth and will only illuminate the facts and allow for thoughtful, substantiated conclusions, not extreme and unfounded opinions, such as those offered in the Freeh Report and relied upon by the NCAA."[454] The scene was set for a second attempt to judge the NCAA for its lack of due process and breaking its own constitution and bylaws in punishing Penn State and, in this case, also Joe Paterno and his family.

The Paterno Family Case and Void *ab Initio*

Ten months after President Rod Erickson signed the Consent Decree, the Paterno Family brought suit against the NCAA. They asked for a declaratory judgment that the NCAA-imposed Consent Decree "was unauthorized, unlawful, and void *ab initio*," that it was never valid.[455] The May 30, 2013 Paterno Family suit made clear its claims against the NCAA, its president Mark Emmert, and Ed Ray, the former head of the NCAA Executive Committee and President of Oregon State University. Ed Ray specifically sought the "death penalty" for Penn State. Void *ab ignitio* is very important in contract law because it means that the contract essentially never existed and had no binding power. This is true if the contract was signed under duress, as in telling Penn State president Rod Erickson that Penn State may receive the "death penalty" if the Consent Decree was not signed.

The Paterno Family case, based in part on void *ab initio*, read that the NCAA:[456]

> circumvented the procedures required by the NCAA's rules and violated and conspired with others to violate Plaintiffs' [Paterno Family] rights, causing Plaintiffs significant harm. Defendants [NCAA] took these actions based on conclusions reached in a flawed, unsubstantiated, and controversial report that Defendants knew or should have known was not the result of a thorough, reliable investigation; had been prepared without complying with the NCAA's investigative rules and procedures; reached conclusions that were false, misleading, or otherwise unworthy of credence; and reflected an improper 'rush to judgment' based on unsound speculation and innuendo.

Void *ab initio*, the Consent Decree was never valid, may have been the most poignant legal point, but the less emphasized claim that "Joe Paterno suffered damage to his good name and reputation, resulting in irreparable and substantial pecuniary harm. . . " was a major reason for the lawsuit.[457] Or as friend of the Paterno Family and board of trustee member, William Oldsey, would later state: "We possess a once in a lifetime legacy that demands complete restoration—Coach Paterno's Legacy."[458]

Unlike the Senator Corman suit, the Paterno Family emphasized from the first the illegality of the Consent Decree. The NCAA was charged with breaching the contract between the NCAA and Penn State and illegally expanding the scope of its authority by "exerting control over matters unrelated to recruiting and athletic competition" as outlined in the NCAA Constitution and Bylaws. Criminal matters stemming from the Sandusky Scandal, the Paternos argued, were to be left to the courts, being "far outside the scope" of NCAA authority. Under NCAA Bylaws, there were only two types of violations, major and secondary, and there were none cited by the NCAA in the Sandusky situation. Furthermore, there was no notice of inquiry to the Penn State president as required by NCAA guidelines, and Penn State needed to be able to respond to allegations of wrongdoing. In addition, the NCAA allegations needed to come, not from President Emmert and the NCAA Executive Committee, but from the NCAA Committee on Infractions. The "Death Penalty" should never have been threatened by Emmert and NCAA officials because it could only be imposed on institutions that were major "repeat violators," and Penn State had never once had a major violation in football or any other sport in its entire history. Thus, the Consent Decree, according to the Paternos, was "unauthorized, unlawful, and void *ab initio*," never valid.[459]

A primary reason why the NCAA Consent Decree was void from the beginning, the Paternos reasoned, was that it was almost completely based on the Freeh Report released less than two weeks before the Consent Decree was signed. The Freeh Report was never intended to replace an investigation by the NCAA. The Freeh investigation said nothing about alleged NCAA rule violations, nor was it intended to do so. The Freeh Report conclusions were not based on evidence as required by NCAA rules, and individuals named in the Report were not given any due process opportunity to challenge conclusions often based on "speculation and innuendo." The Freeh investigators, the lawsuit charged, based their findings on unidentified sources, using "hearsay information," all prohibited by the NCAA Bylaws.[460] In addition. the "rush to judgment" used the Freeh Report as evidence, before criminal charges against Penn State officials were tried in the courts. It was Emmert himself, who stated in his letter to President Erickson on November 17, 2011, that the NCAA would "utilize any information gained from the **criminal** justice process in our review."[461] Emmert failed to be truthful, for as Homer, the Ancient Greek storyteller wrote in the 8th century B.C.E.—"Thy speech was light as in the wind, and rashly made."[462] Emmert had shown his hypocritical side.

The Paternos thus requested relief in their May 30, 2013 lawsuit. First, they wanted a declaratory judgment of unlawful NCAA actions for compensatory damages for "tortious and improper conduct and breach of contract." Second, they claimed punitive damages for "reckless and intentional misconduct" resulting in family losses and damages. Last, the Paternos sought their legal costs to be paid for by the NCAA along with other legal or equitable relief the court might deem just. No specific money amounts were specified.[463]

The Paterno Family lawsuit, however, could have been rejected by the Court, for the NCAA claimed that the Paternos lacked standing before the court. That is, the NCAA claimed the Paterno Family had no connection to, nor were harmed by, the Consent Decree, thus lacked standing to take the NCAA to court. The NCAA also claimed that because Penn State University was not originally brought into the lawsuit, the Paterno Family lacked standing in its Breach of Contract case.[464] Well over a year after the case was filed and after a year of much wrangling and amended versions of the suit, the judge in the case, John Leete, sided with the Paterno Family. He allowed the Paterno Family to charge that the NCAA's Consent Decree was an illegal and unauthorized exercise by the NCAA as found in the "language of the document itself" and not from alleged harm resulting from the Consent Decree. The Paterno family had argued, "The Consent Decree was imposed through an unlawful and unauthorized exercise of the NCAA's enforcement authority, therefore the consent Decree was void, not simply voidable."[465]

Judge Leete used the same reasoning as that found in an 1862 case, the same year Penn State became eligible to be a national Land Grant institution during the Civil War. The 1862 case, first cited earlier by Paterno Family lawyers, concluded, "one who has been fraudulently induced to purchase land may rescind the contract."[466] Thus certain contracts, such as the Consent Decree between the NCAA and Penn State, "are absolutely void, because they have no legal sanction, . . . and even a stranger may raise the objection" to the Consent Decree.[467] The Paterno Family was no "stranger," but was a major irritant to the NCAA, and the lawsuit went forward. It was similar to the Senator Corman lawsuit, in that the judges of the two cases overruled nearly all of the NCAA objections to the case. The loser, the NCAA, lost its attempt to nullify the Paterno Family desire to void the Consent Decree, to which the NCAA said the Paterno Family was neither a party nor a beneficiary.

NCAA Counsel, Donald Remy, lost his argument that "the family of coach Paterno continues to try to scapegoat the NCAA for violations it did not commit, for the firing of a coach it did not do, and for an investigative report it did not write."[468] Strange what a Civil War land dispute lawsuit might say about a fraudulent Consent Decree contract a century and a half later.

Besides helping to restore Joe Paterno's legacy and a finding that the Consent Decree was illegal, the Paterno Family sought specific legal relief from its NCAA lawsuit from the very beginning. It desired an injunction to stop the NCAA from enforcing the Consent Decree, and it wanted the NCAA to pay for the lawsuit. More importantly, the family wanted both compensatory damages "for tortious and improper conduct and breach of contract" and punitive damages for "reckless and intentional misconduct" resulting in losses and damages to the Paterno estate.[469] Compensatory and punitive damages could have reached millions of dollars.

The Deposition Arguments

Once it was finally decided that the case could go forward with discovery, both sides began to gather evidence through under-oath interrogations of key individuals and multiple documents that might reveal relevant information useful in the trial to the Paterno Family or to the NCAA. For instance, the NCAA might wish to question President Rod Erickson or Attorney Gene Marsh under oath on how the Consent Decree was brought about by Penn State agreeing to it. The NCAA might even depose victims of Jerry Sandusky, even those who claimed they were violated years before the first known 1998 incident, some of whom said that Paterno knew about the sexual violations as early as the 1970s. The Paterno Family would logically want to question NCAA president, Mark Emmert, or former head of the NCAA Executive Committee, Ed Ray. They would be asked under oath to tell their side of putting pressure on Penn State to go the route of the Consent Decree rather than the formal investigative process and possible death penalty.

Depositions often reveal information that will tilt a future trial in favor of one side or the other. Following the deposition stage, out-of-court settlements occur in a majority of the cases. That is what happened in the Senator Corman suit against the NCAA. Specifically, because of a deposition of Penn State's hired attorney Gene Marsh, and documents provided to Corman by the NCAA because of the deposition, the Corman side put the NCAA on the defensive with the possibility that the entire Consent Decree might have been illegal under the NCAA's own constitution and bylaws.[470]

The first deposition in the Paterno Family lawsuit available for public consumption was that of Ed Ray, Oregon State University President, who had led the NCAA Executive Committee to a unanimous vote in agreement with the Consent Decree. The December 2014 deposition of President Ray was conducted jointly between the Paterno Family and the Corman lawsuits, and Senator Corman released the deposition legally. Other depositions conducted by the Paterno Family were confidential agreements, not open to the public or were heavily redacted of poignant information.[471] Ed Ray's deposition testimony was an embarrassment to the NCAA, for he admitted that while he and the Executive Committee voted unanimously to accept the Consent Decree, he did not even read the document. When asked by the Paterno Family lawyer if Ray ever saw the Consent Decree, Ray answered, "No, I don't even know when it was signed. . . ."[472]

President Ray acknowledged his ignorance about the Sandusky Scandal. He admitted that he had not read the original Sandusky grand jury presentment nor the original letter of Mark Emmert to President Rod Erickson on November 17, 2011. He didn't read the Freeh Report prior to the Consent Decree, and he did not read the NCAA Constitution and Bylaws, although he did admit, "I have tried to read them." Ray responded to a question about the death penalty only being given to "repeat violators." He stated, "I don't know that as a fact," even though it is clearly stated in the NCAA Bylaws that he neither read nor understood. In addition, Ray did not discuss the legality of bypassing the Committee on Infractions to go directly to the NCAA Board of Directions for action. He didn't even write his own press conference response to the Freeh Report just after its release. Rather, the head of communications at the NCAA, Bob Williams, wrote it for him. Later, it was not surprising when Ray admitted he did not read the Paterno Family *"Critique of the Freeh Report."*[473] In other words, the individual who led the NCAA Executive Committee in voting unanimously to accept the penalties of the Consent Decree knew little about the background of the Sandusky Scandal and had not done due diligence in reading the documents associated with the Scandal and the draconian punishments. No wonder the NCAA officials wanted to distance themselves from the Oregon State University president, who admitted that prior to the Consent Decree he had "no sense that I needed to prep for anything."[474]

If the other depositions from the Paterno Family in its efforts in legal discovery were as revealing of ineptness on the part of the NCAA, it was no wonder that the Paterno Family, as was the situation in the Corman case, believed it would succeed in bringing the NCAA to terms. Even without knowledge of the nature of the closed depositions, it was clear that the NCAA was losing ground in its defense as the case moved through several years of litigation. When the NCAA argued that because Penn State was not an original party in the lawsuit brought by the Paternos, the case should be dismissed. Judge John Leete, however, made Penn State a "nominal defendant," and the NCAA could no longer argue successfully that Penn State was not involved in the lawsuit.[475]

Judge Leete also ruled that the Paterno Family could subpoena the Freeh Report discovery materials of the law firm, Pepper Hamilton, thus allowing the Paternos to see the background used for writing the Freeh Report.[476] The records were held by Penn State. Judge Leete made a "weapon/shield" ruling that Penn State could not use the Freeh Report as a weapon in their public-relations purposes while at the same time shielding the Report from the Paternos' scrutiny. The Paternos had argued that Penn State previously used the Freeh Report "for its own advantage and as a public relations document to appease the NCAA and to take blame away from the university as a whole by pinning it on Coach Paterno and other Appellees," Graham Spanier, Gary Schultz, and Tim Curley.[477]

The judge allowed the Paterno Family to subpoena individuals from the NCAA and others to be deposed, as the plaintiffs desired—a major victory for the Paternos.[478] In addition, all depositions from the Corman suit were available to the Paternos. New depositions were taken of Presidents Eric Barron and Rod Erickson; board of trustees members Ken Frazier, Ira Lubert, Keith Masser, and Paul Silvis; and Penn State lawyers Steve Dunham, Frank Guadagnino, and Gene Marsh.[479] More importantly Louis Freeh, leader of the questionable Freeh Report, was also deposed. His deposition was taken in early 2016, but it revealed little publicly because the deposition released was filled with Freeh responses being redacted. Crossed out of the deposition were Freeh's answer to queries such as a major question of why Joe Paterno was never interviewed in the period from December 2011 and his death toward the end of January 2012. The Paterno Family lawyer questioned Freeh—"Why did you lie about Joe Paterno refusing to meet with you. Was it because you could not afford to hear a more detailed explanation of his actions? Was it because Ken Frazier [Penn State trustee] told you not to interview him?" The Freeh answer was redacted.[480] Freeh was asked whether he interviewed people aware of the McQueary shower incident—including McQueary's father, medical doctor Jonathan Dranov, Penn State attorney Wendell Cortney, and Penn State administrators Tim Curley and Gary Schultz. His answer was "no."

Redactions of Louis Freeh were significant. There were a number of such redactions. One inquiry of Freeh was, "Is it reasonable to conclude your [Freeh] report was neither full, nor fair, nor complete?" The response was redacted. The last major question by Paterno Family lawyers of Freeh was, "Isn't it true that the true purpose of your report was to validate the Penn State board of trustees decision to fire Joe Paterno?" The responses will only be known when the redacted black ink is removed from covering Freeh's answers.[481] They may never be known to the public.

The Chances of a Paterno Family Victory

While few trials are predictable, the chance of the Paterno Family prevailing was looking positive, even with several negatives. In the spring of 2017, a major negative was the sentencing of Joe Paterno's colleagues, President Graham Spanier, Vice President Gary Schultz, and Athletic Director Tim Curley, to prison terms for endangering the welfare of children.[482] Following the state superior court throwing out their perjury, obstruction of justice, and conspiracy charges, Tim Curley and Gary Schultz, just prior to a trial, pleaded guilty of endangerment of the welfare of children. Former president Graham Spanier went to trial and was convicted of the same charge.[483] Each was sentenced to a short time in prison. Despite the fact that Curley and Schultz pleaded guilty, their prison terms were surprisingly longer than that of Spanier, who was convicted in a jury trial.[484] According to one observer, the sentences to Curley and Schultz, the judge's negative comments about Graham Spanier, and "Spanier's guilty verdict ultimately doomed the Paterno lawsuit."[485]

There was an important negative directly related to the *Paterno Family v. NCAA* lawsuit. The Paterno Family asked for materials underlying the

Freeh Report and its influence on the Consent Decree, but at the same time was reluctant to produce pre-trial materials to the NCAA underlying the Paterno Family *"Critique of the Freeh Report."* The Paternos claimed that the materials for the critique were not prepared in anticipation of litigation, and the report was not a legal document.[486] Though the Paternos claimed in the *"Critique"* that a lawsuit was not anticipated, it was a difficult notion to accept, for the Paternos knew they would be contesting the NCAA's Consent Decree shortly after the *"Critique"* was released. The NCAA argued that the Paternos could not refuse to produce the material underlying the *"Critique"* while continuing to press for materials underlying the Freeh Report.[487]

Another negative for the Paterno Family occurred in the spring of 2016, when there were allegations that Joe Paterno knew about child molestations by Jerry Sandusky as early as the 1970s. The revelation came from a lawsuit brought by Penn State against the Pennsylvania Manufacturers' Association Insurance Company to recover money for payment to children (now grown men) molested by Sandusky from the 1970s until the early twenty-first century. It was alleged that Paterno knew of early incidents and did nothing.[488] The Paterno Family denied this, with lawyer son Scott tweeting and calling the charges "bunk."[489] The charges about early knowledge of the incidents, nevertheless, put in the mind of many people that Paterno knew about child molestation well before the first authenticated case in 1998. Whether it was these depositions or others that have been kept under lock and key, the allegations were not positive for the case with the NCAA and importantly Joe Paterno's legacy.

Nevertheless, the lawsuit was proceeding along, if slowly, with the approach of the summer of 2017. Judge Leete ruled that all depositions and dispositive motions and briefs needed to be complete before the fall of 2017.[490] A trial could then ensue by September 2017. But wait. Something happened in a negative way for the Paterno Family. What it was may never be revealed because many of the documents in the case were placed under seal by the Centre County prothonotary under Judge Leete's orders. At the end of June 2017, Sue Paterno withdrew the case "with prejudice"—that is, the same suit could not again be filed. Did Sue Paterno drop the case legally?[491] And more important, why did she withdraw from the case after over four years of litigation in an attempt to help save the legacy of Joe Paterno?[492]

Sue Paterno Withdraws from the NCAA Case

Sue Paterno's justification for concluding the case is telling, but it may not be telling all of the truth. After blaming the Penn State Board of Trustees and Louis Freeh for mishandling the Sandusky Scandal investigation, the coach's wife rationalized that progress had been made in setting "the record straight on Joe" and defending the honor of Penn State. The Consent Decree sanctions were reversed, and, she stated, the victories taken away from Penn State and Paterno were reinstated with the Senator Corman out-of-court settlement. Further, she wrote, it had been shown that Joe Paterno had followed protocol for reporting Sandusky allegations, did not interfere in the investigation, and there was no conspiracy or attempt to cover up. "Our goal" Sue Paterno specified, "has always been to uncover and make transparent the full truth. We have done all we can in this litigation to achieve that end." Nothing new could be revealed in a trial, she pointed out.[493] Yet, wasn't there any more story to the ending of a four-year litigation that was approaching a trial to seek more of the truth? And if the story was rather clear when the Senator Corman case against the NCAA was settled out-of-court in January 2015 with the Consent Decree being thrown out, why didn't the Paterno Family drop the case then? After all, the Corman case had been settled much to the satisfaction of the Paterno Family when the 111 Paterno football victories had been restored and the Consent Decree had been eliminated.[494]

The NCAA, true to its nature, did not let dropping the case rest in peace. The NCAA and its combative counsel, Donald Remy, responded to the Paternos quitting its lawsuit. Remy, retorting with the conceit of any egocentric winner, responded to Sue Paterno's giving up on the case with his statement that the Paternos abandoned the lawsuit "rather than subject those facts [of discovery] to courtroom examination is telling." Further, in Remy's press release, the NCAA believed "that the powerful record developed during discovery overwhelmingly confirmed what the NCAA has believed all along: The NCAA acted reasonably in adopting the conclusions of an eight-month investigation by Louis Freeh." It was not unexpected, Remy stated, that the lawsuit was abandoned only hours before the NCAA was due to file a 100-page summary judgment brief that detailed the discovery results.[495] What was in that 100-page brief that could be damning to Joe Paterno? Was the discovery the key to why the Paternos dropped the lawsuit?

The NCAA rejoinder, however, goaded Sue Paterno into a somewhat greater explanation on why she surrendered to the NCAA. "The fear of discovery being revealed is absurd. . ." retorted Paterno. "At every stage of this litigation we have sought to make a complete record available," she claimed. Well not quite, as the Paternos refused in the NCAA lawsuit to reveal how the Paterno Family *"Critique of the Freeh Report"* was developed through internal memos and discussions. When the NCAA asked for all documents related to the creation of the *"Critique,"* the Paternos declined to turn them over. They claimed the *"Critique"* was protected by attorney-client privilege or as attorney work product, legal ways to protect documents.[496] Eventually, the NCAA won the "sword and shield" argument when the NCAA charged that the Paternos wanted "to achieve a tactical advantage in this litigation by using the critique to support its claims [sword], yet locking any discovery of the facts and analysis that support its self-serving conclusions [shield]." [497] Judge John Leete saw what the Paternos were doing and ordered the Paterno Family to turn over to the NCAA source documents related to the Paterno Family *"Critique of the Freeh Report."*[498]

Sue Paterno may have been more accurate by stating that one of the reasons she gave up on the case against the NCAA was a financial one. In four years, the Paternos may have spent a significant portion of their $20 million or so on the law suit. Several thousand pages of legal documents produced by a highly paid counsel, Wick Sollers, and his assistants would have consumed several million dollars. The financial burden to Sue Paterno may have been one of the reasons why Sollers left as counsel several weeks before Sue Paterno dropped out of the litigation.

Or could it have been that Wick Sollers wanted to settle with the NCAA for money only, negotiating a deal that the Paterno Family did not like? Remember that the desire to attempt to save Joe Paterno's legacy would have been a driving force for his wife to continue the litigation. Yet doing so may have threatened a comfortable retirement and being able to eventually pass on her remaining millions, as a 77-year old, to her five children or, more likely, her 17 grandchildren.

It is not clear if there was any connection between the impact of three guilty administrators, Graham Spanier, Gary Schultz, and Tim Curley, being sentenced to prison and Sue Paterno's decision to drop her suit against the NCAA. That Joe Paterno was the fourth administrator associated with the triad of those guilty of child endangerment may have influenced Sue to drop her suit. "Guilt by association" may not be a legal term or hold legal weight, but it could mean that in the public's mind a negative opinion exists of Paterno's association with the three Penn State administrators sentenced to prison. People's perceptions do have an impact on the legal system. Did the Paterno Family counsel, Wick Sellers, think the Paternos should settle with the NCAA for a sum of money rather than go to a trial, with an uncertain outcome, in an attempt to help save Joe Paterno's legacy? Was there a relationship among Judge John Boccabella's jail term pronouncements of the three administrators in early June 2017, Wick Sollers withdrawal as counsel in mid-June, and Sue Paterno dropping the case two weeks later? Time might reveal a connection.

Nevertheless, there may have been another reason to stop the litigation before a jury trial would determine the outcome. What if in the depositions taken by the NCAA, there was real damning evidence relative to the image of Joe Paterno? For instance, what if there was strong evidence of Paterno having knowledge of Sandusky's sexual involvement with children prior to the first revealed case in 1998? Additionally, what if more damning accusations existed with how Paterno dealt with football player criminal activity that may have broken NCAA Bylaws? Even if these were shown to be unproven accusations, they could further damage the image of Paterno. If the NCAA found compromising activities in the discoveries, they would surely come out in the trial to the detriment of the Paterno legacy, the principal reason for the lawsuit in the first place.

One might recall that Penn State counsel Gene Marsh and President Rod Erickson discussed just such a situation during the Consent Decree negotiations in the summer of 2012. If Penn State had decided not to sign the Consent Decree in favor of a formal NCAA investigation, it was suggested that the NCAA would likely find NCAA violations "picking through all of the football disciplinary player cases." These, Erickson stated to his legal advisors, "could yield much more in the way of problems. . . ."[499] Because the Paterno Family lawsuit depositions were not made available and the 100-page NCAA summary judgment brief of depositions was not submitted before the Paternos dropped the case, it may never be known if the deposition contents were one of the causes for Sue Paterno exiting prior to a jury trial. The three Penn State administrators were, indeed, sentenced to prison for their guilt. Was Paterno guilty by association in the public's mind?

A Penn State alumnus, Linda Berkland, had an interesting take only days after Sue Paterno pulled the plug on the Paterno Family lawsuit. The Marysville, Ohio resident and 1980s graduate of Penn State, sent a letter to the editor of the State College-based *Centre Daily Times* shortly after Sue Paterno dropped the family suit. It tells effectively the story that a number of upset Penn State alumni were feeling:

> By all accounts, the fat lady has sung. Jerry Sandusky is serving a life sentence. Three Penn State administrators stand (wrongfully) convicted of endangering the welfare of children and face prison time. The 'whistleblower' [Mike McQueary] has been awarded $13 million. The Paternos dropped their lawsuit against the NCAA, discovery is sealed, and the likes of Emmert, Ray and Freeh can slither off, unscathed. . . . If Penn State's 'leadership' is celebrating, I would caution them, 'not so fast'. . . . People like me will never move on. The fat lady may have sung but this story doesn't end until the lion roars.[500]

Berkland, a Penn State nutrition major, wrote more like an accomplished English major, and she raised the level of commentary on the Sandusky Scandal, inept Penn State leaders, and hypocritical NCAA officials. Too often the language used by others was like that found in a men's locker room following a loss to an inferior opponent and an unfair official. Raw emotion rather than educated reason regularly dominated any discussion of the Sandusky Scandal that was found on the internet, such as blogs, Facebook, Reddit, Twitter, Tumblr, and YouTube. Communications had changed considerably since Joe Paterno and Sue Pohland were married in the early 1960s, before Linda Berkland was born. Previously, there was generally face-to-face discussion, letters, and the telephone. By the twenty-first century, in an instant, one's views could be transmitted, and often were without real thought going into them. One's legacy can be destroyed much faster than in the past. Berkland, as opinionated as she was on one side of the issue, was rare in placing together a careful commentary before it went out to the world.

Saving Joe Paterno's legacy and condemning the NCAA through a lawsuit seemingly disappeared with the withdrawal of the Paterno Family lawsuit against the national organization controlling most of college sport. It did not mean that the charges against the NCAA for lacking due process and breaking their own constitution and bylaws were not true when it forced the Consent Decree on Penn State with the threat of an illegal "death penalty." What Senator Jake Corman did when he settled out-of-court in 2015 was to allow the NCAA to go on telling the world that what it did to Penn State in 2012 was proper and legal. Had Corman gone to trial and likely won against the NCAA, it would have truly allowed the Paterno Family to end its lawsuit, which in many ways resembled that of Senator Corman. The terminated Paterno Family lawsuit in 2017, with questionable justifications (other than possible financial considerations), was detrimental to the legacy of Joe Paterno and bringing the NCAA to justice in violation of its own bylaws. The NCAA got away with nailing Penn State to the crossbar and not having a court trial conclude that the nails it used were illegal.

In the end, the effort to save Joe Paterno's legacy, while not accomplished, appeared to be more important to Sue Paterno and her family than was the showing of the illegality of the NCAA Consent Decree and the punishment thrust upon Penn State. Justice, even in America, has not always been just.

Afterword

Nothing is more intolerable than to have to be compelled
to accuse one's self of one's own errors.

Ludwig van Beethoven, 1811

It is generally forgotten that the Sandusky Scandal, the Consent Decree, and the illegal actions of Mark Emmert and the NCAA would never have occurred had a psychologist, Alycia Chambers, been listened to when she reported one day after she was informed of the initial 1998 shower incident with Jerry Sandusky. She wrote to Ronald Schreffler, a Penn State police detective, that the actions of Sandusky were that of "a likely pedophile's pattern. . . ."[501] Soon, the police, the Youth Service Bureau, the Department of Public Welfare, and the District Attorney were aware of the incident. The evaluation by Alycia Chambers was rejected by all. The decision by officials was that Jerry Sandusky was not a pedophile. Had Chambers been listened to and her judgment acted upon, the likelihood of a scandal and eventual illegal NCAA actions would have been negligible. Action of a heroic Chambers went for naught.

Denial of Chambers' judgment eventually led to the nailing of Penn State and Joe Paterno to the crossbar by the National Collegiate Athletic Association Consent Decree, resulting in permanent wounds.[502] There was little question that Penn State and its approximately $4 billion annual budget and nearly $4 billion endowment[503] could withstand a future half-billion or even a one-billion dollar NCAA attack on its financial well being. Even Penn State's football team would survive and even flourish after the NCAA attempted to eviscerate it with a $60 million fine, reducing the number of football scholarships, banning bowl games for years, and allowing all members of the squad and incoming freshmen to abandon the team, fleeing to other colleges.[504] This kind of punishment, while the harshest ever handed out, was not entirely unique, for the NCAA had in the early 1950s nailed Kentucky and its iconic coach, Adolph Rupp, to the backboard when it gave a one-year "death penalty" to the Kentucky basketball team. The NCAA also nailed Southern Methodist's football team with a second big-time "death penalty" in the 1980s. Kentucky, like Penn State, soon rallied to maintain its national standing. It rapidly attained an undefeated season. SMU, however, could not recover athletically for the next generation. To the contrary, Penn State recovered, winning a Big Ten championship and going to the Rose Bowl in a half-decade.

No one can accurately judge the psychological cost of the Consent Decree to Penn State for the Sandusky Scandal, either immediately or in the long run. Certainly there was a cost to pay for the damage to Penn State's image. The situation might be compared to the negative image of the U.S. government following the Watergate-Richard Nixon fiasco in the 1970s—a lack of trust in leaders of the government that has continued into the twenty-first century. How much faith could be placed in future Penn State leaders who followed three Penn State administrators sentenced to prison for endangering the institution by a lack of legal and ethical actions? For it was Joe Paterno himself, who at the time of Watergate and the Vietnam War told a graduating class at Penn State: "We shall act, and we shall act with good intentions. Hopefully, we will often be right, but at times, we will be wrong. When we are, let us admit it and immediately try to right the situation."[505] The four Penn State administrators, when they had the opportunity, never did right the situation in the years before the full-blown scandal erupted. Later, Penn State never redressed the negative circumstances when it accepted the Freeh Report without reading it and signed the Consent Decree without a discussion by the full board of trustees. Furthermore, Penn State's administration never challenged the injustices to Penn State by the NCAA.

Beyond the uncalculated image costs to Penn State, the financial burden to the institution may never be known, for many of the extra costs to Penn State are not accounted for by its administrators. The increased costs in hiring tens of additional administrators, faculty, and lawyers were never calculated as Sandusky-induced costs. They were not just a one-time outlay such as the $60 million fine by the NCAA to the athletic department—they will be accumulated expenditures for decades. What is the financial cost of closing buildings to the public, setting up building access computer systems and surveillance cameras, and collecting child molestation data? One must consider the Sandusky Scandal impact on all aspects of running the university that was intended to make Penn State more secure, but at the same time taking freedom away from students, staff, faculty, visitors, and even administrators. Those costs were seldom added to the significant fraction of a billion dollars that had already been paid for fines, such as the penalty for numerous violations of the Clery Act, the payment to those individuals considered to have been violated by Sandusky, and the costs of the dozen or so law suits in which Penn State was involved. It is rather easy to consider a sum of at least $1,000,000,000 to be the financial impact upon Penn State from the Sandusky Scandal over the years.

What about the changing effect upon the national image of Joe Paterno from before the scandal to the immediate reaction and then for a good portion of a decade after? What about the judgment of Mark Emmert, who in this story is the antagonist? The NCAA's head spoke highly of Joe Paterno less than a year before the scandal broke. "For me," Emmert stated praising the coach, "Paterno is the definitive role model of what it means to be a college coach."[506] Following the scandal, Emmert agreed with the Consent Decree that "Joseph V. Paterno failed to protect against a child sexual predator harming children for over a decade."[507] Emmert's change in opinion was dramatic, but not unexpected from someone whose verbal and written acrobatics served him well as he moved from university to university and eventually to lead the NCAA.[508]

Was the NCAA under the leadership of Mark Emmert and his legal counsel Donald Remy able to destroy or permanently damage the coach's image by eradicating 111 of his 409 victories and eliminating his honor for lifetime achievement (the Gerald R. Ford Award) given to him by the NCAA the previous year? Before the Jerry Sandusky scandal in 2011, Paterno's image as a leader in big-time college football and other accomplishments was unmatched. The possible exception would be the historical Walter Camp of Yale, the "father of American football," in the period between 1876 and the second decade of the twentieth century.[509] Camp was considered so ethical and unbiased that he was asked to officiate at football games in which Yale was playing. He was considered the unmatched football authority and as such created the first all-American teams in 1889, even anointing Penn State's first all-American a decade later, Carlton "Brute" Rudolph.[510] Paterno never achieved this level of trust, but he was the first college football coach to be selected "Sportsman of the Year" by *Sports Illustrated*.[511]

Mark Emmert, Donald Remy, and Oregon State University president Ed Ray may well have caused a serious impact on the Paterno legacy by their Consent Decree repudiations of Joe Paterno. When charges that Joe Paterno and other administrators at Penn State hushed up child sexual-abuse for fear of bad publicity, it was reasonable that many people took Louis Freeh charges seriously in the Freeh Report. NCAA officials then included the charges in the Consent Decree. Louis Freeh had the prestige of being former head of the FBI, and Penn State President Rod Erickson signed the Consent Decree, based on the Freeh Report. Louis Freeh claimed that four Penn State administrators, including Joe Paterno, "concealed Jerry Sandusky's activities from the university's board of trustees."[512] Rick Reilly, the *Sports Illustrated* writer, accepted the charges. Reilly had once written in his 1986 *Sports Illustrated* "Sportsman of the Year" article about Paterno that "nobody has stayed truer to the game and at the same time truer to himself. . . ." A quarter-century later, Reilly reversed himself when he penned, "Paterno let a child molester go when he could've stopped him. He let him go and then lied to cover his sinister tracks. . . . Good and decent men protect kids, not rapists."[513]

Others have contemplated the effect upon the legacy of Joe Paterno, one of the most visible individuals in Penn State's history since 1855. Two professors, who were quite knowledgeable of the Paterno situation, had learned perspectives shortly after the firing of Joe Paterno by the board of trustees and publications of the Freeh Report on the Sandusky Scandal. One was Michael Bérubé, the holder of the Paterno Family Liberal Arts Professor in Literature. When the Freeh Report was issued in the summer of 2012, Bérubé decided he must abandon his Penn State Paterno Chair in Literature despite believing that "Penn State became a far stronger institution academically over the course of Paterno's years. . . ." Yet, from an ancient Latin literature standpoint, he reasoned, "it is inconceivable to me that the man who loved the *Aeneid* because he considered it the great epic of honor and duty would not have done more when apprised of Sandusky's behavior than report it up the chain of command." To give up this honored chair was not easy for the literature professor who was "not happy about what happened here in the valley."[514]

Shortly after Joe Paterno was fired, another Penn State academic, George Enteen, offered a three-act picture of Joe Paterno, a heroic tragic figure. "Joe Paterno did what the law required; he informed the higher-ups at the university," wrote Enteen, the emeritus professor of Russian history. "When they did not notify the police, he had an obligation, moral if not legal, to inform them. He failed," stated Enteen, "to do so—an

unforgiveable failure. Hence his fall—a horrible reality, a great tragedy."
Enteen determined that "it was ironic that this congenitally proactive man
should be passive in this crisis." He concluded that Paterno's "egotism
[and] sheer hubris. . . is what . . . aroused the furies."[515] Most individuals,
however, did not have ancient Greek and Latin perspectives to rely on.

From shortly after the scandal broke to years following, individuals
interested in the events generally were found in two groups. One group,
chiefly geographically removed from Happy Valley, believed that what
Penn State or Joe Paterno received in penalties and lowered esteem were
just and deserved. The others, those who lived closer to Penn State or
were closely associated with the institution, such as the alumni and faculty
leaders, were often indignant over the treatment received by the NCAA.
Soon after the penalties were inflicted on Penn State, Scott Kretchmar,
the former NCAA faculty representative from Penn State voiced his
displeasure: "We'll never get over this. It's sort of like the Kent State
shooting [during the student protests of the Vietnam War]." Kretchmar
told *Sports Illustrated*'s S. L. Price, "Everybody, when they hear 'Kent
State,' thinks of a massacre. Whenever they hear 'Penn State,' they're
going to think of this [scandal]."[516] Four years later, another person
affiliated with Penn State and a Happy Valley resident, Patty Kleban,
proclaimed that Joe Paterno and Penn State had been "kicked down and
tainted with an undeserved reputation." She blamed Mark Emmert, who
never apologized to those students or alumni for what seemed to be a
vengeance against our beloved university."[517]

Others, a half-dozen years removed from the first general knowledge
of the Sandusky situation, were not so kind to either Joe Paterno or Penn
State. One was Judge John Boccabella, who sentenced three Penn State
administrators to prison terms and had an opinion on Joe Paterno. Upon
sentencing Graham Spanier, Gary Schultz, and Tim Curley to short terms
in prison, he condemned the long-time Penn State coach stating that
Paterno, following a conversation with whistle-blower Mike McQueary,
"could have made that phone call without so much as getting his hands
dirty. Why he didn't," Boccabella lectured, "is beyond me."[518] Responding
to a *Washington Post* article on the sentencing, a Penn State grad who began
his undergraduate studies the year Paterno became head coach, was harsh
on Paterno. "When this story broke," he began "it became clear that Joe
Paterno knew about this and did nothing." He believed "the damage these
men did to the reputation of the University and themselves is enormous."[519]

Even more damaging to Penn State and Joe Paterno was an *Atlantic Monthly* article on a 2017 Penn State's fraternity hazing death that was compared to Joe Paterno and Penn State's administration dealing with the Sandusky Scandal. In a lengthy article, Caitlin Flanagan believed that the 2017 fraternity pledge death of Tim Piazza and Joe Paterno's actions in 2001 "gestured to a common theme." Both cases, she stated, showed "dark events that had taken place on or near the campus for years, with some kind of tacit knowledge on the part of the university." Flanagan continued, "there is also the sense that at Penn State, both the fraternities and the football team operate as they please. To the extent that this is true," she emphasized, "the person responsible is Joe Paterno." She believed that Paterno, a booster of the fraternity system since his days at Brown University, was not upset with a previous hazing incident in 2007 when Penn State wrestlers engaged in hazing and that it was an accepted part of Greek life on campuses.[520] However questionable her jab at Paterno was, it was contained in a touted periodical and continued the Sandusky story and its negative impact upon Penn State and Paterno.

The story goes on. There has been no resolution of the scandal at Penn State despite the NCAA conceding on the Consent Decree and the Paterno Family giving up on the illegalities of the NCAA and the disparagement of Joe Paterno. There has been no resolution growing out of the Sandusky Scandal between the two factions of the Penn State Board of Trustees between elected alumni members, who opposed nearly all actions of the trustees, and the rest of the board. There has been no resolution on the legacy of Joe Paterno and whether his bronze statue should be brought back to campus once again. There has been no resolution on whether or not Penn State should release closed records of how it dealt with the Freeh Report, the Consent Decree, or the NCAA. After numerous lawsuits and legal maneuvering and after millions of dollars spent by Penn State to attempt to "move forward," many of those who lived through the crisis were not satisfied with the results.

Meanwhile, the NCAA moved on with its inept leadership, not being able to exact penalties against an institution such as the University of North Carolina, which allowed many athletes for nearly two decades to stay eligible to participate in athletics while taking a shadow curriculum. That is, courses with no substance but high grades.[521] The Penn State story goes on unresolved. Only the passage of time makes the scandal and the nailing of Penn State to the crossbar by the NCAA appear to be in the rearview mirror.

After more than a half-dozen years, NCAA leaders, Mark Emmert, Donald Remy, and Ed Ray were still guilty for denying justice to Penn State as they were before the two lawsuits against them were concluded without trials. Just because they got off "scot-free" doesn't mean they weren't culpable for the unlawful breaking of their own constitution and bylaws and bullying Penn State into signing the Consent Decree. Justice is a virtue, and there was nothing virtuous about the leaders of the NCAA or the tainted Consent Decree. For Emmert, trained but not well educated from his Ph.D. degree in public administration, sought power and self aggrandizement over equity and justice in his NCAA administration to the detriment of Penn State and its most visible individual, Joe Paterno. Emmert, individually, following the Machiavellian strategies for ruling princes, used Draco, the ancient Greek, for his Penn State penalties. Draco was the 7th century B.C.E. Athenian lawgiver whose penalty for many crimes was death.[522] Emmert only threatened death to Penn State. Yet, his Consent Decree was "written in blood" more than any Draconian document in the history of the National Collegiate Athletic Association.

One can imagine Mark Emmert dozing off as he sits before his fireplace re-reading Machiavelli's *The Prince* and listening to Beethoven's Eroica Symphony, first called the Bonaparte Symphony.[523] Suddenly Beethoven, who came to despise authoritarian Napoleon, speaks directly to dreaming Emmert: "Nothing is more intolerable than to be compelled to accuse one's self of one's own errors."[524] Especially for an individual, such as Emmert, who remained in a position of power and authority. Justice and plain decency demand more.

Timeline*

February 22, 1855	Birthdate of Penn State University as the Farmers' High School.
April 1, 1863	Penn State becomes the sole land-grant college in Pennsylvania.
June 16, 1866	Penn State's first intercollegiate athletic contest is in baseball.
Fall 1871	First women are admitted into Penn State.
November 12, 1881	First football game, 9-0 win over Bucknell.
1887	An Athletic Association of students is formed at Penn State.
March 18, 1890	The Athletic Association adopts blue and white school colors.
October 1891	Students hire a physical educator and trainer for football and baseball.
January 25, 1892	George Hoskins becomes physical director and football coach.
May 1892	Penn State's football team begins spring practice tradition.
June 9, 1892	The new athletic facility is named Beaver Field for James Beaver, Civil War general and ex-governor.
February 6, 1894	The Alumni Advisory Committee is created by students to help raise money and promote athletics.
November 21, 1894	President Atherton allows a failing football player to continue playing.

*For a 150-page timeline, contact rsmith@eifrigpublishing.com

June 17, 1896	Silvanus Newton replaces George Hoskins as physical director and coach.
Fall 1896	Carlton A. "Brute" Randolph becomes Penn State's first Walter Camp all-American.
July 31, 1900	The Board of Trustees offers athletic scholarship for the first time.
July 31, 1900	W. N. "Pop" Golden is hired as physical educator and coach.
April 1901	Prof. Fred Pattee's "Alma Mater" is published.
July 11, 1903	Trustees agree to build an athletic dorm with a training table.
January 27, 1906	Pop Golden is named the first Penn State athletic director.
Fall 1906	William T. "Mother" Dunn is chosen Penn State's first all-American as a first teamer by Walter Camp.
November 28, 1907	An Alumni Advisory Committee of the Athletic Association recommends a graduate manager of athletics after a loss to Pitt.
January 1908	A graduate manager of athletics is created by the Alumni Association.
1908	The Penn State Faculty Senate votes that it has jurisdiction over athletic contests.
June 15, 1908	Trustees establish the Department of Physical Culture.
May 2, 1909	New Beaver Field for track, baseball, and football is dedicated.
Fall 1909	Bill Hollenback becomes football coach and produces winning teams.
June 1913	The Alumni Advisory Committee proposes eliminating the position of athletic director.
November 1913	A letterman's club, Varsity Club, is organized by alumni.

1918	The Penn State Women's Athletic Association is founded.
August 25, 1918	Hugo Bezdek, manager of the Pittsburgh Pirates, is named football coach and director of physical education.
November 23, 1921	Bezdek's salary is raised to $14,000, more than the president, after winning 30 games without a loss, and athletic scholarships are soon increased from 25 to 75.
January 1, 1923	Proceeds from the Penn State-Southern Cal Rose Bowl game go toward constructing a new athletic dorm, eventually known as Irvin Hall.
January 8, 1926	The Carnegie Foundation begins investigating college athletics including Penn State.
June 14, 1926	An alumni committee in Pittsburgh is appointed to study Penn State athletics, especially the role of Hugo Bezdek in losing to Pitt.
September 24, 1926	Ralph Hetzel is chosen president and leads the Great Experiment failure of attempting to win in big-time athletics without financial aid to athletes.
December 21, 1926	Joseph Vincent Paterno is born in Brooklyn, New York.
August 10, 1927	The Board of Athletic Control ends athletic scholarships.
January 19, 1929	Recreation Hall is opened, receiving a half million dollars from the state for construction.
January 9, 1930	The Board of Athletic Control recommends firing Hugo Bezdek as coach.
January 20, 1930	The Trustees vote to create a new School of Physical Education and Athletics, Bezdek as head, placing athletics within an academic unit.
March 27, 1930	Bob Higgins, all-American in football, becomes head football coach.

September 26, 1931	Alumnus B. C. "Casey" Jones silently begins recruiting and subsidizing in football.
1934	Ridge Riley is hired as the first sports information director.
April 23, 1937	Dr. Carl Schott is chosen Dean of Physical Education and Athletics, replacing Hugo Bezdek.
September 26, 1938	Ridge Riley writes the first Penn State "Football Newsletter."
October 1, 1938	Penn State's radio network for football is established.
March 23, 1939	The School of Physical Education and Athletics opposes women's intercollegiate athletics despite Dorothy Anderson playing on the men's varsity tennis team several years before.
October 12, 1940	The Quarterback Club is organized to raise funds for football.
June 7, 1941	Heinz Warneke is chosen to sculpt a "Lion Shrine" by the Class of '40.
January 26, 1944	Gerald Arthur Sandusky is born in Washington, Pennsylvania.
1944	Joe Paterno translates Virgil's *Aeneid,* a book about courage, endurance, and fate, influencing his life in coaching.
November 17, 1945	Wally Triplett is first African American to start in Penn State football.
November 29, 1946	Penn State players refuse to play the University of Miami when asked to drop two African Americans.
December 1947	"We Are—Penn State" tradition is begun when the team refuses to play Southern Methodist unless Wally Triplett and Dennie Hoggard could play.

January 10, 1948   The NCAA passes the first eligibility and recruiting rules, called the Sanity Code, with the ability to enforce the rules.

March 13, 1949   Joe Bedenk is named head football coach for one year.

May 13, 1949   The Board of Trustees creates 100 athletic scholarships.

April 24, 1950   Charles "Rip" Engle is appointed head football coach.

May 27, 1950   Joe Paterno, Engle's third choice, becomes assistant coach.

November 18, 1950   The Athletic Advisory Board continues policy of no women's intercollegiate athletics at Penn State.

May 5, 1951   The inaugural Blue-White spring football game is held.

July 1952   Ernie McCoy, from the University of Michigan, becomes Dean and Athletic Director of the School of Physical Education and Athletics.

October 1952   The Levi Lamb Fund is created for athletic scholarships.

January 9, 1953   The first "death penalty" is given to Kentucky by the NCAA.

July 15, 1955   Dean McCoy emphasizes there is no distinction made between athletes and others regarding probation and dismissal from Penn State.

April 1959   The Nittany Lion Club is established to support athletics financially.

November 24, 1959   Beaver Field stands are dismantled and moved across campus.

January 28, 1963   The School of Physical Education and Athletics opposes any separation of athletics from an academic unit.

Fall 1963	Jerry Sandusky begins three years of varsity football at Penn State.
June 16, 1964	Joe Paterno is named associate coach and probable successor to Rip Engle.
Fall 1964	Women's intercollegiate athletics begins officially at Penn State.
January 28, 1965	Joe Paterno turns down a head football coaching position at Yale.
February 19, 1966	Joe Paterno is appointed head football coach at $20,000 salary.
May 1966	Jerry Sandusky is named top student in his college.
October 19, 1967	The "Grand Experiment" of Joe Paterno is named in the *Philadelphia Inquirer*.
November 23, 1968	Joe Paterno is offered a head coach position at Michigan.
July 1, 1969	Ed Czekaj becomes Athletic Director.
July 1, 1969	Joe Paterno is granted full professor.
Fall 1969	Jerry Sandusky becomes assistant football coach.
June 11, 1970	The Board of Trustees grants the president the right to create policy.
July 1, 1970	Robert Scannell becomes Dean of Health, Physical Education and Recreation, a position controlling athletics.
January 5, 1973	Joe Paterno turns down New England Patriots coaching position.
June 16, 1973	Joe Paterno delivers Penn State's Commencement Address.
June 7, 1977	Jerry Sandusky creates The Second Mile for at-risk children.

October 12, 1978	A committee to review Dean Bob Scannell's office meets, to determine if he spends too much time on athletics.
January 1, 1979	Paterno's team loses the national championship to Bear Bryant, a devastating blow to Paterno.
March 1979	Penn State, in women's basketball, receives its first ever sanction for illegal recruiting.
May 14, 1979	The report of Dean Scannell's office recommends that athletics remain in the academic unit.
December 1979	Joe Paterno is offered the position of athletic director, demanding that athletics be withdrawn from an academic unit.
January 14, 1980	President John Oswald removes athletics from an academic unit and places it under a business office.
February 6, 1980	President Oswald receives a NCAA notice of recruiting violation by Joe Paterno.
Spring 1980	Joe Paterno asks President Oswald to admit nine football players who can not meet entrance requirements. All are given presidential admits.
January 1, 1983	Paterno wins his first national championship using presidential admits.
January 27, 1983	Paterno asks the Board of Trustees to be more involved in raising money for Penn State.
December 6, 1984	Paterno establishes the Paterno Libraries Endowment with a gift.
June 21, 1985	A special NCAA conventions creates a "death penalty" for institutions with repeat major violations.

June 16, 1986	Rene Portland, basketball coach, announces opposition to lesbians in her program.
December 18, 1986	Joe Paterno is *Sports Illustrated* "Sportsman of the Year."
January 2, 1987	Paterno wins his second national football championship.
January 7, 1987	Southern Methodist University is given the "death penalty."
December 6, 1988	Joe Paterno praises Jerry Sandusky with an "impeccable lifestyle" in a recommendation for Temple's football coaching position.
November 19, 1989	Congress passes the Clery Act requiring reporting of college crime statistics.
June 4, 1990	The Big Ten votes Penn State into the Conference.
November 9, 1990	The Second Mile receives President Bush's 294th Point of Light.
May 16, 1991	The Board of Trustees includes sexual orientation in its anti-discrimination policy.
December 30, 1993	Tim Curley is named Athletic Director.
July 14, 1994	A new library at University Park is named Paterno Library.
January 1, 1995	Gary Schultz is named Senior Vice President for Finance and Business.
January 6, 1996	The Penn State Academic-Athletic Convocation Center (Bryce Jordan Center) is opened.
January 1998	Joe Paterno tells Jerry Sandusky he will not be the next head coach.
May 3, 1998	Jerry Sandusky sexually assaults an 11-year old boy in Lasch Building.

May 4, 1998	Alycia Chambers, a psychologist, calls Sandusky "a likely pedophile."
May 4, 1998	Gary Schultz begins a confidential file on the Sandusky situation.
May 5, 1998	All four administrators, Graham Spanier, Gary Schultz, Tim Curley, and Joe Paterno, are informed of the Sandusky investigation.
June 1, 1998	District Attorney Ray Gricar declines to prosecute Sandusky and Penn State police state "case closed."
June 9, 1999	Jerry Sandusky reaches a retirement agreement and agrees to coach one more year.
December 5, 1999	Jerry Sandusky receives the 1999 Alumni Award and soon is selected Assistant Coach of the Year.
November 28, 2000	Sandusky's book, *Touched: The Jerry Sandusky Story*, is published.
February 9, 2001	Mike McQueary observes Sandusky in a shower room with Victim 2.
February 10, 2001	McQueary reports what he saw the night before to Joe Paterno.
February 11, 2001	Paterno reports McQueary's concerns to Tim Curley.
February 25, 2001	Schultz, Curley, and Spanier exchange emails about Jerry Sandusky, deciding not to report to legal officials.
March 19, 2001	Tim Curley informs The Second Mile of Sandusky allegations.
July 24, 2001	Gary Schultz agrees to sell university property to Sandusky's Second Mile.
November 2, 2001	The Joe Paterno statue is unveiled after his 324th victory as coach.

Fall 2003	Jerry Sandusky becomes a volunteer assistant coach at Central Mountain High School.
February 17, 2004	Mike McQueary becomes a full-time assistant football coach.
November 10, 2004	Graham Spanier, Tim Curley, Gary Schultz, and Steve Garban visit Paterno and inquire about him retiring.
December 21, 2005	Basketball player Jennifer Harris files a sexual discrimination lawsuit against coach Rene Portland.
May 26, 2006	Joe Paterno is elected into the College Football Hall of Fame.
April 1, 2007	A group of football player beat up several students, leading to increased conflict between Paterno and Vicky Triponey, head of Student Affairs.
September 12, 2007	Vicky Triponey leaves Penn State after conflict with Paterno and Spanier.
November 2008	A Central Mountain wrestling coach observes child molestation by Sandusky.
March 3, 2009	The Central Mountain Sandusky molestation case is transferred to Pennsylvania Attorney General Tom Corbett.
May 1, 2009	Tom Corbett initiates the Sandusky Grand Jury investigation.
January 22, 2010	Cynthia Baldwin is appointed General Counsel for Penn State.
November 3, 2010	A "concerned citizen" asks Centre County D.A., Stacy Parks Miller, to interview Mike McQueary about Jerry Sandusky.
December 14, 2010	Mike McQueary tells the Grand Jury about Sandusky's shower incident.

January 12, 2011	Tim Curley, Gary Schultz, and Joe Paterno testify before the Grand Jury, "represented" by Cynthia Baldwin.
March 19, 2011	The Board of Trustees meets, but there is no mention of the Grand Jury.
March 31, 2011	Sara Ganim of the *Harrisburg Patriot-News* reveals contents of the secret Grand Jury Report.
April 13, 2011	Graham Spanier testifies before the Grand Jury, represented, he believes, by Cynthia Baldwin.
May 12, 2012	Spanier downplays the allegations against Sandusky to the Board of Trustees. The Trustees raise no questions.
August 9-10, 2011	NCAA President Mark Emmert convenes a meeting, mostly of presidents, out of which a committee for tougher rules of enforcement results.
October 27, 2011	Penn State receives knowledge of the forthcoming Grand Jury presentment of Gary Schultz and Tim Curley.
October 28, 2011	Spanier, with Cynthia Baldwin, Steve Garban, and Communications staff, plan announcement of Spanier's "unconditional support" for Schultz and Curley.
November 4, 2011	Jerry Sandusky is charged in a Grand Jury presentment of 40 sex crimes involving 8 boys.
November 4, 2011	Charges of perjury are brought against Gary Schultz and Tim Curley.
November 8, 2011	President of the Board of Trustees, Steve Garban, turns the Sandusky Scandal over to Vice-President John Surma.
November 9, 2011	The Trustees receive Graham Spanier's resignation and fire Joe Paterno. Paterno is told with a telephone call.

November 9, 2011	Provost Rod Erickson is appointed Penn State President.
November 9-10, 2011	A State College riot occurs over the firing of Joe Paterno.
November 10, 2011	Mike McQueary is told he will not coach in the next game.
November 11, 2011	Ken Frazier and Ron Tomalis are chosen to lead the Trustees' "Special Investigations Task Force."
November 11, 2011	Mike McQueary is placed on administrative leave.
November 11, 2011	A peaceful candlelight vigil is held focusing on Sandusky victims.
November 13, 2011	Jack Raykovitz, The Second Mile president, resigns.
November 15, 2011	Graham Spanier and Penn State sign a separation agreement.
November 16, 2011	Dave Joyner from the Trustees is appointed acting Athletic Director.
November 16, 2011	Mark Emmert's noted "Mark wants more" statement is made about penalties to Penn State.
November 17, 2011	Mark Emmert sends a kind of condemnation of Penn State to President Erickson asking for answers to four major questions.
November 21, 2011	Former FBI head, Louis Freeh, is chosen by the Trustees to lead an internal investigation of the Sandusky Scandal.
November 23, 2011	Mark Emmert states, "We cannot miss the opportunity to leverage the moment" against Penn State.
December 7, 2011	The Louis Freeh group, NCAA, and Big Ten meet at the Penn State Nittany Lion Inn.

January 5, 2012	NCAA's Donald Remy emphasizes the desire to have the Freeh Group look into "institutional control and ethical conduct."
January 6, 2012	Bill O'Brien is hired as football coach at Penn State.
January 14, 2012	Sally Jenkins of the *Washington Post* interviews Joe Paterno.
January 22, 2012	Joe Paterno dies of lung cancer.
January 26, 2012	The Board of Trustees cancels President Erickson's letter of praise for Joe Paterno.
January 31, 2012	The Pennsylvania Manufacturers' Association Insurance Company files a declaratory judgment lawsuit against Penn State and Sandusky victims.
April 16, 2012	Sara Ganim is winner of a Pulitzer Prize for Sandusky Scandal coverage.
May 4, 2012	Three new Penn State Trustees are elected, all opposed to Paterno's firing.
May 8, 2012	Mike McQueary indicates he will sue Penn State in an employment dispute.
June 6, 2012	A jury of 12 is chosen to hear the Sandusky case.
June 11, 2012	NBC reports emails of Graham Spanier, Gary Schultz, and Tim Curley to be used in the Freeh Report.
June 12, 2012	Mike McQueary testifies at the Sandusky trial.
June 20, 2012	Matt Sandusky, adopted son of Sandusky, reveals that his adopted father abused him.
June 22, 2012	Sandusky is proven guilty on 45 of 48 sexual abuse counts.
June 30, 2012	Cynthia Baldwin, Penn State chief counsel, resigns.

July 11, 2012	Gene Marsh, an Alabama lawyer, is hired by Penn State to deal with the NCAA.
July 2012	The NCAA removes the "death penalty" definition from its website.
July 12, 2012	The Freeh Report, damning to four administrators, is released.
July 12, 2012	The Board of Trustees accepts the Freeh Report without reading it.
July 13, 2012	President Erickson, at a trustees meeting, calls to "move forward" four times.
July 14, 2012	Julie Roe, NCAA Director of Enforcement, reveals that the NCAA was "bluffing" Penn State with the "death penalty."
July 16, 2012	Stephen Dunham begins as General Counsel at Penn State.
July 17, 2012	A plane flies a banner, "Take the Statue Down or We Will," around State College.
July 17, 2012	President Mark Emmert tells President Erickson that "presidents want blood."
July 18, 2012	President Erickson favors moving forward and quickly taking penalties.
July 20, 2012	Trustee member Paul Suhey asks Erickson to remove the Paterno statue.
July 20, 2012	President Erickson tells advisors that the NCAA will pick through all the football disciplinary player cases.
July 21, 2012	President Ed Ray of Oregon State and Harris Pastides of South Carolina favor the NCAA death penalty for Penn State.
July 21, 2012	State Senator Jake Corman suggest due process to President Erickson rather than acting hastily.

July 22, 2012	Joe Paterno's statue is removed on President Erickson's orders.
July 22, 2012	The NCAA-Penn State Consent Decree is signed by Erickson.
July 23, 2012	Graham Spanier sends a letter to the trustees noting errors in the Freeh Report.
August 3, 2012	Wick Sollers, as the Joe Paterno Family lawyer, challenges the NCAA-Penn State Consent Decree.
August 28, 2012	Twenty nine former Penn State Faculty Senate chairs blast the Freeh Report.
September 13, 2012	Penn Staters for Responsible Stewardship issues a 53-page report criticizing the Freeh Report.
September 27, 2012	Victim # 1, Aaron Fisher, signs a book deal, "Silent No More."
October 2, 2012	Mike McQueary sues Penn State for damages to his reputation in a whistleblower suit.
October 9, 2012	Jerry Sandusky is sentenced to 30-60 years in prison.
October 10, 2012	Feinberg Rosen law firm is hired to settle all claims by individuals abused by Sandusky.
October 26, 2012	Cynthia Baldwin illegally testifies to a Grand Jury against President Spanier.
October 26, 2012	Moody's Investors Service downgrades Penn State's credit rating from AA1 to AA2.
October 29, 2012	David Leebron, Rice University president, claims that the NCAA Executive Committee and Board did not fully vet Penn State penalties.
November 1, 2012	Ex-president Graham Spanier is indicted by the Grand Jury for perjury.

January 2, 2013	Governor Tom Corbett files an antitrust lawsuit against the NCAA.
January 4, 2013	State Senator Jake Corman sues the NCAA on its $60 million fine.
January 24, 2013	Julie Del Giorno is hired as Athletics Integrity Officer.
February 2013	Penn State fencer, Kane Gladnick, discards knee tape, taken for a marijuana cigarette, leading to coach Emmanuil Kaidanov's firing.
February 9, 2013	The Paterno Family releases its "Critique of the Freeh Report."
February 20, 2013	The Pennsylvania Endowment bill, to keep the $60 million NCAA fine in state passes 194-2 (House) and 50-0 (Senate), is signed by the Governor.
April 3, 2013	Brent Schrotenboer writes an exposé of Mark Emmert for *USA Today*.
May 30, 2013	The Paterno Family files a lawsuit against the NCAA for violating due process in the Consent Decree.
January 11, 2014	James Franklin is introduced as Penn State football coach.
February 10, 2014	Eric Barron, Florida State president, is chosen Penn State's president.
May 30, 2014	Geoffrey Moulton's "Report to the Attorney General on the Investigation of Gerald A. Sandusky" exonerates Gov. Corbett from investigation delay.
June 5, 2014	Coach Kaidanov, fired fencing coach, files a federal suit for breach of contract and lack of due process.
July 23, 2014	Jay Paterno's book, *Paterno Legacy*, is released.

July 26, 2014	Sandy Barbour is chosen new athletic director.
August 13, 2014	The Trustees vote 19-8 to support the $60 million fine and Consent Decree.
September 8, 2014	The NCAA restores football scholarship for 2015 and bowl eligibility.
September 11, 2014	The Paterno Family is granted standing to challenge the NCAA Consent Decree.
September 19, 2014	The Trustees vote 17-9 not to investigate the Freeh Report.
October 3, 2014	The legality of the Consent Decree becomes part of the Senator Corman suit.
November 5, 2014	Julie Roe's 2012 quote that the NCAA pulled a "bluff" about the death penalty is released to the public.
December 2, 2014	In Mark Emmert's deposition in the Corman suit, he uses "I don't recall, I don't remember," and "I don't know" well over 100 times.
January 15, 2015	Senator Corman announces "the NCAA has surrendered" in the Corman-NCAA out-of-court settlement.
June 17, 2015	The Kaidanov v. Penn State wrongful termination suit is settled out-of-court, presumably in favor of Kaidanov.
June 30, 2015	The "We Are" 10' high sculpture is placed near Beaver Stadium.
January 5, 2016	Painter Michael Pilato restores Joe Paterno's halo on the Heister Street Mural.
January 22, 2016	Because of wrongful actions of Cynthia Baldwin, obstruction, conspiracy, and perjury charges are dropped against Graham Spanier, Gary Schultz, and Tim Curley. Endangering the welfare of children remains.

March 30, 2016	The Pennsylvania Appeals Court agrees that perjury and obstruction charges against Spanier, Schultz, and Curley should be thrown out.
May 24, 2016	The NCAA subpoenas testimony of alleged Sandusky molestations in 1976 and 1987.
September 17, 2016	Penn State honors Joe Paterno at a Temple game, during the 50th anniversary of his first game as head coach.
September 22, 2016	Penn State and the Pennsylvania Manufacturers' Association Insurance Company settle their payment of Sandusky victims' dispute.
October 13, 2016	A judge drops the perjury charges against Tim Curley.
October 27, 2016	A jury awards Mike McQueary $7.3 million for defamation and misrepresentation.
November 3, 2016	The U.S. Department of Education fines Penn State $2.4 million for lack of compliance with the Clery Act.
November 30, 2016	Judge Gavin awards $5 million to Mike McQueary for the whistle-blower portion of the case.
December 7, 2016	Mark Emmert of the NCAA says the Consent Decree was not meant to cripple Penn State.
January 11, 2017	The Paterno Family requests all Senator Corman Consent Decree documents in its case against the NCAA.
March 13, 2017	Tim Curley and Gary Schultz enter guilty pleas in the Sandusky Scandal.
March 24, 2017	Graham Spanier is found guilty of child endangerment.
March 30, 2017	Foreman of the Spanier trial regrets his guilty vote in the Spanier trial.

May 4, 2017	Jay Paterno gains the greatest number of votes in the election to the Penn State Board of Trustees.
June 2, 2017	All three Penn State administrators are sentenced to prison terms.
June 8, 2017	Wick Sollers, Paterno Family counsel, withdraws from the Paterno Family v. NCAA case.
June 30, 2017	Sue Paterno drops the Paterno Family vs. NCAA case with prejudice.
June 30, 2017	NCAA's Donald Remy says Sue Paterno feared discovery materials being revealed in a trial.
July 14, 2017	Tim Curley and Gary Schultz begin their short prison terms in the Centre County Prison.
July 25, 2017	A state Superior Court judge refuses to drop the Paterno Family-NCAA court case.
November 1, 2017	Mike McQueary ends his whistleblower lawsuit with Penn State, likely with a financial settlement.
November 10, 2017	Penn State's pay to Sandusky victims rises to $109 million.
January 10, 2018	An additional Sandusky victim is paid by Penn State.
January 24, 2018	The jailing of Michigan State's Larry Nasser for sexual violations is compared to Jerry Sandusky.
March 26, 2018	Public revelations are released about the illegality of Cynthia Baldwin's testimony and prosecutor Frank Fina questioning in October 2012 leading to guilt of Spanier, Schultz, and Curley.
May 16, 2018	Michigan State will pay 500 million to Nasser sexual assault victims.
June 29, 2018	A review of the Freeh Report by some of the members of the Board of Trustees is presented to the full Board of Trustees.

ENDNOTES

Introduction Notes

1 Edward R. Murrow, "See It Now," 9 March 1954, in condemnation of Senator Joseph McCarthy for his communist, Cold War, witch-hunt.

2 Steven Fink, as quoted by David J. KIetchen, Jr., "How Penn State Turned a Crisis into a Disaster: An Interview with Crisis Management Pioneer Steven Fink," *Business Horizons* (2014), 673.

3 Alycia A. Chambers to Ronald Schraffler, Penn State police, 7 May 1998 [www.msnbcmedia.msn.com/l/msnbc/section/news/chambers_sandusky_report] (accessioned 31 December 2012).

4 *NCAA Division I Manual, Constitution and Bylaws, 2011-2012* [www.ncaapublications.com/productdownloads/D112.pdf] (accessioned 24 August 2015). See particularly Section 19.1, 19.1.2, 19.4.1, 10.01.5, 32.7.l.1, 32.7.1.3,. and 32.8.1. See also "Due Process and the NCAA," Hearing Before the Subcommittee on the Constitution of the Committee on the Judiciary House of Representatives, 108 Congress, 2nd Session, 14 September 2014, pp. 16-20; Joshua J. Despain, "From Off the Bench: The Potential Role of the U. S. Department of Education in Reforming Due Process in the NCAA," *Iowa Law Review*, 100 (2015), 1285-1326; Rodney K. Smith, "A Brief History of the National Collegiate Athletic Association's Role in Regulating Intercollegiate Athletics," *Marquette Sports Law Review*, 11 No. 1 (Fall 2000), 8-22; and Glenn Wong, Kyle Skillman, and Chris Deubert, "The NCAA's Infractions Appeals Committee: Recent Case History, Analysis and the Beginning of a New Chapter," *Virginia Sports and Entertainment Law Journal*, 9 No. 1 (2009), 47-153.

5 Richard H. Rovere, *Senator Joe McCarthy* (Berkeley: University of California Press, 1996), ix-x, showed the demagoguery of McCarthy, and Peter Beinart, "The New McCarthyism of Donald Trump," *Atlantic*, 21 July 2015 [www.theatlantic.com/politics/archive/2015/07/donald...mccarthy/399056] compared the demagoguery of Donald Trump to that of McCarthy well before he was elected president.

6 Erickson told the Board of Trustees multiple times that Penn State needed to "move forward" in his talk on August 12, 2012, justifying why he signed the Consent Decree. In his 2014 deposition during the Corman v. NCAA lawsuit, Erickson emphasized four times the need to "move forward." Rodney Erickson Deposition, 2 December 2014, pp. 127-128, Corman v. NCAA [www.senatorcorman.com/legal-documents-corman-vs-ncaa].

7 After researching in about 80 university archives, I have written five other books on intercollegiate athletics. They include *Sports and Freedom: The Rise of Big-Time College Athletics* (New York: Oxford University Press, 1988); *Big-Time Football at Harvard 1905:*

The Diary of Coach Bill Reid (Urbana: University of Illinois Press, 1994); *Play-by-Play: Radio, Television, and Big-Time College Sport* (Baltimore: Johns Hopkins University Press, 2001); *Pay for Play: A History of Big-Time College Athletic Reform* (Urbana: University of Illinois Press, 2011); and *Wounded Lions: Joe Paterno, Jerry Sandusky, and the Crisis in Penn State Athletics* (Urbana: University of Illinois Press, 2016).

8 "Paternopaterfamilias," *Quest* (September/October, 1978), Joe Paterno Vertical File, Folder "No Name," Penn State University Archives.

9 Research in the Nebraska Archives and over 80 other archives helped me to write *Pay for Play: A History of Big-Time College Athletic Reform* (Urbana: University of Illinois Press, 2011).

10 Notes from meeting with Graham Spanier, Lincoln, Nebraska, 12 April 1995, Ron Smith Personal File.

11 "Statement by Chancellor Graham Spanier, 26 June 1992, Chancellors' Central Files, Box 299, Folder 25, University of Nebraska Archives.

12 I began my research on January 18, 2012, four days before the death of Joe Paterno, searching the papers of Penn State President George W. Atherton, 1882-1906.

13 Ronald A. Smith, *Wounded Lions: Joe Paterno, Jerry Sandusky, and the Crises in Penn State Athletics* (Urbana: University of Illinois Press, 2016).

14 Corman v. NCAA, 4 January 2013, Commonwealth Court of Pennsylvania, No. 1 MD 2013 and Anne E. Covey, Memorandum and Order, 28 January 2015, Commonwealth Court of Pennsylvania, Miscellaneous Docket Sheet, Docket No. 1 MD 2013.

15 *Estate and Family of Joseph Paterno v. NCAA, Mark Emmert, and Edward Ray*, 30 May 2013, Docket No. 2013-2082, Civil Division, Court of Common Pleas of Centre County, Pennsylvania.

16 J. A. Froude, *The Divorce of Catherine of Aragon* (New York: Charles Scribner's Sons, 1891), 79.

17 Charles Dickens, *Life and Adventures of Martin Chuzzlewit* (London: Chapman & Hall, 1843), Chapter 8 [www.gutenberg.org/Files/968/968-h/968-h.htm/#link2HCH0008] (accessioned 10 April 2017).

18 Paul J. Weber, "NCAA Convention: New President Mark Emmert Calls for Tougher Parent Rules, . . ." *Columbus* (Georgia) *Ledger-Enquirer*, 14 January 2011 [www.ledger-inquirer.com/sports/college/sec/auburn-university] (accessioned 13 April 2017).

Chapter One Notes

19 Thucydides, *History of the Peloponnesian War*, Book 5.89 (Thucydides: The Jewett Translations, 411 BCE) [www.classicpersuasion.org/pw.thucydides/thucydides-jowettoc-b.html] (accessioned 31 July 2015).

20 Ibid., Book 5.

21 Niccolò Machiavelli, *The Prince,* XVIII, p. 101 [www.freeclassicbooks.com/nicolo%machiavelli/the%prince.pdf] (accessioned 3 August 2015).

22 One can also draw an analogy of Emmert and Remy and the criticized princes in Biblical times, for in Proverbs 28:16, it states that "a ruler who lacks understanding is a cruel oppressor. . . ." It is possible that wicked individuals strengthen each other in wicked ways. *English Standard Version, Bible,* 28:16.

23 Joseph N. Crowley, *In the Arena: The NCAA's First Century* (Indianapolis, IN: NCAA, 2006), 103.

24 *New York Herald,* 12 October 1905, p. 1. For an insider's view of the White House Conference as a participant, see Ronald A. Smith (ed.), *Big-Time Football at Harvard 1905: The Diary of Coach Bill Reid* (Urbana: University of Illinois Press, 1994), 193-195.

25 For a more nuanced discourse, see Ronald A. Smith, "Brutality, Ethics, and the Creation of the NCAA," *Sports and Freedom: The Rise of Big-Time College Athletics* (New York: Oxford University Press, 1988), 191-208.

26 Ronald A. Smith, "Football, Progressive Reform, and the Creation of the NCAA," and "The NCAA: A Faculty Debating Society for Amateurism," *Pay for Play: A History of Big-Time College Athletic Reform* (Urbana: University of Illinois Press, 2011), 42-59.

27 Ronald A. Smith, "Football, College" in Stephen Riess (ed.), *Sports in America: From Colonial Times to the Twenty-First Century* (Armonk, NY: M. E. Sharpe, 2011), Vol. I, pp. 355-361.

28 NCAA Executive Committee Minutes, 16-18 June 1948, N. W. Dougherty Collection, Box XX, Folder 3, University of Tennessee Archives.

29 The NCAA had never used termination of membership as a punishment for not living up to the ideals of the NCAA in its first four decades of existence. See comments in the NCAA *Proceedings,* 30 December 1941, p. 40.

30 *New York Times,* 21 January 1947, p. 19.

31 Crowley, *In the Arena,* 67-70.

32 Harvey Harman, president of the American Football Coaches Association, quoted a president at the 1949 NCAA convention. NCAA *Proceedings,* 7 January 1949, p. 99. For a more extensive discussion of the Sanity Code, see Smith, "The NCAA and the Sanity Code: A National Reform Gone Wrong," *Pay for Play,* 88-99.

33 NCAA *Proceedings, 1952-53,* p. 261.

34 Albert J. Figone, *Cheating the Spread: Gamblers, Point Shavers, and Game Fixers in College Football and Basketball* (Urbana: University of Illinois Press, 2012), 24-60 and John R. Thelin, Chapter 4, "Schools for Scandals, 1946-1960," in his *Games Colleges Play: Scandals and Reform in Intercollegiate Athletics* (Baltimore: Johns Hopkins University Press, 1994).

35 The sole negative vote was by the University of Tennessee. NCAA *Proceedings, 1952-53,* p. 270.

36 Walter Byers, *Unsportsmanlike Conduct: Exploiting College Athletes* (Ann Arbor:

University of Michigan Press, 1995), 59-61 and NCAA *Proceedings, 1952-53*, January 9-10, 1953, p. 266. Some could later claim that the NCAA used an outside source, the Judge Streit Report, as evidence, but unlike the Penn State case 60 years later, in the Kentucky case, both the Southeastern Conference and the NCAA investigated. In the Penn State case, the NCAA and Big Ten did no investigation before sentencing with severe sanctions, probably much more severe than the Kentucky death sentence. Kentucky played intra-squad games during the 1952-53 season before large crowds, probably more closely contested than against many of its usual opponents.

37 NCAA *Proceedings, 1952-53*, January 9-10, 1953, pp. 268-269. The lone vote against the sanction was by the University of Tennessee representative to insure that his vote was not the vote of Kentucky.

38 Ibid., January 8, 1953, p. 154.

39 Jack Falla, *NCAA: The Voice of College Sports* (Mission, KS: National Collegiate Athletic Association, 1981), 136-138.

40 NCAA *Proceedings, 1955-56*, January 11, 1956, p. 261.

41 Falla, *NCAA*, 139.

42 The charge of bullying by NCAA staff is found in Kenneth Frazier Deposition, 15 December 2014, "Legal Document – *Corman vs NCAA*," [www.senatorcorman.com/legal-documents-corman-vs-ncaa] (accessioned 27 June 2015). Frazier recalled that the NCAA overwhelmed Penn State officials with "a real and imminent threat" of a death penalty. . . "if we did not enter into the consent decree." pp. 75-76. One could argue that the NCAA bullied University of Nevada Las Vegas basketball coach, Jerry Tarkanian in the late twentieth century.

43 "Justices Uphold N.C.A.A.'s Right To Demand Suspension of Coach," *New York Times*, 13 December 1988 [www.nytimes.com/1988/12/13/sports/justices-upheld-ncaa] (accessioned 7 February 2016).

44 See later discussion of the Tarkanian case. The NCAA did not have to follow the due process clause of the U.S. Constitution because the Supreme Court had ruled that universities are not "state actors." See James Potter, "The NCAA as State Actor: Tarkanian, Brentwood, and Due Process," *University of Pennsylvania Law Review*, 155 (2007), 1269-1304 and *NCAA v. Tarkanian, 488 U.S. 179 (1988)*.

45 Falla, *NCAA*, 141-143.

46 The NCAA had passed its most restrictive academic qualification for athletic participation in 1966 with the 1.600 predictive college grade point average criteria. It was based on high school grade point average and standardized test scores, such as the Scholastic Aptitude Test. It lasted until 1973. National turmoil as a result of the Civil Rights Movement, affirmative action, and the Vietnam War led to its demise, but principally because standardized tests were considered racist. See Smith, *Pay for Play*, 127-131.

47 NCAA *Proceedings*, 9 January 1984, p. 101.

48 Smith, *Pay for Play*, 228.

49 David Whitford, *A Payroll to Meet: A Story of Greed, Corruption and Football at SMU* (New York: Macmillan, 1989), 113-135, John S. Watterson, *College Football: History,*

Spectacle, Controversy (Baltimore: Johns Hopkins University Press, 2000), 353-378, and Byers, *Unsportsmanlike Conduct*, 17-36.

50 For instance, the Committee on Infractions contemplated giving the University of Alabama the death penalty following major violations in the first decade of the twenty-first century. Similarly the death penalty was discussed relative to the University of Southern California basketball and football payment of players in which Heisman Trophy winner, Reggie Bush, returned the trophy. So too, the Miami of Florida athletic corruption case of the early twenty-first century was considered for the death penalty, probably until unethical investigative actions taken by NCAA officials interfered with the case. See Glenn Wong, Kyle Skillman, and Chris Deubert, "The NCAA's Infractions Appeals Committee: Recent Case History, Analysis and the Beginning of a New Chapter," *Virginia Sports and Entertainment Law Journal*, 9 No. 1 (2009), 92-99 and Allie Grasgreen, "At Last, Storm Settles at Miami," *Inside Higher Ed*, 23 October 2013 [www.insidehighered. com/news/2013/10/23/ncaa-ends-miami] (accessioned 24 August 2015).

51 VoxMediaUser136261, "The Monday Morning Wash—Contemplating the Death Penalty," [www.uwdawgpound.com/2011/8221275653/the-Monday-morning-wash] (accessioned 26 August 2015).

52 Wilford S. Bailey on Behalf of the NCAA Council, NCAA *Proceedings*, January 15, 1985, p. 162.

53 For a lengthy account of the Tarkanian case and aftermath, see Brian L. Porto, *The Supreme Court and the NCAA: The Case for Less Commercialism and More Due Process in College Sports* (Ann Arbor: University of Michigan Press, 2012), 100-177. See also, Aidan M. McCormack, "Seeking Procedural Due Process in NCAA Infraction Procedures: States Take Action," *Marquette Sports Law Review*, 2 No. 2 (Spring 1992), 261-293 who wrote that "Little can be said for a system that does not grant its own members their fundamental rights." p. 292. It could have been stated in 2012.

54 Charles E. Quirk, "*NCAA v. Tarkanian, 488 U.S. 179 (1988)*, in John W. Johnson (ed.), *Historic U.S. Court Cases: An Encyclopedia*, (New York: Routledge, 2001), vol. 1, 233-236.

55 *Estate and Family of Joseph Paterno v. NCAA, Mark Emmert, and Edward Ray*, Docket No. 2013-2082, Civil Division, Court of Common Pleas of Centre County, Pennsylvania, 29 April 2015, p. 19.

56 "Intercollegiate Sports," Hearings Before the Subcommittee on Commerce, Consumer Protection and Competitiveness of the Committee on Energy and Commerce, House of Representatives, 102d Congress, 1st Session, 19 June 1991.

57 Florida, Illinois, Nebraska, and Nevada passed due process statues in 1991. Joseph N. Crowley, *In the Arena: The NCAA's First Century* (Indianapolis: The NCAA, 2006), 167.

58 Rodney K. Smith, "A Brief History of the National Collegiate Athletic Association's Role in Regulating Intercollegiate Athletics," *Marquette Sports Law Review*, 11 No. 1 (Fall 2000), 18-19 and "Due Process and the NCAA," Hearing Before the Subcommittee on the Constitution of the Committee on the Judiciary, House of Representatives, 108th Congress, 2nd Session, 14 September 2004, p. 30.

59 Smith, "A Brief History," 18-19, and Porto, *The Supreme Court and the NCAA*, 156, 161.

60 "Due Process and the NCAA," Hearings Before the Subcommittee on the Constitution of the Committee on the Judiciary, House of Representatives, 108th Congress, 2nd Session, 14 September 2004, p. 9.

61 In a legal paper in the *Iowa Law Review*, it was claimed that "the NCAA reacted by circumventing ad hoc its own internal mechanism for investigation and enforcement and made an about-face from its original decision to let the criminal justice system run its course." Josha J. Despain, "From Off the Bench: The Potential Role of the U. S. Department of Education in Reforming Due Process in the NCAA," *Iowa Law Review*, 100 (2015), 1288 [ilr.law.uiowa.edu/files/ilr.law.uniowa.edu/files/ILR_100-3_Despain.pdf) (accessioned 7 August 2015).

62 "Auburn Releases Cam Newton Docs," *ESPN College Football*, 5 November 2011 [espn.go.com/college-football/story/_/id/7190987/auburn] (accessioned 2 August 2015).

63 NCAA and Associated Press, "Infractions Decision Stands for USC," *NCAA News*, 27 May 2011. [www.ncaa.com/news/football/2011-05-26/infractions-decision-stands-usc] (accessioned 17 August 2015).

64 "Ohio State Football: Jim Tressel Had Poor History of Reporting Violations," *Chronicle-Telegram Chronicle Online*, 16 July 2011 [chronicle.northcoastnow.com/2011/07/16/ohio-state-football-jim-tressel] (accessioned 4 August 2015).

65 Three years later Tressel became president of Youngstown State University in Ohio.

66 "Alabama Crimson Tide Football," *Wikipedia* [en.wikipedia.org/wiki/Alabama_Crimson_Tide_Football] (accessioned 31 August 2015).

67 Adam Jacobi, "The NCAA's Many Problems: Perception Clouds Alabama Issue," *SB Nation*, 9 October 2013 [www.sbnation.com/college-football/2013/10/9/4819820/alabama] and Jeremy Fowler, "Teflon Tide: Examining Alabama's Recent NCAA Concerns," *CBS Sports*, 28 January 2014 [www.cbssports.com/collegefootball/writer/jeremy-fowler] (accessioned 1 September 2015). The fact that in 2013 Derrick Crawford, an Alabama graduate, was NCAA Director of Enforcement did not help the perception.

68 "Statement from President Donna E. Shalala," 18 February 2013 [www.miami.edu/index/php/news/release] (accessioned 14 August 2015) and Steve Eder, "N.C.A.A. Admits Mishandling Miami Inquiry," *New York Times*, 23 January 2013 [www.nytimes.com/2013/01/24/sports/ncaa-admits-misconduct] (accessioned 6 February 2013).

69 Kenneth L. Wainstein, A. Joseph Jay III, and Colleen Depman Kukowski, "Investigation of Irregular Classes in the Department of African and Afro-American Studies at the University of North Carolina at Chapel Hill," 16 October 2014 [cqh929iorux3fdpl53203kg.wpengine.netdna-cdn.com] (accessioned 1 September 2015). 51% of the athletes in the classes were from football, 12% men's basketball, and 6% women's basketball—all intended to keep athletes eligible for athletic competition.

70 S. L. Price, "How Did Carolina Lose Its Way?" *Sports Illustrated*, 122 (16 March 2015), 67.

71 Aaron Beard, "NCAA Hits UNC Football with 1-Year Postseason Ban," *USA Today,* 13 March 2012 [usatoday330.usatoday.com/sports/college/football/2012-3-12] (accessioned 1 September 2015).

72 Matt Bonesteel and Will Hobson, "After Years-long Investigation, NCAA Finds No Academic Violations at North Carolina," *Washington Post,* 13 October 2017 [www.washingtonpost.com/news/early-lead/wp/2017/10/13] (accessioned 24 November 2017).

73 Ronnie Ramos, "Talk of Change Continues at Summit," 10 August 2011 [www.ncaa.com/news/ncaa/2011-08-10/talk-change-continues-summit] and "Q&A: Emmert on Presidential Retreat," *NCAA News,* 10 August 2011 [www.ncaa.com/news/ncaa/2011-08-10/qa-emmert-presidential-retreat] (accessioned 2 September 2015).

74 Allie Grasgreen, "New Day for Division I Athletes," *Inside Higher Ed,* 28 October 2011 [www.insidehighered.com/news/2011/20/28/ncaa-board] (accessioned 2 September 2015).

75 Edward Ray Deposition, 8 December 2014, p. 151, Legal Documents—*Corman vs NCAA* [www.senatorcorman.com/legal-documents-corman-vs-ncaa].

76 Jerry Jaye Wright, "Irish, Edward Simmons 'Ned,'" in David L. Porter, ed., *Biographical Dictionary of American Sports: Basketball and Other Indoor Sports* (Westport, CN: Greenwood Press, 1989), 140-142; John Christoau, *The Origins of the Jump Shot: Eight Men Who Shook the World of Basketball* (Lincoln: University of Nebraska Press, 1999), 13-15; and Neil D. Issacs, *A History of College Basketball* (Philadelphia: J. B. Lippincott, 1975), 111-115.

77 NCAA *Proceedings,* 1939, p. 117.

78 Ibid., 1963-64, p. 180.

79 For the impact of TV on basketball see, Ronald A. Smith, "Basketball: From Madison Square Garden to a Televised Final Four," *Play-by-Play: Radio, Television, and Big-Time College Sport* (Baltimore: Johns Hopkins University Press, 2001), 176-191.

80 NCAA *Proceedings,* "Financial Reports," 1951-52, 1965-66, and 1966-67.

81 Steve Berkowitz, "NCAA Nearly Topped $1 Billion in Revenue in 2014," *USA Today,* 11 March 2015 [www.usatoday.com/story/sports/college/2015/03/11/ncaa-financial] (accessioned 8 September 2015).

82 It took years for the NCAA to even consider settling out-of-court for activities that were challenging the 1890 Sherman Antitrust Act. The NCAA first lost the 1984 Oklahoma v. NCAA case in which the U. S. Supreme Court found the NCAA a monopoly in the telecasting of football games. It lost another antitrust case in 1998 when its rule to limit certain assistant coaches' salaries was monopolistically illegal resulting in an original $66 million fine. In 2005, the antitrust case against the NCAA for antitrust actions against the National Invitational Tournament was settled out-of-court when the NCAA purchased rights to the NIT tournament for $56.5 million. The NCAA lost the 2014 O'Bannon v. NCAA case in which antitrust laws were violated by the NCAA relative to illegal use of players' images in video games. The 2014 Senator Corman case against the NCAA for violations in the Penn State Consent Decree, including disbursement of a $60 million fine, was settled out-of-court in 2015 to save the NCAA from losing the case to the Pennsylvania state senator.

Chapter Two Notes

83 I was informed of this by the assistant to Dean Ernie McCoy, Glenn "Nick" Thiel, when I was interviewing in April 1968 for a position at Penn State. Thiel told me this, after I raised a question whether there would be any pressure on a professor for athlete's grades, something not uncommon in intercollegiate athletics in the 1960s across the nation. In 2015, for essentially doing what Paterno did, Rutgers' head football coach, Kyle Flood, was fined $50,000 of his $1.25 million salary and suspended for three games, including the Penn State game. "Report of the Factual Findings of the Investigation into Alleged Improper Contact by the Rutgers Head Football Coach with a Faculty Member," 15 September 2015 [president.Rutgers.edu/sites/president/files/Final%Report.pdf] (accessioned 19 September 2015) and "Rutgers Coach Kyle Flood Suspended Three Games, Fined $50,000," *USA Today Sports*, 16 September 2015 [www.usatoday.com/story/sports/ncaa/2015/09/16] (accessioned 19 September 2015).

84 Following his track coaching at Penn State, my colleague in sport history from 1968-1996 recounted this incident several times during our careers in what became the Department of Kinesiology.

85 There is good evidence that the so-called "Grand Experiment" of Joe Paterno was in existence well before Paterno became head coach. For instance, Professor Sparks wrote to Coach Rip Engle in 1956 that Engle had "inaugurated a new era in football" and would "attract smart players who are not only good athletes but also good students," reflecting what Paterno would preach about the "Grand Experiment," beginning in 1967. Even John Cappelletti in his Heisman Trophy winner address in 1973 noted Rip Engle for the "great tradition at Penn State. . . . " N. R. Sparks to Rip Engle, ca. October 1956, Charles Rip Engle Papers, Box 05.20, Folder "Ohio State Congratulatory Letters, 1956," Penn State University Archives and "John Cappelletti Heisman Acceptance Speech," Penn State University Archives.

86 Students originated athletics in the nineteenth century, while alumni often came to their rescue financially and then took over control outside the university administration. At Penn State this occurred in the late 1800s and early 1900s. See Ronald A. Smith, *Sports and Freedom: The Rise of Big-Time College Athletics* (New York: Oxford University Press, 1988), 118-120, 132, 212, 214-215.

87 Joseph V. Paterno to President Oswald, ca. fall 1979, President Oswald Papers, Box 10290, Folder "Athletics Relating to Admission, Policies, Etc. 1979-1982," Penn State University Archives. For a lengthy discussion, see my *Wounded Lions: Joe Paterno, Jerry Sandusky, and the Crises in Penn State Athletics* (Urbana: University of Illinois Press, 2016), Chapter 8.

88 See my *Wounded Lions*, passim.

89 William Ulerich, the Penn State Trustee liaison to the Athletic Department, gave a lengthy report on the incident to the Trustees. Penn State Board of Trustees Minutes, 25 May 1979, Penn State University Archives.

90 "Penn State is Placed on Year's Probation: Damage to Reputation Feared," *New York Times*, 5 April 1979, p. D21 and Denise Bachman and Joe Saraceno, "Meiser

Wonders, 'Why Penn State?'" [Penn State] *Daily Collegian*, 9 April 1979, pp. 1, 10-11. Meiser resigned at Penn State in 1980 and eventually became Assistant Athletic Director at the University of Connecticut and headed the committee that hired a dominating coach, Geno Auriemma, as the women's basketball coach. See Avi Salzman, "UConn Basketball Then and Now," *New York Times*, 18 April 2004. [www.nytimes.com/2004/04/18/nyregion/uconn-basketball] (accessioned 12 September 2015).

91 For a discussion of the AIAW losing power to the NCAA, see Ronald A. Smith, *Pay for Play: A History of Big-Time College Athletic Reform* (Urbana: University of Illinois Press, 2011), 141-150 and Ying Wushanley, *Playing Nice and Losing: The Struggle for Control of Women's Intercollegiate Athletics, 1960-2000* (Syracuse, NY: Syracuse University Press, 2004), 126-141.

92 Robert A. Stein, Big 10 Conference Compliance Committee, to Charlene Morett-Newman, 20 June 1991, Office of the Senior V.P. For Finance Records, Box 03086, Folder "Intercollegiate – Big 10-1," Penn State University Archives; Kathryn M. Statz, NCAA Eligibility Representative, to Carol Iwaoka, Big Ten Assistant Commissioner, 6 January 1994, President Joab Thomas Papers, Box 10449, Folder "NCAA(2)," Penn State University Archives; Cynthia J. Gabel, NCAA Enforcement Representative, to Timothy M. Curley, Penn State Athletic Director, 19 June 1995 and 24 March 1995, President Joab Thomas Papers, Box 10449, Folder "NCAA (2)," Penn State University Archives; and Gabel to Charles Waddell, Big Ten Assistant Commissioner, 16 March 1994, President Joab Thomas Papers, Box 10449, Folder "NCAA (2)," Penn State University Archives, and Gabel to James Tarman, Penn State Athletic Director, 8 December 1993, President Joab Thomas Papers, Box 10449, Folder "National Collegiate Athletic Association," Penn State University Archives.

93 Cynthia J. Gabel, NCAA Enforcement Representative, to Carol Iwaoka, Assistant Big Ten Commissioner, 24 March 1995, President Joab Thomas Papers, Box 10449, Folder "NCAA," and Gabel to Charles Waddell, Big Ten Assistant Commissioner, 16 March 1994, President Joab Thomas Papers, Box 10449, Folder "NCAA(2)," Penn State University Archives.

94 *Daily Collegian*, 28 February 1985, p. 8.

95 S. David Berst, NCAA Director of Enforcement, to President John W. Oswald, 6 February 1980, John Oswald Papers, Box 10338, Folder "Athletes-NCAA-CFA-TitleIX-2," Penn State University Archives.

96 Taped interview with Paterno, 14 April 1992, in Jodi Weber, "Joe Paterno in the NCAA," Ex Sci 444 paper, 21 April 1992, Penn State University Archives, "Paterno Violated Rule in Signing of Quintus McDonald," *Los Angeles Times*, 28 February 1985 [articles.latimes.com1985-02-28/sports/sp-12890] (accessioned 14 September 2015), and Michael O'Brien, *No Ordinary Joe: The Biography of Joe Paterno* (Nashville, TN: Rutledge Hill Press, 1998), 170-171.

97 Bill Brubaker, "Dear Chris," *Sports Illustrated* (26 November 1984), 120-136.

98 David Whitford, *A Payroll to Meet: A Story of Greed, Corruption and Football at SMU* (New York: Macmillan, 1989), 113-135, Walter Byers, *Unsportsmanlike Conduct: Exploiting Athletes* (Ann Arbor: University of Michigan Press, 1995), 17-26, and John S. Watterson, "Sudden Death at SMU: Football Scandals in the 1980s," in his *College*

Football: History, Spectacle, Controversy (Baltimore: Johns Hopkins University Press, 2000), 17-36.

99 Darren Everson and Hannah Karp, "The NCAA's Last Innocents," *Wall Street Journal*, 22 June 2011 [www.wsj.com/articles/SB10001424052704570005212286390] (accessioned 15 September 2015).

100 "NCAA Legislative Services Database—LSDBi" [wwb1.ncaa/exec/misearch] (accessioned 15 September 2015). Football and men's basketball have been involved in 635 of the 744 major violations from 1953 to 2012.

101 Marta Lawrence, "Penn State's Paterno Wins Ford Award: NCAA Honors Advocate for Intercollegiate Athletics During Career," *NCAA News*, 30 December 2010 [www.ncaa.com/news/football/2010-12-22/penn-states-paterno] (accessioned 16 September 2015).

102 Charles de Montesquieu, *Consideration on the Causes of the Grandeur and Decadence of the Romans,* Translation, Jehu Baker (New York: D. Appleton, 1882), Chapter XIV, p. 179.

103 Joe Paterno to Charles Theokas, 6 December 1988, Paterno Papers, Box 07574, Folder "Recommendations 1970-1980," Penn State University Archives.

104 "The Paterno Report: Critique of the Freeh Report," 10 February 2013, *Centre Daily Times*, 11 February 2013, p. 4.

105 Freeh Report, 12 July 2012, pp. 41-44.

106 Sara Ganim, "Former Centre County DA Ray Gricar's Reasons for Not Pursuing Case Against Jerry Sandusky," *Harrisburg Patriot-News*, 6 November 2011 [www.pennlive.com/midstate/index.ssf/2011/11/former_centre_county] (accessioned 22 September 2015).

107 Freeh Report, 12 July 2012, p. 48.

108 Joe Paterno Appointment Book (1998), Paterno Papers, Box 07574, Folder "Appointment Book," Penn State University Archives and Tim Curley, email to Gary Schultz, 13 May 1998, "Report of the Special Investigative Counsel Regarding the Actions of the Pennsylvania State University Related to the Child Sexual Abuse Committed by Gerald A. Sandusky," [Freeh Report] 12 July 2012, p. 49.

109 Ronald L. Schreffler, "Penn State Department of University Safety Incident Report," 3 June 1998 [notpsu.blogspot.com/2013/07/when-did-ray-gricar-close-his-sandusky] (accessioned 13 February 2014).

110 *Centre Daily Times*, 16 July 2012, p. A3.

111 Transcript of Proceedings Preliminary Hearings, 12 January 2011, Commonwealth of Pennsylvania v. Timothy Mark Curley, Court of Common Pleas, Dauphin County, Pennsylvania No. CP-MD-1374-2011; "The Freeh Report," 12 July 2012; and *Centre Daily Times*, 13 November 2011, p. A7.

112 Barry Petchesky, "When Current PSU President Rodney Erickson Bent the Rules for Jerry Sandusky," 12 July 2012 [deadspin.com/5925561/when-current-penn-state] (accessioned 21 August 2012).

113 "The Freeh Report," 12 July 2012, pp. 68-71.

114 *Monsieur Verdoux (1947) Movie Script* [www.springfield.co.uk/movie_script. php?movie=monsieur-verdoux] (accessioned 12 April 2017).

115 "The Freeh Report," 12 July 2012, pp. 71-79.

116 "Report of the Special University Faculty Committee to Review President Thomas' Proposed Amendment to the University's Non-Discrimination Policy," 19 March 1991, Board of Trustees Minutes, 16 May 1991, Penn State University Archives.

117 Bill Figel, "Lesbians in World of Athletics," *Chicago Sun-Times,* 16 June 1986 [www.clubs.psu.edu/up/psupride/articles/chicago%20times] (accessioned 25 September 2015).

118 Jennifer E. Harris v. Maureen T. Portland, et al., Civil Action No. 1:05-CV-2648, U. S. District Court, Harrisburg, PA, 3 January 2006 and Penn State Press Release, "University Concludes Investigation of Claims Against Women's Basketball Coach," 18 April 2006 [www.clubs.psu.edu/up/psupride/article/press$release%404182006. pdf] (accessioned 5 March 2014).

119 For a more extensive account of the Portland situation, see Ronald A. Smith, *Wounded Lions: Joe Paterno, Jerry Sandusky, and the Crises in Penn State Athletics* (Urbana: University of Illinois Press, 2016), 140-149.

120 Joe Paterno to President Oswald, ca. fall 1979, President Oswald Papers, Box 10290, Folder, "Athletics Relating to Admissions, Policies, Etc. 1979-1982," Penn State University Archives.

121 Board of Trustees Executive Committee Minutes, 20 January 1979, Penn State University Archives.

122 Ibid., 20 January 1930. It should be noted that the alumni still continued to have significant control of athletics as it had for several decades before the School of Physical Education and Athletics was created. This continued until Ernie McCoy was made Dean in 1952. He was successful, with the help of President Eric Walker, in eliminating most alumni from direct influence over athletics.

123 For the letter of administrators recommending Czekaj's ouster, see R. J. Scannell and R. A. Patterson, memo to President John Oswald and J. V. Paterno, 23 November 1979, John Oswald Papers, Box 10290, Folder "Athletic Relating to Academics, Admission, Policies, Etc. 1979-1982-1," Penn State University Archives.

124 Of the four, Paterno was least likely to have been charged of a crime, for he not only reported the 2001 incident to his superior, and had no email trace, but he died shortly after the Sandusky Scandal broke. The other three either pleaded guilty in early 2017 of child endangerment (Tim Curley and Gary Schultz) or were proven guilty of child endangerment in a trial (Graham Spanier).

Chapter Three Notes

125 "Sandusky Press Conference," 7 November 2011 [cumberlink.co/sports/ penn-state-fb/sandusky-press-conference] (accessioned 18 September 2015).

126 Statement from President Spanier," *Penn State News,* 5 November 2011 [news.

psu.edu.story/story/153819/2011/11/05/statement] (accessioned 28 September 2015). Before Spanier released his statement, he contacted Curley's attorney, Caroline Roberto, and Schultz's attorney, Tom Farrell, to make sure they agreed with his statement and met with the Penn State public relations staff, Trustee President, Steve Garban, and PSU Counsel, Cynthia Baldwin. See Mark Scolforo, "Lawyer Says Defense Attorney Helped Penn State Edit Release," 18 October 2016 [www.wrex. com/story/33418176/lawyer-says] (accessioned 24 October 2016).

127 Six years later, Judge Robert Eby, in the Graham Spanier v. Penn State case, called the Penn State administration an example of "conscious ignorance" in how it dealt with Spanier and his Separation Agreement of November 15, 2011. *Graham B. Spanier v. Penn State University*, No. 2016-0571, Court of Common Pleas of Centre County, Pennsylvania, Civil Action-Law, 9 November 2017, p. 32.

128 For fuller accounts, see Aaron Fisher, Michael Gillum, and Dawn Daniels, *Silent No More: Victim # 1's Fight for Justice Against Jerry Sandusky* (New York: William Morrow, 2012) and Ronald A. Smith, "Insularity, The Second Mile, and Sandusky's On-Campus Incidents," in his *Wounded Lions: Joe Paterno, Jerry Sandusky, and the Crises in Penn State Athletics* (Urbana: University of Illinois Press, 2016),127-139.

129 Bill Keisling IV, "Busted: Behind the Sandusky Arrest," 22 January 2014 [www/yardbird.com/busted_nacrotics_agent] (accessioned 26 February 2014).

130 H. Geoffrey Moulton, Jr., Special Deputy Attorney General, "Report to the Attorney General on the Investigation of Gerald A. Sandusky," 30 May 2014 [www. scribd.com/doc/230973065/Report] (accessioned 29 September 2014).

131 Ibid., p. 130.

132 Ibid., p. 123.

133 Sara Ganim, "Sandusky Faces Grand Jury Probe," *Harrisburg Patriot-News*, 31 March 2011 [www.pulitizer.org/files/2012/local-responding/local01.pdf] (accessioned 19 February 2014).

134 Moulton, "Report," p. 17.

135 Sara Ganim, "Penn State Athletic Director Tim Curley, Senior Official Charged in Jerry Sandusky Investigation," *Penn Live*, 5 November 2011 [www.pennlive.com/ midstate/index.ssf/2011/11/sandusky_investigation_sources.html] (accessioned 30 September 2015).

136 Over five years after the ouster of Graham Spanier, it was not clear if Spanier had resigned or been fired. In the Spanier v. Penn State lawsuit of 13 March 2017, "Penn State denies that Dr. Spanier resigned from the Presidency of Penn State, to the contrary, he was terminated without cause. . . ." *Spanier v. Penn State*, Court of Common Pleas of Centre County, Pennsylvania Civil Division, Docket No. 2016-0571, 13 March 2017, p. 4.

137 *New York Times*, 19 January 2012 [www.nytimes.com/2012/01/19/sports/ncaafootball/penn-state-trustees] (accessioned 9 February 2012).

138 No formal vote was registered when Paterno was fired. Steve Garban had not even read the Grand Jury Report before the first meeting of the board of trustees on November 6th, showing his lack of leadership as president of the Board. Garban

had been on the Penn State staff as Vice President for Finance and Business, in charge of athletics, prior to becoming a trustee member. This "revolving door of insiders" was highly criticized by the Auditor General, Eugene DePasquale in his "Performance Audit Report" in 2017 for it "did not represent good governance practice as it promoted a culture of insider influence that squelched transparency and accountability." See Eugene DePasquale, "Performance Audit Report: The Pennsylvania State University, June 2017 [www.paauditor.gov/Media/Default/Reports/PSU%Audit%20Report.pdf] (accessioned 21 July 2017).

139 Don van Natta, Jr., "Fight on State: In Wake of Scandal Power Struggle Spread from Penn State Campus to State Capital," *ESPN The Magazine*, 4 April 2012 [espn.go.com/espn/tol/story/_/id/7770996/in-wake-joe-paterno] (accessioned 4 April 2012).

140 Steven Fink, "Say It Ain't So, Joe!—The Penn State Crisis," in his *Crisis Communications: The Definitive Guide to Managing the Message* (New York: McGraw Hill, 2013), 142, 144-145.

141 By 2012, Purple Nations Solutions, a strategic communications and public relations firm in Washington, D.C, was hired and suggested a crisis management plan for Penn State's Board of Trustees. See Purple Nations Solutions memorandum, email to Committee on Outreach and Community Affairs, 23 February 2012 [www.penstatesunshinefund.org/results/download/20111] (accessioned 10 December 2016).

142 "Joe Paterno to Retire; President Out?" *ESPN.com*, 9 November 2011 [espn.go.com/college-football-story/_/id/72311281/penn-state] (accessioned 15 March 2012).

143 *New York Times*, 19 January 2012 [www.nytimes.com/2012/01/19/sports/ncaafootball/penn-state-trustees] (accessioned 9 February 2012).

144 Tom Conner, Gainesville, VA, to Jennifer Branstetter, Board of Trustees, 30 January 2012 [www.pennstatesunshinefund.org/results/download/20111 (9 December 2016).

145 Solesbee v. Balkcom, page 339 U.S. 16 (1950) [supreme.justia.com/cases/federal/us/339/9/case.html] (accessioned 20 February 2017).

146 The U.S. Supreme Court in *NCAA v. Tarkanian*, 488 U.S. 179 (1988) in a 5-4 vote determined that coach Jerry Terkanian's University of Nevada Las Vegas was not bound by the U.S. Constitution's 14th amendment stating "No state shall. . . deprive any person of life, liberty, or property, without due process of law. . . ." Thus, UNLV was not a state actor needed to comply with the 14th amendment, nor would the NCAA need to comply with the 14th amendment in the Penn State case.

147 In 2017, President Donald Trump placed Frazier on his 2017 Manufacturing Council, but Frazier resigned following Trump's failure to denounce neo-nazi and white supremacist in a Charlottesville white nationalist rally that ended in a riot and the death of a protestor. Sally Persons, "Trump Slams Merck CEO for Quitting Manufacturing Council Over Charlottesville Reaction," *Washington Times*, 14 August 2017 [www.washingtontimes.com/news/2017/aug/13/donald-trump-slams-ken-frazier (accessioned 21 August 2017).

148 Ronald Tomalis, Pennsylvania Secretary of Education, email to Stephen Aichele, General Council Office, 8 November 2011 and Tomalis to Frazier, 17 November 2011 [www.penstatesunshinefund.org/results/download/2011] (accessed 16 August 2016). The third firm recommended from the governor's office was Kevin O'Connor, while Rudy Guiliani, a New York City politician, former mayor, 1983-2001, offered his services.

149 Kenneth Frazier Deposition, 15 December 2014, "Legal Documents – *Corman vs NCAA*," pp. 30-31 [www.senatorcorman.com/legal-documents-corman-vs-ncaa] (accessed 27 June 2015).

150 Charles Thompson, "Penn State Trustee Ken Frazier Fires Back at Freeh Report Critics," *Penn Live*, 14 March 2013 [www.pennlive.com/midstate/index.ssf/2013/penn-state-trustees-Ken_Frazier.html] (accessed 1 October 2015).

151 Kenneth Frazier Deposition, 15 December 2014, "Legal Documents – *Corman vs NCAA*," p. 39. [www.senatorcorman.com/legal-documents-corman-vs-ncaa] (accessed 27 June 2015).

152 Kenneth C. Frasier to Paula Ammerman and cc: Steve Garban, John P. Surma, and Cynthia Baldwin, 12 November 2011 quoted in *Graham B. Spanier v. Penn State University*, Docket No. 2015-0571, Court of Common Pleas of Centre County, Pennsylvania, Civil Action, 14 November 2016, p. 23.

153 *New York Times*, 20 December 1996 [http:www.nytimes.com/1996/12/20/us/head-of-fbi] (accessed 1 August 2014) and Adam Bernstein, "Richard A. Jewell; Wrongly Linked to Olympic Bombing," *Washington Post*, 30 August 2007 [www.washingtonpost.com/wp-dya/content/article/2007/08/09] (accessed 4 November 2015).

154 "Arbitral Award Delivered by the Court of Arbitration for Sport," CAS 2011/A/2625 Mohamed Bin Hammam v. FIFA, Lausanne, Switzerland, 19 July 2012 [www.taqs-cas.org/fileadmin/user_upload/Award20262520-FIN] (accessed 6 November 2015).

155 Eric Bochlert, "Judging Louis Freeh," *Salon*, 4 June 2002 [www.salon.com/2002/06/04/freeh] (accessed 7 November 2015) and Charles Thompson, "Penn State Trustees Ken Frazier Fires Back at Freeh Report Critics," *Penn Live*, 14 March 2013 [www.pennlive.com/midstate/index.ssf/2013/03/penn-state_trustees-Ken_Frazier.html] (accessed 1 October 2015).

156 Andrew W. Griffin, "Will Freeh Bungle Penn State Child-Sex Abuse Investigation Too?" *Red Dirt Report*, 21 November 2011 [www.reddirtreport.com/red-dirt-grit/will-freeh-bungle] (accessed 6 November 2015).

157 Kenneth Frazier, "Update on Special Investigations Task Force Activities," 4 May 2012 [www.pennstatesunshinefund.org/results/download/20111] (accessed 12 December 2016).

158 The letter was written principally by NCAA Counsel, Donald Remy, according to NCAA insider, Shep Cooper. See Cooper, email to Joe McGormley, NCAA administrator, 12 June 2012 [www.pennstatesunshinefund.org/results/download/2020601221 (accessed 13 December 2016).

159 David Berst, email to Jim Delany, Big Ten Commissioner, 16 November 2011,

"Legal Documents – *Corman vs NCAA*," Emmert, Exhibit 4 [www.senatorcorman.com/legal-documents-corman-vs-ncaa] (accessioned 9 June 2015]. Emphasis is mine.

160 Shepard Cooper, NCAA Director of the Committee on Infractions, claimed that the Consent Decree "was exclusively the product of the VP for legal affairs," Counsel Donald Remy. Shepard Cooper Deposition 13, p. 81, November 2014, "Legal Documents – *Corman vs NCAA*" [www.senatorcorman.com/legal-documens-corman-vs-ncaa] (accessioned 21 June 2015).

161 Bob Williams, 4 November 2014, "Legal Documents – *Corman vs NCAA*," Exhibit 13 [www.senatorcorman.com/legal-documents-corman-vs-ncaa] (accessioned 17 June 2015).

162 Julie Roe Lach Deposition, 11 December 2014, "Legal Documents – *Corman vs NCAA*," [www.senatorcorman.com/legal-documents-corman-vs-ncaa] (accessioned 7 July 2015). Recently married, Lach generally was called Julie Roe.

163 Mark Emmert to Rodney Erickson, 17 November 2011, in the writer's possession.

164 As quoted in Bob Williams, Vice President for Communications, to Mark Emmert, 10 November 2011, "Legal Documents – *Corman vs NCAA*," Williams Exhibit 2 [www.senatorcorman.com/legal-ducuments-corman-vs-ncaa] (accessioned 21 July 2015).

165 Proverbs 3:27, *The Holy Bible*, King James Version.

166 Proverbs 28:16, *English Standard Bible*.

167 David Berst Deposition, 12 November 2014, "Legal Documents – *Corman vs NCAA*," [www.senator corman.com/legal-documents-corman-vs-ncaa] (accessioned 17 June 2015).

168 Rod Erickson Deposition, 2 December 2014, "Legal Documents – *Corman vs NCAA*," [www.senatorcorman.com/legal-documents-corman-vs-ncaa] (accessioned 15 June 2015).

169 Cynthia A. Baldwin to Mark A. Emmert, 6 December 2011, Berst Exhibit 4, "Legal Documents – *Corman-vs-NCAA*," [www.senatorcorman.com/legal-documents-corman-vs-ncaa] (accessioned 20 August 2015).

170 Jonathan A. Barrett, Big Ten Counsel, email to Omar Y. McNeill, lead Freeh investigator, 5 December 2011, McNeill Exhibit 3, "Legal Documents – *Corman vs NCAA*," [www.senatorcorman.com/legal-documents-corman-vs-ncaa] 5 December 2011 [www.pacourts.us/assets/files/setting-4002/file-4011.pdf] (accessioned 13 July 2015).

171 Untitled Document, 10 February 2012, McNeill Exhibit 9, "Legal Documents – *Corman vs NCAA*" [www.senatorcorman.com/legal-documents-corman-vs-ncaa] (accessioned 13 July 2015).

172 Michael Garrett, "Freeh Investigator: NCAA Had No Influence on Investigation or Content of Freeh Report," *StateCollege.com*, 31 January 2015 [www.statecollege.com/news/local-news/freeh-investigator] (accessioned 1 April 2016).

173 Tommie Walls, NCAA, email to Louis Freeh, Eugene Sullivan, Omar McNeill,

Barbara Mather, Donald Remy, Julie Roe, and Jon Barrett, 1 December 2011, Roe Exhibit 6, "Legal Documents – *Corman vs NCAA*" [www.senatorcorman.com/legal-documents-corman-vs-ncaa] (accessed 20 June 2015).

174 Julie Roe Lach Deposition, 11 November 2014, "Legal Documents – *Corman vs NCAA*" [www.senatorcorman.com/legal-documents-corman-vs-ncaa] (accessed 7 July 2015).

175 Donald Remy, email to Omar McNeill, 5 January 2012 [www.pennstatesunshinefund.org/results/download/20111] (accessed 9 December 2016).

176 Omar McNeill Deposition, 17 December 2014, "Legal Documents – *Corman vs NCAA*" [www.senatorcorman.com/legal-documents-corman-vs-ncaa] (accessed 13 July 2015) and Donald Remy Deposition, 20 November 2014, "Legal Documents – *Corman vs NCAA*" [www.senatorcorman.com/legal-documents-corman-vs-ncaa] (accessed 14 July 2015).

177 According to the Freeh Group contract, the file of correspondence, pleadings, agreements, depositions, exhibits, physical evidence, expert reports including work product may be destroyed in 10 years. See "Engagement to Perform Legal Services of Freeh Sporkin & Sullivan by Penn State University Board of Trustees," 2 December 2011 [ps4rs.files.wordpress.com/2015/03/freehsporkinsullivanengage] (accessed 13 October 2015).

178 Donald Remy email to Omar Y. McNeill, 28 December 2011, Roe Lach Exhibit 7, "Legal Documents – *Corman vs NCAA*" [www.senatorcorman.com/legal-documents-corman-vs-ncaa] (accessed 7 July 2015).

179 Kevin Lennon Deposition, 4 November 2014, "Legal Documents – *Corman vs NCAA*," [www.senatorcorman.com/legal-documents-corman-vs-ncaa] (accessed 9 July 2015).

180 Using Freeh Report footnotes and information within the document, these names were logically assumed. Chief investigator Omar McNeill told of a run-in with a likely inebriated Anthony Lubrano shortly after Lubrano was interviewed by the investigative team. See Omar McNeill email to Ken Frazier, 17 February 2012 in Paula Ammerman, Director, Penn State Board of Trustees, email to Board of Trustees and the Freeh Special Investigations Task Force, 17 February 2011 [www.pdf-archive.com/2014/10/19/aslkjaslkdjasldjlkj/preview] (accessed 16 August 2016). Keith Masser indicated that all members of the Trustees were interviewed. Masser, email to Karen Peetz and Ken Frazier, 5 May 2012 [www.pennstatesunshinefund.org/results/download/20111] (accessed 12 December 2016).

181 "Review of the Freeh Report Concerning Joseph Paterno by Dick Thornburgh," 6 February 2013 [Paterno.com/Resources/Docs/THORNBURGH_FINAL_REPORT_2-7-2013.pdf] (accessed 17 November 2015), and Curtis Everhart, Criminal Defense Investigator, in Joe Amendola Law Office, Commonwealth of Pennsylvania vs. Gerald A. Sandusky case, undated or redacted [www.framingpaterno.com/sites/default/files/interview_Vic_2_Redacted.pdf] (accessed 7 November 2016), and *Graham B. Spanier v. Louis J. Freeh and Freeh Sporkin & Sullivan, LLP*, Docket No. 2013-2707, Court of Common Pleas of Centre County, Pennsylvania Civil Action, 14 October 2016.

Chapter Four Notes

182 Baldwin resigned as counsel on June 30, 2012 following the Sandusky trial, having announced five months earlier of her decision to do so. In 2016, Superior Court Judge ruled that Baldwin breached attorney-client privilege after Graham Spanier, Gary Schultz, and Tim Curley believed she was representing them before the Sandusky Grand Jury. *Commonwealth of Pennsylvania v. Graham B. Spanier*, "Appeal from the Order Entered January 14, 2015 in the Court of Common Pleas of Dauphin County Criminal Division at No(s): CP-22-CR-00e615-2013 in the Superior Court of Pennsylvania, No. 304 MDA 2015, 22 January 2016.

183 Paula Ammerman, quoting Lisa Powers, Penn State spokeswoman, email to Board of Trustees, 16 April 2012 [www.pennstatesunshinefund.org/results/download/20111) (accessioned 11 December 2016).

184 Rod Erickson, message to Board of Trustees, 25 January 2012, sent by Paula Ammerman [www.pennstatesunshinefund.org/results/download/20120125] (accessioned 9 December 2016).

185 For a cogent discussion of the Penn State crisis by an expert in the area, see Steven Fink, "Say It Ain't So, Joe!—The Penn State Crisis," in his *Crisis Communications: The Definitive Guide to Managing the Message* (New York: McGraw Hill, 2013), 138-172.

186 "Richard Edelman Public Relations Strategy for Penn State Post-Sandusky," *You Tube*, 30 June 2014 [www.youtube.com/watch?v=t3KDnaLr50] (accessioned 27 October 2016) and Tarum Luna, "Penn State Hires PR Firm to Address Scandal," *Pittsburgh Post-Gazette*, 26 April 2012 [www.post-gazette.com/news/education/2012/04/26/penn-state] (accessioned 27 October 2016).

187 Paula Ammerman, email and attachment to Board of Trustees, 4 May 2012 [www.pennstatesunshinefund.org/results/download/20111] (accessioned 12 December 2016).

188 Anonymous, 27 April 2012 response to "A Curious Assignment—Hiring Public Relations Firms to Manage Communications with Faculty?!" Monitoring University Governance blog, 27 April 2012 [lebpsusenate.blogspot.com/2012/04/curious-assignment-hiring-public/html] (accessioned 17 February 2017].

189 Rod Erickson Deposition, 2 December 2014, "Legal Documents – Corman vs NCAA," pp. 140-143 [www/senatorcorman.com/legal-documents-corman-vs-ncaa].

190 *Centre Daily Times,* 20 February 2012, p. A1; 1 March 2012, p. A1; 2 March 2012, p. A1, A3; 20 April 2012, p. A6; 9 May 2012 p. A1, A6; and 26 May 2012, p. A1.

191 Ibid., 12 June 2012, p. A3 and 13 June 2012, p. A1, A6.

192 See Abby Minor's letter to the editor in the *Centre Daily Times*, 26 June 2012, p. A6, for what she considered inappropriate crowd cheering.

193 Shep Cooper, Director of the NCAA Committees on Infractions, email to Jerry Parkinson, law professor at the University of Wyoming, 27 July 2012, Shepard Cooper Exhibit 7, "Legal Documents – Corman vs NCAA," [www.senatorcorman.com/legal-documents-corman-vs-ncaa].

194 Brad Wolverton, "Freeh Group Member Criticizes NCAA's Use of Investigative Report," *Chronicle of Higher Education*, 27 July 2012 [chronicle.com/article/Freeh-Group-Member-Criticizes/133213] (accessioned 9 December 2015).

195 "Report of the Special Investigating Counsel Regarding Activities of the Pennsylvania State University Related to the Child Sexual Abuse Committee by Jerry Sandusky [Freeh Report], 12 July 2012, pp. 14-17. Emphasis was added.

196 Ibid., 12 July 2012, p. 20.

197 Michael Bangs, head examiner of the Pennsylvania State Employees Retirement System, reported: "The terrifically significant disparity between the findings in the Freeh Report and the actual truth is disturbing." Quoted in *Graham B. Spanier v. Penn State University*, Docket No. 2016-0571, Court of Common Pleas of Centre County, Pennsylvania, Civil Action, 14 November 2016, p. 42.

198 "Report of the Special Investigating Counsel," 12 July 2012, p. 17.

199 William Shakespeare, "King Lear," 11.2.

200 Alan Cowell, "After 350 Years, Vatican Says Galileo Was Right," *New York Times*, 31 October 1992 [www.nytimes.com/1992/19/31/world/after-350-years] (accessioned 17 October 2016).

201 Later, Rod Erickson admitted that parts of the Freeh Report were "inaccurate and unfortunate." See *Graham B. Spanier v. Penn State University*, Docket No. 2016-0571, Court of Common Pleas of Centre County, Pennsylvania, Civil Action, 14 November 2016, p. 42.

202 Don Van Natta, Jr., "Inside the Negotiations that Brought Penn State Football to the Brink of Extinction," *ESPN Magazine*, 4 August 2012, "Legal Documents – Corman vs NCAA," Marsh Exhibit 3 [www.senatorcorman.com/legal-documents-corman-vs-ncaa].

203 "Report of the Special Investigating Counsel Regarding Activities of the Pennsylvania State University Related to the Child Sexual Abuse Committed by Jerry Sandusky, [Freeh Report], 12 July 2012, footnotes 180, 326, 479, p. 53, 73, and 90. Spanier was interviewed on June 6, 2012. Later, Spanier indicated that he was in the United Kingdom from June 8-16, 1998 where he did not have access to emails and may have not have seen them in over 1000 emails awaiting him when he returned. See *Spanier v. Penn State*, Court of Common Pleas of Centre County, Pennsylvania Civil Action – Law, Docket No. 2016-571, 10 February 2016.

204 See Justin Sievert's insightful "Revamping the NCAA's Penalty Structure Through Sentencing Guidelines," *Law Insider*, 22 December 2011 [www.thelawinsider.com/insider-news-ncaa-penalty-structure] (accessioned 4 August 2015) and George Dohrman, "An Inside Look at the NCAA's Secretive Committee on Infractions," *Sports Illustrated*, 18 February 2010 [www.si.com/more-sports/2010/02/18/suc-coi] (accessioned 18 August 2015).

205 Jonathan Mahler, "Student-Athlete Equation Could be a Win-Win," *New York Times*, 10 August 2011, B13.

206 Edward Snowden, quoted by Ewen MacAskill in "Edward Snowden, NSA Files Source: 'If They Want to Get You, in Time They Will,'" *The Guardian*, 10 June

2013 [www.theguardian.com/world/2013/jun/09/nsa-whistleblower] (accessioned 13 February 2017).

207 Mark Emmert to Rodney Erickson, 17 November 2011, "Legal Document – *Corman vs NCAA*," Emmert Exhibit 6 [www.senatorcorman.com/legal-documents-corman-vs-ncaa].

208 David Berst Deposition, 12 November 2014, "Legal Documents – *Corman vs NCAA*," [www.senatorcorman.com/legal-documents-corman-vs-ncaa].

209 David Berst, email to Jim Delany, 16 November 2011, "Legal Documents – *Corman vs NCAA*," Emmert Exhibit 4 [www.senatorcorman.com/legal-documents-corman-vs-ncaa].

210 As quoted by Peter Thamel, "N.C.A.A. Begins Penn State Inquiry," *New York Times*, 18 November 2011 [www.nytimes.com/2011/11/19/sports/ncaafootball/ncaa] (accessioned 30 July 2014).

211 Penn State Board of Trustees Minutes, 13 July 2012, Penn State University Archives.

212 Ken Frazier, email to Jennifer Thompson, Keith Masser, and Karen Peetz, cc; Mark Dambly and Rod Erickson [www.pennstatesunshinefund.org/results/download/20120606 (accessioned 13 December 2016).

213 "Penn State Issues Statement on Freeh Report," 12 July 2012, "Legal Document – *Corman vs NCAA*, " Erickson Exhibit 6 [www.senatorcorman.com/legal-documents-corman-vs-ncaa].

214 Steven Fink, *Crisis Communications: The Definitive Guide to Managing the Message* (New York: McGraw Hill, 2013), 159-160.

215 Penn State Board of Trustees Minutes, 13 July 2012, Penn State University Archives. Less than two years later, on May 9, 2014, Rod Erickson, by a unanimous Board vote, was given the honor of having a building named after him, the Rodney Erickson Food Science Building, constructed in 2006 and housing the famed ice cream parlor with the "Peachy Paterno Alumni Swirl" ice cream.

216 Rodney Erickson Deposition, 2 December 2014, p. 238, " Legal Documents – *Corman vs NCAA*," [www.senatorcorman.com/legal-documents-corman-vs-ncaa].

217 "Preliminary Report: Transforming Intercollegiate Athletics Working Group on Collegiate Model—Enforcement," January 2012, in Ed Ray Exhibit 12, 8 December 2014, "Legal Documents–*Corman vs NCAA*," [www.senatecorman.com/legal-documents-corman-vs-ncaa].

218 Edward Ray, "Remarks Before the Northwestern States Higher Education Internal Auditors," 15 August 2012, "Legal Documents – *Corman vs NCAA*," Ray Exhibit 2 [www.senatorcorman.com/legal-documents-corman-vs-ncaa].

219 Quoted in Nancy Armour, "From UConn to USC, Corruption in College Sports Spotlight," *Mass Live*, 10 September 2011 [www.masslive.com/sports/indexssf/2011/09/from_uconn] (accessioned 2 February 2016).

220 Ed Ray, email to Julie Roe, cc: Jim Isch, Mark Emmert, 12 July 2012, "Legal Documents–*Corman vs NCAA*," Julie Roe Exhibit 15 [www.senatorcorman.com/legal-documents-corman-vs-ncaa].

221 Ed Ray, email to Julie Roe, cc: Mark Emmert, Jim Isch, 13 July 2012, "Legal Documents – *Corman vs NCAA*," Julie Roe Exhibit 18, [www.senatorcorman.com/legal-documents-corman-vs-ncaa] and Rick Reilly, "The Sins of the Father," *ESPN*, 12 July 2012 [espn.go.com/espn/story/_/id/8162972/joe-paterno-true-legacy] (accessioned 12 December 2015).

222 Ed Ray Deposition, 8 December 2014, "Legal Documents – *Corman vs NCAA*," [www.senatorcorman.com/legal-documents-corman-vs-ncaa].

223 "Interview with Paul Dee," 10 June 2010, *Todd McNair v. NCAA*, 6 February 2015, Court of Appeals of the State of California, Second Appellate District, Division 3 [dl.dropboxusercontent.com/u/75728002/B245475%20Appendix%20Pu] (accessioned 10 August 2015).

224 Bob Williams Deposition, 5 November 2014, "Legal Documents–*Corman vs NCAA*" [www.senatorcorman.com/legal-documents-corman-vs-ncaa].

225 Julie Roe, email to Kevin Lennon, 14 July 2012, "Legal Documents–*Corman vs NCAA*," Kevin Lennon Exhibit 8 [www.senatorcorman.com/legal-documents-corman-vs-ncaa]. Emphasis was added. Later, new Penn State president Eric Barron and Board of Trustee president Keith Masser wrote: "We find it deeply disturbing that NCAA officials in leadership positions would consider bluffing one of their member institutions, Penn State, to accept sanctions outside of their normal investigative and enforcement process." In Kevin Horne, "Internal Emails Show NCAA Questioned Authority to Sanction Penn State," *Onward State*, 5 November 2014 [onwardstate.com/2014/11/05/internal-emails-show-ncaa] (accessioned 5 October 2016).

226 Julie Roe, email to Kevin Lennon, 14 July 2012, "Legal Documents–*Corman vs NCAA*," Kevin Lennon Exhibit 8 [www.senatorcorman.com/legal-documents-corman-vs-ncaa].

227 Report by President Rod Erickson, Penn State Board of Trustees Minutes, 12 August 2012, Penn State University Archives. All but two of the 20 members of the NCAA Division I Board of Directors were presidents and all of the NCAA Executive Committee were presidents. Two key presidents who voted to give the "death penalty" were on both groups, Ed Ray and Harry Pastides of the University of South Carolina.

228 Stephen Dunham Deposition, 21 November 2014, "Legal Documents–*Corman vs NCAA*," [www.senatorsenatorcorman.com/legal-documents-corman-vs-ncaa] (accessioned 25 June 2015).

229 "Dunham Named as Vice President and General Counsel," Press Release, 23 May 2012 [www.pennstatesushinefund.org/results/download/20111] (accessioned 12 December 2016).

230 James Wright, "10 Years After 'Mission Accomplished,' the Risks of Another Intervention," *The Atlantic*, 1 May 2013 [www.theatlantic.com/international/archives/2013/05/10-years] (accessioned 28 December 2015).

231 Aristotle, trans. Benjamin Jowett, *Politics* (Kitchener, Ontario: Batoche Books, 1999, original ca. 340 BCE), Book 1, Part 2.

232 Rod Erickson Deposition, 2 December 2014, "Legal Documents – *Corman vs*

NCAA," [www.senatorcorman.com/legal-documents-corman-vs-ncaa].

233 Michael DiRaimo, email to Rod Erickson, 18 July 2012, "Legal Documents – *Corman vs NCAA*," Erickson Exhibit 2 [www.senatorcorman.com/legal-documents-corman-vs-ncaa].

234 Ibid.

235 Paul Suhey, email to Rod Erickson, Mark Dambly, Paul Silvis, Karen Peetz, Ken Maser, 20 July 2012, "Legal Documents – *Corman vs NCAA*," Erickson Exhibit 5 [www.senatorcorman.com/legal-documents-corman-vs-ncaa].

236 Rodney Erickson, email to Gene Marsh, Frank Guadagnino, Stephen Dunham, and William King III, 20 July 2012 [www.pennstatesunshinefund.org/results/download/20120780095erickson] (accessed 21 December 2015).

237 The U. S. Department of Education investigation of the Clery violations was not concluded until late 2016, when Penn State was fined $2.4 million for, among other violations, over 300 crimes not reported. U. S. Department of Education, "Final Program Review Determination," 3 November 2016 [studentaid.ed.gov/sa/sites/default/files/fsawg/datacenter/cleryact/pennstate) (accessed 4 November 2016).

238 Rod Erickson, email to Steve Dunham and Frank Guadagnino, 20 July 2012, "Legal Document – *Corman vs NCAA*," Erickson Exhibit 7 [www.senatorcorman.com/legal-documents-corman-vs-ncaa].

239 Several years after the Sandusky Scandal broke and well after leaving Penn State, Triponey wrote to me that the "backlash (mostly anonymous)" to her "from some of the most loyal Joe Paterno fans has been quite brutal (including death threats)." Vicky Triponey, email to Ron Smith, 13 January 2016, in Ron Smith Personal Collection.

240 For a story of the Triponey-Paterno controversy, see Ronald A. Smith, "Shaping Reality: Saving Joe Paterno's Legacy," in *Wounded Lions: Joe Paterno, Jerry Sandusky, and the Crises in Penn State Athletics* (Urbana: University of Illinois Press, 2016), 112-126.

241 Gene Marsh, email to Frank Guadagnino, Steve Dunham, William King III, and Rodney Erickson, 19 July 2012 [av.pasentegop.com/ncaa/discovery/rodney-erickson/exhibits/exhibit-15.pdf] (accessed 21 June 2015).

242 Kathy Redmond, National Coalition Against Violent Athletes, email to Mark Emmert, 18 November 2011, "Legal Documents – *Corman vs NCAA*," Emmert, Exhibit 24 [www.senatorcorman.com/legal-documents-corman-vs-ncaa]. Redmond suggested that Emmert contact Vicky Triponey for her testimony. Redmond had been raped by a University of Nebraska football player in a case settled in 1997. Later, Redmond became embroiled in the Michigan State Larry Nassar Scandal in 2018 when she reported that she advised Mark Emmert in November 2010 about rapant sexual abuse by athletes at Michigan State. See Nicole Auerbach, "NCAA President Mark Emmert Was Alerted to Michigan State Sexual Assault Reports in 2010," *The Athletic*, 27 January 2018 [theathletic.com/223555/2018/01/26/ncaa] (accessed 23 March 2018).

243 Gene Marsh, email to Rodney Erickson, Stephen Dunham, Frank Guadagnino, cc: William H. King, III, 22 July 2012, "Legal Documents – *Corman vs NCAA*," Marsh Exhibit 6 [www.senatorcorman.com/legal-documents-corman-vs-ncaa] (accessed 13 July 2015). Erickson downplayed the role of athlete's disciplinary infractions in his deposition, 2 December 2014, "Legal Documents – *Corman vs NCAA*," [www.

senatorcorman.com/legal-documents-corman-vs-ncaa].

244 A reader of this book manuscript suggested that "Joe Paterno was neither villain nor hero but basically a man whom time had passed by. What he did/thought/ said was perfectly acceptable by 1950s and 60s norms, but everything around him changed after that. He did not change and more importantly, he failed to recognize that things had changed." Private email correspondence to Ron Smith, 5 September 2017, in the Ron Smith Personal collection.

245 Montesquieu, *The Spirit of the Laws* (London, England: Crowder, Ware, and Payne, 1748, 1773 English edition) Book XI, Chapter 3.

246 Gene Marsh, email to Rodney Erickson, Stephen Dunham, Frank Guadagnino, cc: William H. King, III, 22 July 2012, "Legal Documents – *Corman vs NCAA*," Marsh Exhibit 6 [www.senatorcorman.com/legal-documents-corman-vs-ncaa].

247 Bylaws 19.01.5, 19.1, 19.1.2, 19.5.2(g), 19.5.2.2, 27.7.1, and 32.5.1, *NCAA 2011-12 NCAA Division I Manual, Effective August 1, 2011*, NCAA Constitution and Bylaws, 2011-2012 [www.ncaapublications.com/productdownloads/D112.pdf] (accessioned 21 December 2015).

248 A statement by King of Thebes, Creon, in Jean Anouilh, *Antigone: A Tragedy* (New York: Random House, 1946), 44.

249 Bill Levinson, Penn State '78, response to Charles Thompson, "NCAA Responds to Senator Jake Corman's Accusations of 'Manipulation and Deception' Regarding Penn State Sanctions," *Penn Live*, 11 February 2015 [www.pennlive.com/midstate/index.ssf/2015/02/ncaa_respond] (accessioned 1 September 2016).

250 NCAA Special Convention *Proceedings*, 20-21 June 1985, p. 56. See specifically the Bylaws: Article 4, Section 6-(d), p. 34; Article 9, Section 5, p. 126; Section I-(1), pp. 206-207; and Section 7, pp. 211-213 for actions of the Committee on Infractions including "giving notice of any specific charges" and the "Committee shall impose an appropriate penalty." Emmert did not recognize the previous policies, nor did he abide by the current ones.

251 NCAA Special Convention *Proceedings*, 20-21 June 1985, p. 56.

252 As quoted by Kevin Lennon, NCAA Vice President, in an email to NCAA Management, 29 October 2012, "Legal Documents – *Corman vs NCAA*," Emmert Exhibit 26 [www.senatorcorman.com/legal-documents-corman-vs-ncaa].

253 Stated NCAA Counsel, Donald Remy, "I think [Emmert] made clear that the death penalty was in play and Penn State's cooperation helped avoid it." See Donald Remy, email to Gene Marsh, Penn State liaison to the NCAA, 24 July 2012 [www.pennstatesunshinefund.org/results/download/2012072 (accessioned 14 December 2014).

254 As quoted by Erickson in Rodney Erickson Deposition, 2 December 2014, p. 110, "Legal Documents – *Corman vs NCAA*," [www.senatorcorman.com/legal-documents-corman-vs-ncaa] and Penn State Board of Trustees Minutes, 12 August 2012, Penn State University Archives.

255 Erickson argued with a good deal of certainty that if he had gone to the entire board of trustees to discuss the Consent Decree, it would have been leaked to

the press, and the Consent Decree would have been taken off the table by Emmert. That, in itself, would have called the "bluff" by Emmert. See Rodney Erickson Deposition, 2 December 2014, p. 114, 116, "Legal Documents—*Corman vs NCAA*," [www.senatorcorman.com/legal-documents-corman-vs-ncaa].

256 Katie Murt, "Through the Storm: Rodney Erickson's Career at Penn State," *Daily Collegian*, 2 May 2014 [www.collegian.psu.edu/news/campus/article_24dc6288-d18f-11e3-aead-0017a43b2370.html] (accessioned 22 December 2015).

257 Dennis Dodd, "No Bluffing—NCAA Has Lost All of Its Credibility with Penn State, USC, etc.," *CBS Sports*, 7 November 2014 [www.cbssports.com/collegefootball/writer/dennis-dodd/247888247 (accessioned 10 November 2014).

258 William Shakespeare, *Merchant of Venice*, ca. 1596, Act IV, Scene 1.

259 "Bombing of Dresden," *History* [www.history.com/topic/world-war-ii/battle-of-dresden] (accessioned 13 October 2016).

260 When Mark Emmert testified before a U.S. Senate Committee in 2014, he stated, "Neither I nor any member of my staff have a vote on association policy or **infraction decisions**." He didn't need to in 2012 when he skirted association policy and the infraction process to bully Penn State into signing the Consent Decree. "Promoting the Well-Being and Academic Success of College Athletes," Hearing Before the Committee on Commerce, Science, and Transportation, U.S. Senate, 113th Congress, 2nd Session, 9 July 2014. See also Anthony C. Campbell, "An Impact Analysis of the NCAA's Handling of the Pennsylvania State University's 2011-2012 Case," Ph.D. dissertation, Creighton University, 2014, who concluded, p. 7, "The NCAA was unable to use the Penn State penalty as an effective deterrent against other schools."

Chapter Five Notes

261 Steven Fink, "Say It Ain't So, Joe!—The Penn State Crisis," *Crisis Communications: The Definitive Guide to Managing the Message* (New York: McGraw Hill, 2013), 159-160.

262 Michael Bezilla, *Penn State: An Illustrated History* (University Park: Penn State University Press, 1985), 294-309.

263 Penn State Board of Trustees Minutes, 23 April 1970, Penn State University Archives.

264 Jerry M. Lewis and Thomas R. Hensley, "The May 4 Shootings at Kent State University," *Ohio Council for the Social Studies Review*, 34 #1 (Summer, 1998), 9-21 and ""Jackson State: A Tragedy Widely Forgotten," 3 May 2010 [www.npr.org/templates/story/story.php?storyId=126426361] (accessioned 14 June 2016).

265 Penn State Board of Trustees Minutes, 10 June 1970, Penn State University Archives.

266 Discussion with Prof. John Swisher, 11 November 2014, Lemont, Pennsylvania.

267 Joe Paterno, memo to John Oswald, ca. December 1979, John Oswald Papers, Box 10290, Folder "Athletics Relating to Academic, Admissions, Policies, Etc., 1979-

1982," Penn State University Archives and Ronald A. Smith, "The Joe Paterno, Steve Garban, John Oswald Coup d'état," in his *Wounded Lions: Joe Paterno, Jerry Sandusky, and the Crises in Penn State Athletics* (Urbana: University of Illinois Press, 2016), 75-88.

268 Smith, *Wounded Lions*, 89-99.

269 Joel N. Myers to Board of Trustees, 18 December 1989, Office of Senior Vice President for Finance Records, Box 03085, Folder "The Big Ten Conference," Penn State University Archives.

270 This judgment came after hours and hours of reading Board of Trustees Minutes in the Penn State Archives from 2012 to 2016.

271 Carol Hermann, Penn State Executive Assistant to the President, memo to J. Lloyd Huck, 11 January 1990, Joab Thomas Papers, Box 10435, Folder "Big Ten Con.," Penn State University Archives.

272 *The Holy Bible*, Proverbs 3:27, King James Version.

273 Penn State Board of Trustees Minutes, 10 June 1970, Penn State University Archives.

274 "Athletic Candidates Submitted to J. W. Oswald for 1980 Admission," John Oswald Papers, Box 10290, Folder "Athletics Relating to Academic, Admissions, Policies, Etc., 1979-1982," Penn State University Archives.

275 C. W. Heppenstall to J. B. Warriner, W. L. Affelder, and F. H. Gyger, Board of Trustees Committee, 9 March 1929; President R. D. Hetzel to J. B. Warriner, 3 July 1929; J. B. Warriner, W. L. Affelder, Furman H. Gyger, "Report of Special Committee to Confer with Pittsburgh Alumni," ca. 1929-1930, to Executive Committee of the Board of Trustees, and Board of Trustee Minutes, 7 June 1930, John Oswald Papers, Box 10290, Folder "Athletics Relating to Academics, Admission, Policies, Etc. 1979-1982," Penn State University Archives. It is clear that Oswald wanted the facts, despite breaking Trustee precedent, before making a major change in athletic and Penn State policy.

276 This was the conclusion of Steve Garban, Vice President for Finance and Business at Penn State, when I was on a committee with him in 1979. After studying big-time college athletics for over a half century, I believe Garban's statement was true.

277 For a lengthy discussion of the early Grand Experiment, see Ronald A. Smith, "The Ernie McCoy-Rip Engle Era and the Beginning of the Grand Experiment in College Football," *Wounded Lions: Joe Paterno, Jerry Sandusky, and the Crises in Penn State Athletics* (Urbana: University of Illinois Press, 2016), 64-74.

278 The term "Grand Experiment" was evidently first written by sportswriter Bill Conlin of the *Philadelphia Daily News* and then allowed to be reprinted for Penn State football fans in the *Beaver Stadium Pictorial*, 25 November 1967. See Bill Conlin, "The Grand Experiment," *Beaver Stadium Pictorial*, 25 November 1967, p. 25, Penn State University Archives.

279 Quoted in Douglas S. Looney, " A Lot of People Think I'm Phony," *Sports Illustrated*, 52 (17 March 1980), 45.

280 President Oswald announced the P.E. program being ranked # 1 based on the ranking of members of the American Academy of Physical Education. Two other

Big Ten institutions were ranked second and third, Iowa and Illinois. Penn State Board of Trustees Minutes, 22 March 1980, Penn State University Archives.

281 The Dean Scannell Review Committee consisted of Howard Thoele, College of Agriculture, Walter Bahr in Athletics and Physical Education, Ronald Smith in Physical Education, Patricia Ferrell in Recreation and Parks, Ben Niebel in Industrial Engineering, and Steve Garban, Controller and Assistant to the Senior Vice President for Finance and Operations.

282 Howard W. Thoele, memo to Walter Bahr, Patricia Farrell, Steve Garban, Ben Niebel, and Ronald Smith, 14 May 1979, John Oswald Papers, Box 10290, Folder "Athletics Related to Academics, Admission, Policies, Etc., 1979-1982," Penn State University Archives. Emphasis is added. Garban emphasized his desire to move athletics into the business office a number of times in the committee—my observation from being on the committee.

283 R. J. Scannell and R. A. Patterson, memo to President John Oswald and J. V. Paterno, 23 November 1979, President Oswald Papers, Box 10290, Folder "Athletics Relating to Academics, Admission, Policies, Etc., 1979-1982-1," Penn State University Archives.

284 Joe Paterno to President Oswald, ca. December 1979, President Oswald Papers, Box 10290, Folder "Athletics Relating to Admission, Policies, Etc., 1979-1982," Penn State University Archives.

285 Penn State Board of Trustees Minutes, 20 January 1979, Penn State University Archives. Emphasis is added.

286 "Statement of Dr. John W. Oswald, President the Pennsylvania State University, THE MISSION OF THE DEPARTMENT OF INTERCOLLEGITE ATHLETICS AND RESPONSIBILITIES AND AUTHORITY OF ITS ADMINISTRATIVE OFFICER AND DIRECTOR OF ATHLETICS," 14 January 1980, Ron Smith Personal File.

287 Ronald A. Smith, "The Rise of Basketball for Women in American Colleges," *Canadian Journal of History of Sport and Physical Education*, 1 (December 1970), 18-36.

288 For more complete documentations, see Ronald A. Smith, "Rene Portland and the Culture of Athletic Silence," in his *Wounded Lions: Joe Paterno, Jerry Sandusky, and the Crises in Penn State Athletics* (Urbana: University of Illinois Press, 2016), 140-149.

289 "Title IX, Education Amendments of 1972," United States Department of Labor [www.dol.gov/oasam/regs/statues/titleix.htm] (accessioned 1 January 2016).

290 Milt Ford, "A Brief History of Homosexuality" [www.gvsu.edu/allies/a-brief-history-of-homosexuality] (accessioned 1 January 2015).

291 Bill Figel, "Lesbians in World of Athletics," *Chicago Sun-Times*, 16 June 1986 [Chicago%20sun%20times/02006261986.pdf] (accessioned 4 March 2014).

292 *Jennifer E. Harris v. Maureen T. Portland, et al.,* Civil Action No. 1:05-CV-2648, U. S. District Court for the Middle District of Pennsylvania, Harrisburg, PA, 3 January 2006.

293 For a lengthy discussion of the Portland case, see Ronald A. Smith, "Rene Portland and the Culture of Athletic Silence," in his *Wounded Lions: Joe Paterno, Jerry*

Sandusky, and the Crises in Penn State Athletics (Urbana: University of Illinois Press, 2016), 140-149.

294 "Report of the Special University Faculty Committee to Review President Thomas's Proposed Amendment to the University's Non-Discrimination Policy," 19 March 1991 and 16 May 1991, Board of Trustees Minutes, Penn State University Archives. There were over 10 pages of discussion on this important topic, far more than almost any other in its history.

295 *Jennifer E. Harris v. Maureen T. Portland*, Case No. 1:05-CV-2648, United States District Court for the Middle District of Pennsylvania, Harrisburg, PA, 21 December 2005. The complaint is recorded.

296 Penn State Board of Trustees Minutes, 12 May 2006, Penn State University Archives.

297 Ibid., 4 November 2005.

298 Ibid., 17 March 2006. This was found rather hidden in Trustees material in a statement of the Committee on Finance and Physical Plant and not raised by President Spanier in his "Report of the President of the University."

299 "Coach Joe Paterno Press Conference," 15 October 2002, *GoPSUsports*, Joe Paterno Vertical File, Folder "2000s," Penn State University Archives.

300 "Rene Portland Named 2005 Renaissance Person of the Year," Press release, 23 July 2005 [www.clubs.psu.edu/up/psupride/article/press%207232005. pdf.] (accessioned 8 March 2014).

301 Penn State Press Release, "University Concludes Investigation of Claims Against Women's Basketball Coach, 18 April 2006 [www.clubs/psu.edu/up/psupride/articles/press%20release%404182006.pdf] (accessioned 5 March 2014).

302 *Jennifer E. Harris v. Maureen T. Portland, et al.*, Civil Action No. 1:05-CV-2648, U. S. District Court, Harrisburg, PA, 3 January 2006 and Kristine E. Newhall and Erin E. Buzuvis, "Sexuality and Race, Law and Discourse in Harris v. Portland," *Journal of Sport and Social Issues,* 32 No. 4 (November 2008), 345-346.

303 U. S. Department of Education, "Final Program Review Determination," 3 November 2016, p. 8 [studentaid.ed.gov/sa/sites/default/files/fsawg/datacenter/cleryact/pennstate] (accessioned 4 November 2016). Penn State was fined $2.4 million for, among other things, failure to report 331 campus crimes. The damage to Penn State could have been far worse if federal aid had been cut, helping to ruin research funds needed to uphold the status of Penn State.

304 Sara Ganim, "Sandusky Faces Grand Jury Probe," *Harrisburg Patriot-News*, 31 March 2011 [www.pulitizer.org/files/2012/local.reporting/local.01.pdf] (accessioned 12 January 2017] and Pete Thammel and Mark Viera, "Penn State's Trustees Recall Painful Decision to Fire Paterno," *New York Times,* 19 January 2012 [www.pennstatesunshinefund.org/results/download/201201192215letter] (accessioned 9 December 2016).

305 Personal discussion with Trustee David Jones, Garden Restaurant, Penn State University, University Park, PA, 6 May 2016.

306 Ken Frazier told the Trustees that former Federal Judge and FBI Director Louis Freeh "has unimpeachable credentials. . . ." Yet, the FBI, under Freeh, botched

the Atlanta Olympic Games of 1996 bombing investigation of Richard Jewell; the Waco, Texas incident with the Branch Davidians; the Los Alamos National Laboratory Scientist investigation of Wen Ho Lee in 1999; and failed to deliver thousands of documents in the Timothy McVeigh Oklahoma City Bombing in 1995. See *New York Times,* 20 December 1996 [www.nytimes.con/1996/12/20/us/head-of-fbi] (accessioned 1 August 2014); Adam Bernstein, "Richard A. Jewell: Wrongly Linked to Olympic Bombing," *Washington Post,* 30 August 2007 [www.washingtonpost.com/wp-dya/content/article/2007/08/29] (accessioned 4 November 2015); and Charles Thompson, "Penn State Trustee Ken Frazier Fires Back at Freeh Report Critics," *Penn Live,* 14 March 2013 [www.pennlive.com/midstate/index.ssf/2013/03/penn_state_trustees_Ken_Frazier.html] (accessioned 1 October 2015). Freeh and Tomalis did spend several hours interviewing both Freeh and Michael Chertoff of the Covington Law Firm. Kenneth Frazier Deposition, 15 December 2014, "Legal Documents – *Corman vs NCAA*" [www.senatorcorman.com/legal-documents-corman-vs.ncaa] (accessioned 27 June 2015).

307 One could argue that there was pressure on the trustees by, among others, the Faculty Senate of Penn State and irate alumni, who felt that the trustees might alter the Freeh Report before it became public if it were not released to the public immediately. Ken Frazier warned, a week before the Report was released, against an immediate release by the Freeh group without the board discussing it: "I would think our initial communications should say that we are looking over the Report, and the Board will provide its responses after we have a chance to meet to digest and discuss the findings and recommendations." Ken Frazier, email to Jennifer Thompson, Keith Masser, Karen Peetz, cc: Mark Dambly, Rod Erickson, 6 June 2012 [www.pennstatesunshinefund.org/results/download/20120606] (accessioned 13 December 2016).

308 "Posts Tagged 'Paul Silvis,'" *The Penn Stater,* 7 March 2014 [pennstatermag.com/tag/paul-silvis] (accessioned 26 October 2016).

309 "Penn State Issues Statement on Freeh Report," 12 July 2012, Erickson, Exhibit. 6. "Legal Documents – *Corman vs NCAA*" [www.senatorcorman.com/legal-documents-corman-vs-ncaa] (accessioned 16 June 2015).

310 Notes were taken at a meeting of the Trustees Executive Committee on the evening President Erickson signed the Consent Decree. The notes stated: "'Crippling' Consent Decree (have Erickson and Peetz sign" and "share PSU statement with full board.") "Notes from Board of Trustees Executive Committee Meeting, 22 July 2012. Guadagnino Exhibit 15, "Legal Documents – *Corman vs NCAA*," [www.senatorcorman.com/legal-documents-corman-vs-ncaa] (accessioned 29 June 2015). At the meeting were Trustees Alexander, Broadhurst, Dambly, Eckel, Erickson, Frazier, Hintz, Masser, Peetz, and Surma. Also attending were attorneys Dunham and Guadagnino, and Vice-President Poole. Later, Karen Peetz, President of the Trustees, stated: "I absolutely support President Erickson and his decision to accept the Consent Decree. . . ." Penn State Board of Trustees Minutes, 12 August 2012, Penn State University Archives.

311 Joseph F. O'Dea, Jr., Penn State attorney, letter to Edward B. Brown, II, Barbara L. Doran, Robert C. Jubelirer, Anthony P. Lubrano, Ryan J. McCombie, William F. Oldsey, and Alice W. Pope, 17 April 2015 [www.psu.edu/ur/2014/Response_Letter.pdf] (accessioned 6 August 2016).

312 In the case of the merger of Penn State's Hershey Medical system with that of the Geisinger group, called the Penn State Geisinger Health System, the $100,000,000 breakup was euphemistically called "unwinding of the affiliation." No one of the board of trustees raised a question of President Spanier when he gave his report on the merger. "Report of the President of the University," 11 July 1997, Penn State Board of Trustees Minutes, Penn State University Archives. See also, Chapter 6.

Chapter Six Notes

313 Rick Reilly, "The Sins of the Father," *ESPN*, 13 July 2012 [espn.go.com/espn/story/_/id/8162972/joe-paterno-true-legacy] (accessed 24 December 2015).

314 "Binding Consent Decree Imposed by the National Collegiate Athletic Association and Accepted by the Pennsylvania State University," 23 July 2012 [www.ncaa.com/content/penn-state-conclusions] (accessed 19 December 2015).

315 Some of the additional costs to Penn State include the massive paperwork throughout the university caused by the Scandal; removing Gary Schultz's name from a new building; continuing to pay President Spanier's salary as a continuing member of the Penn State faculty, and loss of Joe Paterno likeness merchandise revenue. Despite Consent Decree agreement for transparency, this kind of cost information is not available.

316 William T. Mallon, "The Alchemist: A Case Study of a Failed Merger in Academic Medicine," *Strategic Alliances in Academic Medicine* (2003), 26-37 [journals.lww.com/academicmedicine/documents/mallon.pdf] (accessed 30 December 2015).

317 Baltasar Gracian, *The Act of Worldly Wisdom* (London, England: Macmillan, 1904), 129.

318 "Binding Consent Decree Imposed by the National Collegiate Athletic Association and Accepted by the Pennsylvania State University," 23 July 2012 [www/ncaa/com/content/penn-state-conclusions] (accessed 19 December 2015). The Consent Decree statement read: "If the NCAA determines, in its sole discretion, that the University materially breached any provision of the AIA, such action shall be considered grounds for extending the term of the AIA or imposing additional sanctions, up to and including, a temporary ban on participation in certain intercollegiate athletic competition and additional fines." Penn State was running scared.

319 "Athletics Integrity Agreement Between the National Collegiate Athletic Association and the Big Ten Conference, and the Pennsylvania State University," 28 August 2012 [www.psu.edu/ur/2012/Athletics_Integrity_Agreement.pdf] (accessed 9 January 2016).

320 Caitlin Gailey, "Julie Del Giorno: The Life Behind the Athletics Integrity Officer," *Onward State*, 19 March 2015 [onwardstate.com/2015/03/19-julie-del-giorno] (accessed 9 January 2016).

321 Eric Shutz, "Fencer Reveals More Information Surrounding Kaidanov's Departure," *Daily Collegian*, 10 September 2013 [www.collegian.psu.edu/sports/fencing] (accessed 8 January 2016).

322 Kaidanov v. Pennsylvania State University, Pennsylvania Eastern District Court, Case No. 2:14-cv-03191, District Judge Gene E. K. Pratter presiding.

323 Zack Berger, "Kaidanov, Penn State Resolve Wrongful Termination Suit," *Onward State,* 12 December 2015 [onwardstate.com/2015/12/12/kaidanov] (accessed 9 January 2016).

324 "Joyner Retires," *Penn State News,* 17 June 2014 [news.psu. edu/318567/2014/06/17/athletics/joyner] (accessed 26 January 2016).

325 Ron Smith, email to Jan Bortner, 30 August 2013 and Bortner to Smith, 3 September 2013, Ron Smith Personal Collection.

326 Del Giorno, a lesbian, would not likely have been hired by those in the previous athletic administration when the Sandusky Scandal broke. She would not have been admitted into the U.S. Military Academy at West Point had her sexual orientation been known in the 1980s. Many attitudes and policies had changed at Penn State and in the nation since the 1980s.

327 See William D. Cohan, *The Price of Silence: The Duke Lacrosse Scandal, the Power of the Elite, and the Corruption of Our Great University* (New York: Scribner, 2014) and Elizabeth Nix, "What Was the Dreyfus Affair?" *History* (14 January 2015) [www. history.com/news/ask-history/what–was-the-dreyfus-affair] (accessed 5 July 2016).

328 The 20 were: Rob Bolden (to Louisiana State), Justin Brown (to Oklahoma), Zack Bradshaw (to Virginia), Tim Buckley (to N.C. State), Ross Douglas (to Michigan), Anthony Fera (to Texas), Khairi Fortt (to California), Will Fuller (to Notre Dame), Luke Graham (remain PSU), Kevin Haplea (to Florida State), Dorian Johnson (to Pittsburgh), Paul Jones (to Robert Morris), Shawney Kersey (to Marshall), Ryan Kowicki (to Illinois), Matt Marcincin (remain PSU), Jamil Pollard (to Rutgers), Silas Redd (to Southern California), Dakota Royer (remain PSU), Derrick Thomas (to West Virginia), Greg Webb (to North Carolina). Thomas transferred just before Consent Decree penalties.

329 John U. Bacon, *Fourth and Long: The Fight for the Soul of College Football* (New York: Simon & Schuster, 2013), pp. 78-80, 83-84.

330 Darren Rowell, "Penn State's Attendance Down Again," *ESPN,* 25 November 2012 [espn.go.com/college-football/story/_/id/8671564] (accessed 2 February 2016), "Football Fans Boost Home Attendance by 5,000," 2 December 2014 [news. psu.edu/story336808] (accessed 2 February 2016), Chris Kwiencinski, "Big Ten Schools Enjoy High Attendance" [www.landof10.com/big-ten/big-ten-football-home-attendance] (accessed 17 February 2017) and Mark Wogenrich, "Penn State Attendance Up 6 percent for 2017," *The Morning Call,* 19 November 2017 [www.mcall. com/sports/college/psu/mc-spt-penn-state] (accessed 26 November 2017).

331 "Binding Consent Decree Imposed by the National Collegiate Athletic Association and Accepted by the Pennsylvania State University," 23 July 2012, p. 5.

332 "Equity in Athletics" (2011, 2012, 2013, 2014) Penn State Survey [publicaccess. psu.edu/docs/financial_year] (accessed 29 January 2016), and Mark Wogenrich, "A Look at Penn State's Athletic Budgets," *Morning Call,* 16 March 2014 [blogs.mcall. com/nittany_lines/2014/03/a-look] (accessed 29 January 2016). The shortened

tenure of swimming coach John Hargis may also have been due to possible violations of NCAA rules concerning the amount of practice time.

333 Raymond Flandez, "Penn State Grapples with Angry Donors," *The Chronicle of Philanthropy*, 21 November 2011 [philanthropy.com/article/penn-state-grapples] (accessioned 29 January 2016).

334 Lee Stout and Harry H. West, *Lair of the Lion: A History of Beaver Stadium* (University Park: Penn State University Press, 2017), 74-79.

335 "'We Are' Sculpture Spells It Out for Penn State Community," *Penn State News*, 1 July 2015 [news.psu.edu/story/362033/201/15/07/01] (accessioned 17 February 2017).

336 "Penn State at a Glance—A Statistical Snapshot," ca. January 2016 [stats.psu.edu] (accessioned 30 January 2016).

337 Ed Czekaj was a member of the 1948 Sugar Bowl football team (AD-1970); Joe Paterno was the football coach (AD-1980); Jim Tarman was a sports information man working for Joe Paterno (AD-1982), and Tim Curley was Joe Paterno's pick for AD (1993).

338 David Jones, "Sandy Barbour Far From Perfect Fit as New Penn State AD But Has Personal Tools to Adapt," *Penn Live*, 5 August 2014 [www.pennlive.com/sports/index.ssf/2014/08/sandy_barbour] (accessioned 1 February 2016).

339 John Cummins and Kirsten Hextrum, "The Management of Intercollegiate Athletics at UC Berkeley: Turning Points and Consequences," November 2013, Center for Studies in Higher Education, University of California, Berkeley [www.eshe.berkeley.edu/sites/default/files/shared/publications/docs/ROSP.CSHE_12.1] (accessioned 1 February 2016).

340 Ronald A. Smith, "Far More than Commercialism: Stadium Building from Harvard's Innovations to Stanford's 'Dirt Bowl,'" *International Journal of the History of Sport*, 25 (September 2008), 1462-1463.

341 Jon Wilner, "Cal Stadium Plan Financially Flawed," *San Jose Mercury News*, 24 June 2013 [www.mercurynews.com/ci_23528258/cal-stadium-plan-financially-flawed] (accessioned 1 February 2016).

342 "Athletic Department Estimated Income and Expenses, 1979-1980," Box 10290, Folder "Athletics – Budget – 1980-1982," and Robert A. Patterson to President John W. Oswald, 10 June 1981, President Oswald Papers, Box 10290, Folder "Athletics Relating to Admission, Policies, Etc., 1979-1982," Penn State University Archives.

343 Wilner, "Cal Stadium Plan Financially Flawed." The University of California had already forgiven athletics over $30 million of indebtedness during Barbour stint at Berkeley and over the past two decades forgiven $170 million. See Cummins and Hextrum, "The Management of Intercollegiate Athletics."

344 "Director of Intercollegiate Athletics Appointment Terms," News release, 26 July 2014 [www.psu.edu.ur/2014/Barbour.pdf] (accessioned 29 January 2016).

345 Audrey Snyder, "Penn State Athletic Director Sandy Barbour Backs Off 409 Sticker Stance," *Pittsburgh Post Gazette*, 20 January 2015 [www.post-gazette.com/sports/psu/2015/01/20/Penn-State] (accessioned 2 February 2016).

346 For a discussion of needed improvements, indeed a history of Beaver Stadium, see Lee Stout and Harry H. West, *Lair of the Lion: A History of Beaver Stadium* (University Park, PA: Penn State University Press, 2017), 160-161.

347 Replies to Mike Poorman, "Penn State Football: What is the Future of Beaver Stadium," *Statecollege.com* [www.statecollege.com/news/columns/penn-state-football-what-is-the-future] (accessioned 3 February 2016).

Chapter Seven Notes

348 Alison Boston and Lori Falce, "Corman Announces End to Penn State Sanctions; Paterno Wins Restored," *Centre Daily Times,* 16 January 2015 [www.centredaily.com/news/local/education/penn-state/jerry-sandusky/article42901299.html] (accessioned 6 February 2016).

349 Senate Bill 187, Regular Session 2013-2014, Pennsylvania General Assembly [www.legis.state.pa.us/cfdocs/billinfo/billinfo.cfm?syear=203&sind=0&bo] (accessioned 4 March 2016).

350 Zach Berger, "Judge in Corman Lawsuit Criticizes NCAA, Elaborates on Landmark Case," *Onward State*, 2 April 2015 [onwardstate.com/2015/04/02/judge-in-corman-lawsuit-criticizes-ncaa] (accessioned 4 March 2016).

351 "Executive Summary, NCAA Motion to Dismiss Corman v. NCAA," [www.ncaa.org/sites/default/files/Cormansummary.pdf.](4 March 2016).

352 Jeré Longman, "A Boost from the State Capitol Helped Penn State Escape N.C.A.A. Penalties," *New York Times,* 4 February 2015 [www.nytimes.com/2015/02/05/sports/ncaafootball/how-one-legislator-helped] (accessioned 4 March 2016).

353 *Corman v. NCAA,* 15 October 2014, Commonwealth Court of Pennsylvania, No. 1 M.D. 2013 [www.pacourts.us/assets/files/setting-4002/file-3944.pdf?cb=501121] (accessioned 23 February 2016).

354 Mark Emmert, letter to Rodney Erickson, 17 November 2011 (www.psu.edu/ur/2011/ncaa.pdf] (accessioned 5 March 2016).

355 Kathy Redmond, email to Mark Emmert, 18 November 2011 and Emmert to Redmond, 23 November 2011, Mark Emmert Exhibit No. 24, 12 December 2014, "Legal Documents – *Corman vs NCAA,*" [www.senatorcorman.com/legal-documents-corman-vs-ncaa] (accessioned 5 March 2016). Emphasis is added.

356 Longman, "A Boost From the State Capitol."

357 "NCAA Reaches Proposed Settlement in Corman Lawsuit," 16 January 2015 [www.ncaa.org/about/resources/media-center/news/ncaa-reaches] (accessioned 5 March 2016).

358 The NCAA depositions were from Mark Emmert, president; Ed Ray, former chair of the NCAA Executive Committee; Donald Remy, NCAA counsel; David Berst, long-time NCAA executive; Julie Roe Lach, former Vice-President of NCAA Enforcement; Shep Cooper, Director of the NCAA Infractions Committee; Kevin

Lennon, NCAA Vice President of the Academic and Membership Affairs; Bob
Williams, Vice President of NCAA Communications; and Omar McNeill, Freeh
Group head investigator, to whom Donald Remy communicated. The Penn State
depositions were from Rodney Erickson, Penn State president; Stephen Dunham,
Penn State Counsel; Frank Guadagnino, Penn State legal staff; Keith Masser, Penn
State Board of Trustees; Ken Frazier, Penn State Board of Trustees, and Gene Marsh,
Penn State's liaison to the NCAA. Jake Corman represented the *Corman vs. NCAA*
case.

359 Quoted in Don Van Natta, Jr., "Docs: NCAA, Freeh Worked Together,"
ESPN News, 12 November 2014 [espn.go.com/espn/tol/story/_/11863293/court]
(accessioned 1 April 2016).

360 As quoted in Jeré Longman, "A Boost From the State Capitol Helped Penn
State Escape N.C.A.A. Penalties," *New York Times*, 4 February 2015 [www.nytimes.
com/2015/02/05/sports/ncaafootball] (accessioned 21 December 2016).

361 Mark Emmert Deposition, 2 December 2014, "Legal Documents – *Corman vs.
NCAA* [www.senatorcorman.com/legal-documents-corman-vs-ncaa] (accessioned
23 February 2016).

362 Shakespeare, *Julius Caesar*, ca. 1599, Act 3 Scene 2. Julius Caesar's friend, Mark
Anthony, spoke as Caesar's body was returned: "Friends, Romans, Countrymen, lend
me your ears; I came to bury Caesar, not to praise him. The evil that men do lives after
them; the good is often interred with their bones."

363 Donald Remy, email to Gene Marsh, 18 July 2012, "Legal Documents – *Corman
vs NCAA*," Berst Exhibit 16 [www.senatorcorman.com/legal-documents-corman-vs-
ncaa] and Stephen Dunham, email to Gene Marsh, 21 July 2012, "Legal Documents
– *Corman vs NCAA*," Stephen Dunham Deposition, 21 November 2014 [www.
senatorcorman.com/legal-documents-corman-vs-ncaa].

364 "Statement of Findings," News release, 11 February 2015 [www.senatorcorman.
com/files/2015/02/News-Release-Statement-of-Findings-pdf] (accessioned 6 March
2016).

365 The quote that Penn State "is so embarrassed they will do anything. . ." is from
the email of NCAA's Kevin Lennon to Julie Roe, 14 July 2012, Julie Roe, Exhibit
17, "Legal Documents – *Corman vs NCAA*," [www.senatorcorman.com/legal-
documents-corman-vs-ncaa].

366 Statement of Findings," 11 February 2015 [www.senatorcorman.com/
files/2015/02/News-Release-Statement-of-Findings-pdf] (accessioned 6 March
2016].

367 Ibid.

368 "NCAA Reaches Proposed Settlement in Corman Lawsuit," 16 January
2015" [www.ncaa.org/about/resources/media-center/news/ncaa-reaches-proposed-
settlement] (accessioned 4 March 2016).

369 *Estate of Joseph Paterno v. NCAA*, Docket No. 2013-2082, 16 April 2014,
Amended Complaint [online.swj.com/public/resources/documents/0521-paterno]
(accessioned 16 March 2016).

370 Ray was questioned by lawyers from both the Paterno Family and Senator Corman. Wick Sollers for Paterno and Matthew Haverstick for Corman. Edward Ray Deposition, 8 December 2014, "Legal Documents – *Corman vs NCAA*," Exhibit 13 [www.senatorcorman.com/legal-documents-corman-vs-ncaa] (accessioned 16 March 2016).

371 Wick Sollers, letter to Mark Emmert and NCAA, 3 August 2012, Estate of Joseph Paterno v. NCAA, Docket No. 2013-2082, 15 October 2014, Exhibit 3 [www.centredaily.com/latest-news-article40942935.ece/BIN] (accessioned 17 March 2016).

372 *George Scott Paterno and Family of Joe Paterno, et al. v. NCAA*, Court of Common Pleas of Centre County, PA, 30 May 2013 and *Centre Daily Times*, 31 May 2013, p. A1, A3.

373 Pete Thamel, "Sanctions Decimate the Nittany Lions Now and for Years to Come," *New York Times*, 23 July 2012 [www.nytimes.com/2012/07/13/sports/ncaafootball/penn-state-penalties-include-60] (accessioned 12 October 2017).

374 *"Critique of the Freeh Report: The Rush To Injustice Regarding Joe Paterno," ESPN.com*, 6 February 2013 [ESPN.go.com/pdf/2013/02/10/espn_OTL_FINAL%KING&S] (accessioned 18 March 2016).

375 Ibid.

376 Ibid.

377 "Text of Louis Freeh Response to Paterno Report," *Centre Daily Times*, 10 February 2013, p. A3.

378 "The Freeh Report," 12 July 2012, pp. 47-49 [www.nytimes.com/interactive/2012/07/12/sports/ncaafootball/13pennstate] (accessioned 14 July 2012).

379 "Statement by the Paterno Family Regarding Settlement with the NCAA," 16 January 2015 [www.paterno.com/family-statements/post/Statement-by-the-Paterno-Family-Regarding-Settlement] (accessioned 11 July 2017).

Chapter Eight Notes

380 "Binding Consent Decree Imposed by the National Collegiate Athletic Association and Accepted by the Pennsylvania State University," 23 July 2012 [www.ncaa.org/sites/default/files/Binding%20Consent%20Decree.pdf] (accessioned 24 December 2016).

381 For a fuller account, see "Hugo Bezdek's Saga—Alumni, Trustees, and Presidents," in Ronald A. Smith, *Wounded Lions: Joe Paterno, Jerry Sandusky, and the Crises in Penn State Athletics* (Urbana: University of Illinois Press, 2016), 43-52.

382 As quoted by J. Brady McCollough, "Death of Joe Paterno Created Deep Void for Penn Staters," *Pittsburgh Post-Gazette*, 29 January 2012 [www.post-gazette.com/frontpage/2012/01/29/Death-of-Joe-Paterno] (accessioned 24 December 2016).

383 As quoted in Dennis Alan Booher, "Joseph Vincent Paterno, Football Coach: His Involvement with the Pennsylvania State University and American Intercollegiate Athletics," Ph.D. dissertation, Penn State University, 1985, p. 23.

384 Joe Paterno's Speech at the AFCA (American Football Coaches Association),'' [www.gospusports.com/sports/m-footbl/spec-rel/011801aaa.html] (accessioned 16 March 2016).

385 Joe Paterno with Bernard Asbell, *Paterno by the Book* (New York: Random House, 1989), 72, 87.

386 Joe Paterno Third Amended and Restated Employment Contract, 27 January 1978, John Oswald Papers, Box 10290, Folder "Athletics Relating to Academics, Admission Policies, Etc. 1979-1982," Penn State University Archives. In 1978, his salary rose from $46,128 to $55,000.

387 "Statement of Coach Joe Paterno," 6 January 1973, Joe Paterno Papers, Box 07594, Folder "Sports Illustrated Issue," Penn State University Archives.

388 Ray McAllister, "Paterno Bought a Million Dollar Night, *Daily Collegian*, 2 April 1973, p. 13, and Michael O'Brien, *No Ordinary Joe: The Biography of Joe Paterno* (Nashville, TN: Rutledge Hill, 1998), unpaginated on Google. The dinner also raised $7,500 for the Levi Lamb, Penn State athletic scholarship fund.

389 Smith, *Wounded Lions*, p. 45.

390 "Penn State Commencement Speech by Head Football Coach Joe Paterno," 16 June 1973 [pennstatermag.files.wordpress.com/2012/01/paterno1973commencementspeech (accessioned 30 January 2012).

391 Ibid.

392 Ibid.

393 "Joe Paterno Interview: Sally Jenkins Discusses Her Talk with Ex-Penn State Coach," *Washington Post*, 16 January 2012 [live.washingtonpost.com/joe-paterno-speaks-to-sally-jenkins.html] (accessioned 22 April 2017).

394 "Penn State Commencement Speech by Head Football Coach Joe Paterno," 16 June 1973 [www.pennstatemag.files.wordpress.com/2012/01/paterno1973commencementspeech (accessioned 30 January 2012).

395 "John Cappelletti Heisman Acceptance Speech," 13 December 1973, Penn State University Archives, *Chicago Tribune*, 14 December 1973, p. S1, and Paterno with Bernard Asbell, *Paterno by the Book*, 171-173.

396 Bill Lyon, "Italian 'Invasion' Takes Over City," *Philadelphia Inquirer*, January 1974, Ridge H. Riley Papers, Box 03.01, Folder "34," Penn State University Archives.

397 Rick Reilly, "Not An Ordinary Joe," *Sports Illustrated*, 22 December 1986 [www.si.com/vault/1986/12/22/114570] (accessioned 28 April 2017).

398 Ibid.

399 Douglas Looney, "There Are a Lot of People Who Think I'm a Phony and Now They Think They Have the Proof," *Sports Illustrated*, 17 March 1980 [www.si.com/vault/1980/03/17/824489/there-are-a-lot-of-people] (accessioned 4 January 2016).

400 The most egregious effort for presidential admits was 1980 when he asked President John Oswald for nine rejected athletes by Penn State admissions to be admitted. See "Candidates Submitted to J. W. Oswald for 1980 Admissions," John Oswald Papers, Box 10290, Folder "Athletics Relating to Academics, Admissions,

Policies, etc., 1979-1982," Penn State University Archives.

401 Thomas Fuller, *Introduction: Or, Directions, Counsels, and Cautions, Tending to Prudent Management of Affairs in Common Life* (London: Taylor and Hessey, 1815, 6th ed.) Adage # 686.

402 His contract for 1978 showed $15,000 for a TV program; $25,000 bonus for a major bowl game, a supplementary pension for life of $12,000/year, and a salary of $55,000 that was increasing at 5% a year. The contract included the statement "Such cash bonus or bonuses as may be awarded to him from time to time by the University acting through its President." Joe Paterno Third Amended and Restated Employment Contract, 27 January 1978, John Oswald Papers, Box 10290, Folder "Athletics Relating to Academics, Admission Policies, Etc. 1979-1982," Penn State University Archives.

403 Thomas Ferraro, "In the World of College Athletics. . . : He Is Not an Average Joe," *Los Angeles Times*, 17 May 1987 [articles.latimes.com/1987-05-07/sports/sp-774_1_Joe-Paterno] (accessioned 29 December 2016) and Paterno with Bernard Asbell, *Paterno By The Book*, 205, 233-237.

404 "Joe Paterno's Speech to the BOT Following His First National Championship," 22 January 1983 [docs.google.com/document/d/lvm/vpkrt7KrmyZ1qjisepf8] (accessioned 22 January 2014). In that speech he said that Penn State had some "lazy profs who are only concerned with tenure. Some. . . would make Happy Valley Sleepy Valley. . . ." He also said Penn State needed a better library. Paterno might have noted that his own Kinesiology department, of which he was a full professor, was rated # 1 in the nation well before his team was rated # 1.

405 Ibid.

406 Paterno wrote Stuart Forth stating that "your leadership in the Libraries set the stage for the excitement this new addition will provide, and if it wasn't for you, I wouldn't be part of this critically important effort." Paterno to Forth, 29 October 1992, Paterno Papers, Box 07574, Folder "Library Project Correspondence, 1993-1998), Penn State University Archives.

407 "Solicitation Strategies for Joe Paterno Prospects," 1992, and Dave Gearhart, Vice President for Development, to Cheryl Norman, Secretary to Joe Paterno, 27 November 1992, Joe Paterno Papers, Box 07574, Folder "Library Campaign Feasibility Study 1993-1998," Penn State University Archives.

408 When my daughter Penny and I in 1998 created a Penn State game, "Memento: A Game of Recollection," it was promoted with a photo of Joe Paterno, signature, and his quote on the box cover and several photos of Paterno among the 48 duplicate recollection photos. I asked and Paterno agreed to donate his royalties (20 percent of the retail price) to the Penn State Archives from which many of the game photos were obtained.

409 Joseph V. Paterno to Drew Lewis, Chair, Union Pacific Corporation, Bethlehem, PA, 5 April 1995, Joe Paterno Papers, Box 07574, Folder "Union Pacific Corporation, 1995-1996," Penn State University Archives.

410 Jan Murphy, "Paternos Gave Another $100,000 Donation to Penn State in December," *Penn Live*, 14 January 2012 [www.pennlive.com/midstate/index/ssf/2012/01/paternos-gave] (accessioned 17 April 2017). In addition, $50,000 was

added to the Paterno Liberal Arts Undergraduate Fellows Program.

411 "Paternos Pledge $3.5 Million to Penn State," *Penn State News*, 15 January 1998, Joe Paterno Vertical File, Folder "2000s," Penn State University Archives and Susan Welch, "Farewell to Joe Paterno, a Legendary Liberal Arts Leader," College of the Liberal Arts, ca. February 2012 [www.la/psu.edu/news/farewell-to-joe-paterno-a-legendary-liberal-arts-leader] (accessioned 23 March 2012).

412 Michael Bérubé, "Why I Resigned the Paterno Chair," *Chronicle of Higher Education*, 15 October 2012 [chronicle.com/article/Why-I-Resigned-The-Paterno/134944] (accessioned 27 April 2017). He relinquished the Paterno Family chair after the Sandusky Scandal broke and Sandusky was convicted of child abuse crimes. He felt that Paterno had not done enough to protect the abused children.

413 Discussion with Paul Harvey, Classics Department head from 2006-2013. 22 January 2014, Ron Smith Personal File.

414 Bert Schoff, Allentown, PA to President Joab Thomas, 6 December 1991, Office of Vice President for Finance Records, Box 03086, Folder "Intercollegiate Athletics-Beaver Stadium," Penn State University Archives.

415 Penn State athletics has denied the 9-0 victory over Bucknell in a game played on November 12, 1881 in Lewisburg. At the time, the game of rugby was about to be transformed into American football, principally by the work of Yale's Walter Camp in the early 1880s. It definitely was Penn State's first football game and acknowledged by those who played in it. See I. P. McCreary, class of 1882, Erie, PA, to Mr. Sullivan, undated, ca. 1923, "Story of the 1881 and 1887 Teams," *Penn State Alumni News*, 10 (December 1923), 10-12.

416 "Paternos Pledge $3.5 Million to Penn State."

417 Chip Minemyer and Chris Rosenblum, "'Joe's Legacy:' Almost a Year After His Death, Paterno's Image Still Debated, Defended," *Centre Daily Times*, 19 January 2013 [www.centredaily.com/news/special-reports/joe-paterno/article42815778.html] (accessioned 28 April 2017).

418 Ibid.

419 Paterno with Bernard Asbell, *Paterno By The Book*, 226-227.

420 Denise Bachman, "The Truth About Joe: A Saint He Certainly Ain't," *Daily Collegian*, 21 March 1980, Joe Paterno Papers, Box 07594, Folder "Newspaper Clippings, 1980-1989," Penn State University Archives.

421 *Centre Daily Times*, 5 August 2012, p. A8.

422 Joe Posnanski, *Paterno* (New York: Simon and Schuster, 2012), 304; Gene Wojciechowski, "Paterno a Study in Contradictions," *ESPN*, 22 January 2012 [espn.go.com/college-football/story/_/7488723/former-Penn-State]; Michael O'Brien, *No Ordinary Joe: The Biography of Joe Paterno* (Nashville, TN: Rutledge Hill Press, 1998), ix; Peter Thammel, "For Paterno, Lover of Classics, Tragic Flaw to a Legacy," *New York Times*, 22 January 2012 [http//www.nytimes.com/2012/01/23/sports/ncaafootball/joe-paterno-leaves-a-complicated-legacy.html] (accessioned 21 March 2012); Jonathan Mahler, *Death Comes to Happy Valley: Penn State and the Tragic Legacy of Joe Paterno* (San Francisco: Byliner, 2012), 65; Frank Fitzpatrick, *Pride of the Lions: The Biography of*

Joe Paterno (Chicago, Triumph Books, 2011), 223; and Ron Bracken, "Ron Bracken: Climate of Secrecy Led to Crumbling of Camelot," *Centre Daily Times*, 11 November 2011 [www.centredaily.com/news/special-reports/joe-paterno/article42806880.html] (accessed 3 May 2017). Bill Lyon of the Knight-Ridder Newspapers, called Paterno an "emotional bully." See *Centre Daily Times*, 16 January 1983, p. D2

423 Russell Frank, "Oral History Interview with Ron Bracken," 16 June 2009, pp. 9-10 [comm.psu.edu/assets/uploads/brackeninterview.pdf] (accessed 3 May 2017).

424 A Big Ten study revealed that athletes at Penn State had nearly 20 percent of all physical assaults and sexual assaults on its campus while being only 2 percent of the student body. "Big Ten Discipline Data Comparisons," [ca. 2004] and "Penn State Student Athlete Data Compared to Non-Student Athlete Data," Office of the Vice President for Student Affairs Papers, Box 12016, Folder "Football," Penn State University Archives.

425 Douglas S. Looney, "A Lot of People Think I'm Phony," *Sports Illustrated*, 52 (17 March 1980), 334-48; Lou Prato, *The Penn State Football Encyclopedia* (Champaign, IL: Sports Publishing, 1998), 260-261; Ron Bracken, "Nittany Lions Not Used to Off the Field Turbulence," *Centre Daily Times*, 18 August 1992, p. D1. Prato, a friend of Penn State athletics and instrumental in creating the Penn State All-Sports Museum, once called the "The Grand Experiment" of Paterno "The Grand Debacle." p. 260.

426 Frank, "Oral History," pp. 11-12 and Bracken, "Nittany Lions Not Used," p. D1.

427 Kelly Whiteside, "Paterno Isn't All Smiles in Happy Valley," *USA Today*, 19 April 2003, Joe Paterno Papers, Box 07594, Folder "Newspaper Clippings, Magazine Articles," Penn State University Archives and Ron Bracken, "Paterno Refuses to Answer Questions About Phillips," *Centre Daily Times*, 27 March 2003, p. B1, B4.

428 David McCullough, *The Path Between the Seas: The Creation of the Panama Canal, 1870-1914* (New York: Simon & Schuster, 1978), 360-397.

429 For a fuller account of the Triponey-Paterno conflict, see Smith, *Wounded Lions*, pp. 119-126.

430 Reed Albergotti, "A Discipline Problem: Paterno Fought Penn State Official Over Punishment of Players, *Wall Street Journal*, 22 November 2011 [www.wsj.com/articles/SB100] (accessed 4 May 2017).

431 Matt Miller, "Judge Slams Paterno, McQueary as He Sends Spanier, Curley and Schultz to Jail Over Sandusky Child-Sex Case," *Penn Live,* 25 March 2017 [www.pennlive.com/news/2017/06/judge_slams_paterno] (accessed 7 September 2017).

432 Associated Press, "Paterno Says He Should Have Done More," *Scranton Times-Tribune*, 9 November 2011 [thetimes-tribune.com/paterno-says-he-should-have-done-more (accessed 8 May 2012) and Sally Jenkins, "Conversations," *Washington Post*, 16 January 2012 [live.washingtonpost.com/joe-paterno-speaks-to-sally-jenkins.html] (accessed 8 February 2012).

433 As quoted by Dennis Dodd, "Joe Paterno's Loyal Son Refuses to Let His Father's Legacy Wilt," *CBS Sports*, 14 May 2013 [www.cbssports.com/collegefootball/story/222437678/joe-paternos-loyal-son] (accessed 16 March 2016).

434 Andrew Cohen, "Thus Begins the Rehabilitation of Joe Paterno," 15 January 2012 [www.pennstatesunshinefund.org/results/download/20120116249] (accessed 9 December 2016).

435 Marian V. Liautaud, "Success, Honor, and the Legacy of Joe Paterno," *Christianity Today*, 16 November 2011 [www.christianitytoday.com/women/2011/november/success-honor] (accessed 12 September 2016).

436 Florida 727, response to Ben Kercheval, "What the Paternos' Critique of the Freeh Report Didn't Do, and What It Did," *NBC Sports*, 10 February 2013 [collegefootballtalk.nbcsports.com/2013/02/10/what-the-paterno] (accessed 3 August 2016).

437 "Sue Paterno Defends JoePa in Letter to Former Penn State Players," *Huffington Post*, 8 February 2013 [www.huffingtonpost.com/2013/02/08/sue-paterno-defends-joe] (accessed 31 December 2016).

438 Bob Hammel, "Student-Athletes: Tackling the Problem," *Phi Delta Kappan*, 62 (September 1980), 7-13 [www.jstor.org/ezaccess.libraries.psu.edu/stable/2038471=29?se] (accessed 5 May 2017).

439 Joe Paterno, "Speech to the AFCA Clinic," 1987, Bernie Asbell Papers, 1950-2000, Box 07835, Folder "Coaching Summary Thoughts," Penn State University Archives.

440 "Ike and Tina Turner – I Can't Believe What You Say Lyrics," *Songlyrics* [www.songlyrics.com/ike-tina-turner] (accessed 24 March 2018).

441 "PS4RS—Penn Staters for Responsible Stewardship" [ps4rs.org] (accessed 5 May 2017).

442 "The Hoover Legacy, 40 Years After," 4 May 2012 [www.fbi.gov/news/stories/the-hoover-legacy] (accessed 5 May 2017).

443 As quoted by Ron Cook, "Paterno's Legacy at Penn State Long Will be Debated," *Pittsburgh Post-Gazette*, 9 May 2016 [www.post-gazette.com/sports/ron-cook/2016/05/09/Ron-Cook] (accessed 31 December 2016).

444 LDavis5 response to Melinda Henneberger, "What Paterno Admitted He Knew: Sandusky Couldn't Have Done Without Him," *Washington Post*, 3 July 2012 [www.washingtonpost.com/blogs/she-the-people/post/what] (accessed 7 July 2012).

445 As quoted by Rick Reilly, "Joe Paterno's True Legacy," *ESPN*, 23 January 2012 [espn.go.com/espn/story/_/id/7492873/rick-reilly-paterno-true-legacy] (accessed 22 January 2014).

446 Pentinental, in reaction to Maxwell Edison, "Sara Gamin and Sally Jenkins at ASPE," *Black Shoe Diaries*, 11 April 2012 [www.blackshoediaries.com/2012/4/11/29400213/sara-gamin-and-sally-jenkins] (accessed 1 February 2014).

447 Francis D. Cogliano, *Thomas Jefferson: Reputation and Legacy* (Charlottesville: University of Virginia Press, 2006), 187-190 and Thomas Jefferson Heritage Society, "Group of Defenders of Thomas Jefferson's Reputation Settle Lawsuit Brought by Owners of Monticello," *P R Newswire*, 5 September 2000 [www.prnewswire.com/news-releases/group-of-defenders] (accessed 6 May 2017).

Chapter Nine Notes

448 Carol Ross Joynt and Marisa M. Kashino, "Who Ya Gonna Call? Joe Paterno Looks to Washington for Legal Counsel, PR Help," *Washingtonian,* 11 November 2011 [www.washingtonian.com/2011/11/11/who-ya-gonna-call] (accessed 8 July 2017).

449 See "Wick Sollers," [www.kslaw.com/people/JSedwick-Sollers] (accessed 3 January 2017).

450 Associated Press, "PSU Pays Paterno Estate $5M-plus," *ESPN,* 20 April 2012 [www.espn.com/college/football/story/_id/7834352/penn-state-pays]; "Joe Paterno Net Worth," *The Richest,* undated [www.therichest.com/celebnetworth/athletes/coach/joe-paterno-net-worth; and Charles Thompson, "Joe Paterno's New Record: $13.4 Million in Pension from Penn State," *Penn Live,* 23 May 2012 [www.pennlive.com/midstate/index.ssf/joe_paternos_new_record] (accessed 17 August 2017).

451 Joe Paterno began contract negotiations with Penn State in January 2011 at the time he learned the state was investigating Jerry Sandusky sexual abuse and would be testifying before the attorney general grand jury. His contract was signed in September 2011 indicating that he would retire at the end of the football season. He was to be given a coaching bonus of $425,000, debt forgiveness of $250,000, a career bonus of $3,000,000. With a bowl bonus, TV and radio revenue, and other considerations such as the use of the university's private plane and a luxury box at Beaver Stadium, the value was more than $5.5 million. "Question 38, Facts About the University's Payments to the Estate and the Paterno Family and Coach Paterno's Contract with the University," 13 February 2012 [openness-psu.edu/faz.html] (accessed 18 September 2014) and Doug Mataconis, "Joe Paterno Struck Lucrative Contract Deal Months Before Sandusky Story Broke," *Outside the Beltway,* 14 July 2012 [www.outsidethebeltway.com/joe-paterno-struck-lucrative-contract] (accessed 13 December 2013).

452 Gene J. Puskar, "Paterno's Wife to Receive $13.4 Million Pension from Penn State," *USA Today,* 22 May 2012 [usatoday30.usatoday.com/sports/college/football/story] (accessed 27 June 2017). Paterno never took money from his pension before dying at age 85.

453 Michael R. Sisak, "Joe Paterno's Dying Secret," *Citizens Voice,* 10 June 2012 [citizensvoice.com/news/joe-paterno-s-dying-secret-1.1327633] (accessed 27 June 2017).

454 King & Spalding, Washington, D. C., facsmilie/email, to Mark A. Emmert, NCAA, 3 August 2012 [a.espncln.com/pdf/2012/0723/pennstateconclusions.pdf] (accessed 13 July 2014).

455 *Estate and Family of Joseph Paterno v. NCAA, Mark Emmert, and Edward Ray,* 30 May 2013, Docket No. 2013-2082, Court of Common Pleas of Centre County, Pennsylvania.

456 Ibid.

457 Ibid.

458 Bill Oldsey, Letter of Intent to Maribeth Roman Schmidt and PS4RS Board of Directors, 28 January 2016 [ps4rs.files.wordpress.com/2016/02/2016-bill-oldsey-letter] (accessioned 1 January 2017).

459 Estate and Family of Joseph Paterno v. NCAA, Mark Emmert, and Edward Ray, 30 May 2013, Docket No. 2013-2082, Civil Division, Court of Common Pleas of Centre County, Pennsylvania.

460 Ibid.

461 Mark Emmert to Rodney Erickson, 17 November 2011, "Legal Documents – Corman vs. NCAA," Emmert, Exhibit 6 [www.senatorcorman.com/legal-documents-corman-vs-ncaa] (accessioned 9 June 2015). Emphasis was added.

462 William Cowper (trans.), *The Iliad of Homer* (New York: D. Appleton, 1860), Book 4, lines 420-421.

463 *Estate and Family of Joseph Paterno v. NCAA, Mark Emmert, and Edward Ray*, 30 May 2013, Docket No. 2013-2082, Civil Division, Court of Common Pleas of Centre County, Pennsylvania.

464 Ibid.

465 *Estate and Family of Joseph Paterno v. NCAA, Mark Emmert, and Edward Ray*, 11 September 2014, Docket No. 2013-2082, Civil Division, Court of Common Pleas of Centre County, Pennsylvania and Mark Dent, "Paterno Family Granted Standing to Challenge NCAA Consent Decree with Penn State," *Pittsburgh Post-Gazette*, 11 September 2014 [www.post-gazette.com/local/region/2014/09/11/paterno] (accessioned 10 August 2016).

466 Pearsoll v. Chapin, 44 Pa 9 (1862), Assumpsit, Action of, III. Grandes (E) Torts, *Century Edition of the American Digest: A Complete Digest of All Reported American Cases From the Earliest Times to 1896*, Vol. 20: Evidence-Excavations (St. Paul, MN: West Publishing, 1900), 57.

467 *Estate and Family of Joseph Paterno v. NCAA, Mark Emmert, and Edward Ray*, 16 April 2014, p. 24, Docket No. 2013-2082, Civil Division, Court of Common Pleas of Centre County, Pennsylvania.

468 Kelly Knaub, "NCAA Says Paterno Can't Elbow in to Penn State Sanctions," *QLAW360*, 7 May 2014 [www.law360.com/articles/535435/ncaa-says-paterno] (accessioned 10 August 2016).

469 *Estate and Family of Joseph Paterno v. NCAA, Mark Emmert, and Edward Ray*, Docket No. 2013-2081, Civil Division, Court of Common Pleas of Centre County, Pennsylvania, 30 May 2013.

470 For a more thorough discussion, see Max Mitchell, "NCAA-Penn State Settlement Turned on Court Ruling," *The Legal Intelligencer*, 17 February 2015 [www.conradobrien.com/news/ncaa-penn-state-settlement] (accessioned 12 August 2016).

471 Ed Ray Deposition, *Estate of Joseph Paterno vs. NCAA*, and *Corman vs. NCAA*, 8 December 2014, Court of Common Pleas of Centre County, Pennsylvania, Civil Action, No. 2013-2082.

472 Ed Ray Deposition, "Legal Documents—*Corman vs NCAA*," 8 December 2014,

p. 151 [www.senatorcorman.com/legal-documents-corman-vs-ncaa] (accessioned 16 March 2016].

473 Ed Ray Deposition, *Estate of Joseph Paterno vs. NCAA*, and *Corman vs. NCAA*, 8 December 2014, p. 14, 37, 47, 151, 155, Court of Common Pleas of Centre County, Pennsylvania, Civil Action, No. 2013-2082; *Estate and Family of Joseph Paterno v. NCAA, Mark Emmert, and Edward Ray*, Docket No. 2013-2082, Civil Division, Court of Common Pleas of Centre County, Pennsylvania, 15 January 2015, p. 6; and "Preliminary Report: Transforming Intercollegiate Athletics Working Group on Collegiate Model—Enforcement," January 2012, in Ed Ray, Exhibit 12, 8 December 2014, Legal Documents—*Corman vs. NCAA* [www.senatorcorman.com/legal-documents-corman-vs-ncaa] (accessioned 2 June 2015).

474 *Estate and Family of Joseph Paterno v. NCAA, Mark Emmert, and Edward Ray*, 15 January 2015, Docket No. 2013-2082, Civil Division, Court of Common Pleas of Centre County, Pennsylvania. President Ray could explain his lack of preparation on the fact that he was vacationing in Hawaii with his grandson during much of the Penn State-NCAA negotiations.

475 *Estate and Family of Joseph Paterno v. NCAA, Mark Emmert, and Edward Ray*, 23 July 2013, Docket No. 2013-2082, Civil Division, Court of Common Pleas of Centre County, Pennsylvania.

476 Exhibit 23, *Estate and Family of Joseph Paterno v. NCAA, Mark Emmert, and Edward Ray*, 11 September 2014, 30 December 2014 and 8 May 2015, Docket No. 2013-2082, Civil Division Court of Common Pleas of Centre County, Pennsylvania.

477 Exhibit 17, *Estate and Family of Joseph Paterno v. NCAA, Mark Emmert, and Edward Ray*, 30 October 2015, Docket No. 2013-2082, Civil Division, Court of Common Pleas of Centre County, Pennsylvania, 30 December 2015.

478 *Estate and Family of Joseph Paterno v. NCAA, Mark Emmert, and Edward Ray*, 30 March 2015, Docket No. 2013-2082, Civil Division, Court of Common Pleas of Centre County, Pennsylvania.

479 Dunham, Erickson, Frazier, Guadagnino, Marsh, and Masser had been deposed in the Corman case.

480 "Louis Freeh Deposition in *Paterno Family v. NCAA* Lawsuit," March 2016 [www.jmmyw.wordpress.com/2016/03/03/freeh-deposition] (accessioned 6 August 2016).

481 *Paterno Family v. NCAA*, "Memorandum of Law in Support of Motion to Quash Third-Party Deposition Subpoena Directed Toward Eric J. Barron and for Protective Order," 30 March 2016, Court of Common Pleas of Centre County, Pennsylvania, Docket No. 2013-2082, and "Louis Freeh Deposition in *Paterno Family v. NCAA* Lawsuit," 1 March 2016 [jimmyw.wordpress.com/2016/03/03/freeh-deposition] (accessioned 6 August 2016).

482 Matt Miller, "Judge Slams Paterno, McQueary as He Sends Spanier, Curley and Schultz to Jail Over Sandusky Child-Sex Case," *Penn Live*, 3 June 2017 [www.pennlive.com/news/2017/06/judge_slams] (accessioned 3 June 2017).

483 *Centre Daily Times*, 14 March 2017, p. 1A, 3A and 25 March 2017, p. 1A, 3A.

484 Ibid.,, 3 June 2017, p. 1A, 3A.

485 "Bdgan" reply to "Paterno's Drop Lawsuit vs NCAA," *BlueWhite Illustrated*, 30 June 2017 [bwi.forums.rivals.com/threads/paternos-drop-lawsuit] (accessioned 1July 2017).

486 *Estate and Family of Joseph Paterno v. NCAA, Mark Emmert, and Edward Ray*, Docket No. 2013-2082, Civil Division, Court of Common Pleas of Centre County, Pennsylvania, 1 March 2016.

487 Ibid.

488 *Penn State v. Pennsylvania Manufacturers' Association Insurance Co.*, No. 131103195, 4 May 2016; Raymond Williams, Jr., "Expert Report," to Steven J. Engelmyer, PMA, 8 September 2015, Exhibit H, *Penn State v. Pennsylvania Manufacturer's Association Insurance Company*, Case No. 1311103195, Filed 6 November 2015 [fjdefile.phila.gov/efs/temp/ YaDM716N.pdf]; John Doe 75 Deposition, 29 September 2015, Exhibit J, *Penn State v. Pennsylvania Manufacturers' Association Insurance Company*, Case No. 131103195, filed 12 June 2015 [fjdefile.phila.gov/efs/temp/S5EQdD8L.pdf]; John Doe 102 Deposition, 21 November 2014, Exhibit L, *Penn State v. Pennsylvania Manufacturers' Association Insurance Company*, Case No. 131103195, Filed 15 July 2016 [fjdefile.philoa.gov/efs/ temp/WaFL9H8L.pdf]; John Doe 150 Deposition, 13 October 2014, Exhibit I, *Penn State v. Pennsylvania Manufacturers' Association Insurance Company*, Case No. 131103195, Filed 15 July 2016 [fjdefile.phila.gov/efs/temp/S5EQdD81.pdf]; and John Doe 200 Deposition, 8 July 2015, Exhibit 7, *Penn State v. Pennsylvania Manufacturers' Association Insurance Company*, Case No. 131103195, Filed 12 January 2015 [fjdefile.phila.gov/efs/ temp/Z7_L5R9H.pdf].

489 Matt Bonesteel, "Joe Paterno's Son Says Newly Revealed Allegations Are 'Bunk'," *Washington Post*, 6 May 2016 [www.washingtonpost.com/news/early-lead/ wp/2016-05-06/joe-paterno] (accessioned 24 July 2017).

490 *Estate and Family of Joseph Paterno v. NCAA, Mark Emmert, and Edward Ray*, Docket No. 2013-2082, Civil Division, Court of Common Pleas of Centre County, Pennsylvania, 7 June 2017. Judge John Leete ruled that all dispositive motions, supporting briefs, responsive briefs, and reply briefs in support of dispositive motions were to be filed by June 30, 2017 and the final reply briefs by 28 August 2017.

491 A three judge Superior Court panel, led by Victor P. Stabile, ruled in late July 2017 that "The Paterno Parties' discontinuance, and any trial court order permitting a discontinuance, were a nullity" because appeals from the Centre County lawsuit were still being acted upon by the state Superior Court. Until the appeals have been dealt with, the case cannot be abandoned. See *Estate of Paterno, J., v. NCAA*, No. 877 MDA 2015, *The Supreme Court Reporter*, 25 July 2017 [www.pacourts.us/courts/ superior-court/court-opinions] (accessioned 1 August 2017).

492 Much of what follows is speculation on my part, since many of the facts are missing. Isaac Asimov has stated that "Where any answer is possible, all answers are meaningless." However, I agree more with Charles Darwin, who in his *On the Origin of Species* stated, "After five years' work I allowed myself to speculate on the subject. . . ." After researching on this topic of Paterno and the Sandusky Scandal for more than a half-decade, I am comfortable in believing that speculation is an attempt to make sense of things, even when many facts are missing. Isaac Asimov, "Fifty Million Big Brothers," *Magazine of Fantasy and Science Fiction*, 55 No. 5 (November 1978), 86 and Charles Darwin, *On the Origin of Species* (New York: D. Appleton, 1861), 9.

493 Steve Connelly, "Sue Paterno Releases Statement on Family's Decision to Drop Lawsuit Against NCAA," *Onward State*, 30 June 2017 [onwardstate.com/2017/06/30/sue-paterno-releases-statement] (accessioned 8 July 2017).

494 Zach Berger, "Corman: 'Today Is a Victory for Penn State Nation,' Paterno Family Reacts to Settlement News," *StateCollege.com*, 16 January 2015 [www.statecollege.com/news/local-news/corman] (accessioned 24 March 2018).

495 "Paterno Family Abandons All Claims Against NCAA," NCAA press release, 30 June 2017 [www.ncaa.org/about/resources/media-center/news/paterno-family-abandons] (accessioned 1 July 2017).

496 Exhibit 32, Patricia L. Maher, Washington, D. C. Counsel to the Paternos, to Brian E. Kowalski, Washington, D. C. 10 November 2015, *Estate and Family of Joseph Paterno v. NCAA, Mark Emmert, and Edward Ray*, Docket No. 2013-2082, Civil Division of Common Pleas of Centre County, Pennsylvania, 30 December 2015.

497 *Estate and Family of Joseph Paterno v. NCAA, Mark Emmert, and Edward Ray*, 30 December 2015, Docket No. 2013-2082, Civil Division, Court of Common Pleas of Centre County, Pennsylvania.

498 Max Mitchell, "Defamation Suits Tied to Freeh Report Heating Up," *The Legal Intelligencer*, 30 March 2016 [www.thelegalintelligencer.com/id=1202753674045/defamation] (accessioned 29 June 2016).

499 Rod Erickson, email to Steve Dunham and Frank Guadagnino, 20 July 2012, Erickson Deposition, Exhibit 8 "Legal Documents—*Corman vs NCAA*," [www.senatorcorman.com/legal-documents-corman-vs-ncaa].

500 Linda Berkland, Marysville, OH, letter to the editor, *Centre Daily Times*, 8 July 2017, p. 6A.

Afterword Notes

501 Alycia A. Chambers to Ronald Schreffler, 7 May 1998 [msnbemedia.msn.com/msnbc/sections/news/chambers_sandusky_report] (accessioned 31 December 2012).

502 The term "nailed to the cross" (with the addition of "bar" to "cross") comes from Colossians 2:14 which states: "Blotting out the handwriting of ordinances that was against us, out of the way, nailing it to his cross." *King James Bible*.

503 Penn State was 27th among the world's universities in endowment money in 2017 with about $3.8 billion; third in the Big Ten behind Michigan's $9.7 billion and Northwestern's $9.6 billion. Harvard and Yale were first and second with $34.5 and $25.4 billion respectively. "The 100 Richest Universities: Their Generosity and Commitment to Research 2017" [thebestschools.org/features/richest-universities-endowments] (accessioned 18 October 2017).

504 "Binding Consent Decree Imposed by the National Collegiate Athletic Association and Accepted by the Pennsylvania State University," 23 July 2012 [www.ncaa.com/content/penn-state-conclusions] (accessioned 19 December 2015).

505 Joe Paterno "Commencement Address, *Penn State Magazine*, 16 June 1973"

[pennstatemag.files.wordpress.com/2012/01/paterno1973commencementspeech. pdf] (accessed 31 January 2012).

506 Quoted in Marta Lawrence, "Penn State's Paterno Wins Ford Award: NCAA Honors Advocate for Intercollegiate Athletics During Career," *NCAA Newsletter*, 30 December 2010 [www.ncaa.com/news/football/2010-12-22/penn-state-paterno] (accessed 16 September 2015).

507 "Binding Consent Decree Imposed by the National Collegiate Athletic Association and Accepted by the Pennsylvania State University," 23 July 2012 [www/ ncaa/com/content/penn-state-conclusions] (accessed 19 December 2015).

508 For a devastating article on Emmert, see Brent Schrotenboer, "Digging into the Past of NCAA President Mark Emmert," *USA Today*, 3 April 2013 www.usatoday. com/story/sports/ncaa/2013/04/02/ncaa-president] (accessed 21 November 2014).

509 Walter Camp was recognized as the "father" of American football, being principally responsible for changing the rules of rugby football in the early 1880s into a game with the retention of the ball by one team, a scrimmage line, yards to be gained in a certain number of attempts, calling of specific plays, and the position of quarterback. See Ronald A. Smith, "Walter Camp, Father of American Football," in his *Sports and Freedom: The Rise of Big-Time College Athletics* (New York: Oxford University Press, 1988), 83-88.

510 William "Mother" Dunn, 1906, is often credited as being the first Penn State all-American. Dunn was Penn State's original first team all-American, while Rudolph was on Camp's third string all-American in 1898.

511 Rick Reilly, "Not an Ordinary Joe," *Sports Illustrated*, 23 December 1986 [www.si.com/ vault/1986/12/22/114570/sportsman-of-the-year] (accessed 20 October 2017).

512 "Binding Consent Decree Imposed by the National Collegiate Athletic Association and Accepted by the Pennsylvania State University, 23 July 2012 [www/ ncaa/com/content/penn-state-conclusions] (accessed 19 December 2015), and *Estate and Family of Joseph Paterno v. NCAA, Mark Emmert, and Edward Ray*, Docket No. 2013-2082, Civil Division, Court of Common Pleas of Centre County, Pennsylvania, 9 May 2013, pp. 6-7.

513 Rick Reilly, "Not an Ordinary Joe," *Sports Illustrated*, 23 December 1986 and Rick Reilly, "The Sins of the Father," *Sports Illustrated*, 13 July 2012 [espn.go.com/ espn/story/_/id8162972/joe-paterno-true-legacy] (accessed 10 August 2012).

514 Michael Bérubé, "Why I Resigned the Paterno Chair," *Chronicle of Higher Education*, 15 October 2012 [chronicle.com/article/Why-I-Resigned-the-Paterno/134944] (accessed 15 October 2012).

515 George Enteen, "A Penn State Dialogue," email to friends, 30 November 2011, Ron Smith Personal File.

516 S. L. Price, "We Are Still Penn State," *Sports Illustrated*, 5 November 2012 [www.si/com/vault/2012/11/05/106252298/we-are-still-penn-state] (accessed 2 October 2017). Price wrote: "Few outside of Happy Valley would argue that the sanctions weren't just."

517 Patty Kleban, "Open Letter to Mark Emmert," *StateCollege.com*, 5 December 2016 [www.statecollege.com/news/columns/a-letter-to-mark-emmert-1472039] (accessioned 2 October 2017).

518 Will Hobson, "Former Penn State President Graham Spanier Sentenced to Jail for Child Endangerment in Jerry Sandusky Abuse Case," *Washington Post*, 2 June 2017 [www.washingtonpost.com/news/sports/wp/2017/06/02] (accessioned 11 October 2017).

519 Ibid.

520 Caitlin Flanagan, "Death at a Penn State Fraternity," *Atlantic Monthly* (November 2017) pp. 17-18 [www.theatlantic.com/magazine/archive/2017/11/a-death-at-penn-state/540657] (accessioned 13 October 2017).

521 Mark Tracy, "N.C.A.A.: North Carolina Will Not Be Punished for Academic Scandal," *New York Times,* 13 October 2017 [www.nytimes.com/2017/10/13/sports/unc] (accessioned 16 October 2017). It will be interesting to see if the NCAA takes actions against Michigan State, or threatens it with a "death penalty" for the 2017-2018 case of a medical doctor treating gymnasts at Michigan State and sexually abusing over 300 of them.

522 Antonios Loizides, "Draco's Law Code," *Ancient History Encyclopedia* [www.ancient.eu/dracos] (accessioned 18 October 2017). Draco created the first written law codes in Athens, ca. 621 B.C.E., to help reduce arbitrary punishments and blood feuds between parties. The laws of the famous Solon in 594 B.C.E. replaced Draco's laws.

523 Beethoven, who in 1803, praised Napoleon Bonaparte for his leadership in the French Revolution later turned against the authoritarian leader, and the symphony was no longer the "Bonaparte Symphony."

524 Ludwig van Beethoven, Teplitz, Czech Republic, letter to poet Christopher August Tiedge, Dresden, Germany, 6 September 1811, Friedrich Kerst and Henry Edward Krehbiel (eds.), B. W. Hueback (trans.), *Beethoven: The Man and the Artist as Revealed in His Own Words,* # 267 [www.gutenberg.org/files/3528/3528-h/3528-h-html] (accessioned 28 October 2017).

BIBLIOGRAPHY

Books

Anouilh, Jean. *Antigone: A Tragedy*. New York: Random House, 1946.

Aristotle, trans. Benjamin Jowett. *Politics*. Kitchener, Ontario: Batoche Books, 1999.

Bacon, John U. *Fourth and Long: The Fight for the Soul of College Football*. New York: Simon & Schuster, 2013.

Bezilla, Michael. *Penn State: An Illustrated History*. University Park: Penn State University Press, 1985.

Byers, Walter. *Unsportsmanlike Conduct: Exploiting College Athletes*. Ann Arbor: University of Michigan Press, 1995.

Christoau, John. *The Origins of the Jump Shot: Eight Men Who Shook the World of Basketball*. Lincoln: University of Nebraska Press, 1999.

Cogliano, Francis D. *Thomas Jefferson: Reputation and Legacy*. Charlottesville: University of Virginia Press, 2006.

Cohan, William D. *The Price of Silence: The Duke Lacrosse Scandal, the Power of the Elite, and the Corruption of Our Great University*. New York: Scribner, 2014.

Cowper, William (trans.). *The Iliad of Homer*. New York: D. Appleton, 1860.

Crowley, Joseph N. *In the Arena: The NCAA's First Century*. Indianapolis: NCAA, 2006.

Darwin, Charles. *On the Origin of Species*. New York: D. Appleton, 1861.

Dickens, Charles. *Life and Adventures of Martin Chuzzlewit*. London: Chapman & Hall, 1843.

Falla, Jack. *NCAA: The Voice of College Sports*. Mission, KS: National Collegiate Athletic Association, 1981.

Figone, Albert J. *Cheating the Spread: Gamblers, Point Shavers, and Game Fixers in College Football and Basketball*. Urbana: University of Illinois Press, 2012.

Fina, Steven. *Crisis Communications: The Definitive Guide to Managing the Message*. New York: McGraw Hill, 2013.

Fisher, Aaron, Michael Gillum, and Dawn Daniels. *Silent No More: Victim # 1's Fight for Justice Against Jerry Sandusky*. New York: William Morrow, 2012.

Fitzpatrick, Frank. *Pride of the Lions: The Biography of Joe Paterno*. Chicago: Triumph Books. 2011.

Ford, Milt. *A Brief History of Homosexuality*. www.gvsu.edu/allies/a-brief-history-of-homosexuality.

Froude, J. A. *The Divorce of Catherine of Aragon*. New York: Charles Scribner's Sons, 1891.

Thomas Fuller. *Introduction: Or, Directions, Counsels, and Cautions. Tending to Prudent Management of Affairs in Common Life*. London: Taylor and Hessey, 1815, 6th ed.

Gracian, Baltasar. *The Act of Worldly Wisdom*. London: Macmillan, 1904.

Hueback, B. W. (trans.). *Beethoven: The Man and the Artist as Revealed in His Own Words*. www.gutenberg.org/files/6546/6546-readme.txt.

Isaacs, Neil D. *A History of College Basketball*. Philadelphia: J. B. Lippincott, 1975.

Machiavelli, Niccolo. *The Prince*. www.freeclassicbooks.com/nicolo%20 machiavelli/the%20prince.pdf.

Mahler, Jonathan. *Death Comes to Happy Valley: Penn State and the Tragic Legacy of Joe Paterno*. San Francisco: Byliner, 2012.

McCullough, David. *The Path Between the Seas: The Creation of the Panama Canal, 1870-1914*. New York: Simon & Schuster, 1978.

Montesquieu, Charles de. *Consideration on the Causes of the Grandeur and Decadence of the Romans*. Trans. Jehu Baker. New York: D. Appleton, 1882.

Montesquieu, Charles de. *The Spirit of the Laws*. London: Crowder, Ware, and Payne, 1748.

O'Brien, Michael. *No Ordinary Joe: The Biography of Joe Paterno*. Nashville, TN: Rutledge Hill Press, 1998.

Paterno, Jay. *Paterno Legacy: Enduring Lessons from the Life and Death of My Father*. Chicago: Triumph Books, 2014.

Paterno, Joe with Bernard Asbell. *Paterno by the Book*. New York: Random House, 1989.

Porto, Brian L. *The Supreme Court and the NCAA: The Case for Less Commercialism and More Due Process in College Sports*. Ann Arbor: University of Michigan Press, 2012.

Posnanski, Joe. *Paterno*. New York: Simon and Schuster, 2012.

Rovere, Richard H. *Senator Joe McCarthy*. Berkeley: University of California, 1966.

Prato, Louis. *The Penn State Football Encyclopedia*. Champaign, IL: Sports Publishing, 1998.

Shakespeare, William. *Julius Caesar*. shakespeare.mit.edu/julius_caesar/full.html.

Shakespeare, William. *King Lear*. shakespeare.mit.edu/lear/full.html.

Shakespeare, William. *Merchant of Venice*. www.folger.edu/merchant-of-venice.

Smith, Ronald A. *Big-Time Football at Harvard: The Diary of Coach Bill Reid*. Urbana: University of Illinois Press, 1994.

Smith, Ronald A. *Pay for Play: A History of Big-Time College Athletic Reform.* Urbana: University of Illinois Press, 2011.

Smith, Ronald A. *Play-by-Play: Radio, Television, and Big-Time College Athletic Reform.* Baltimore: Johns Hopkins University Press, 2001.

Smith, Ronald A. *Sports and Freedom: The Rise of Big-Time College Athletics.* New York: Oxford University Press, 1988.

Smith, Ronald A. *Wounded Lions: Joe Paterno, Jerry Sandusky, and the Crises in Penn State Athletics.* Urbana: University of Illinois Press, 2016.

Stout, Lee and Harry H. West. *Lair of the Lion: A History of Beaver Stadium.* University Park: Penn State University Press, 2017.

Thelin, John R. *Games Colleges Play: Scandals and Reform in Intercollegiate Athletics.* Baltimore: Johns Hopkins University Press, 1994.

Thucydides. *History of the Peloponnesian War.* www.classicpersuasion.org/pw.thucydides/thucydides-jowettoc-htm.

Watterson, John S. *College Football: History, Spectacle, Controversy.* Baltimore: Johns Hopkins University Press, 2000.

Whitford, David. *A Payroll To Meet: A Story of Greed, Corruption and Football at SMU.* New York: Macmillan, 1989.

Articles and Book Chapters

"Alabama Crimson Tide Football." *Wikipedia.* en.wikipedia.org/wiki/Alabama_Crimson_Tide_Football.

Armour, Nancy. "From UConn to USC, Corruption in College Sport Spotlight," *Mass Live,* 10 September 2011. www.masslive.com/sports/indexssf/2011/09/from_uconn.

Asimov, Isaac. "Fifty Million Big Brothers." *Magazine of Fantasy and Science Fiction.* 55 (November 1978): 86.

Associated Press. "Infractions Decision Stands for USC." *NCAA News.* May 27, 2011 www.ncaa.com/news/football/2011-05-16/infractions-decision-stands-usc.

Associated Press, "PSU Pays Paterno Estate $5M-plus." *ESPN.* 20 April 2012. www.theriches.com/celebnetworth/athletes/coach/joe-paterno-net-worth.

"Auburn Releases Cam Newton Docs." *ESPN College Football.* November 5, 2011. espn.go.com/college-football/story/_/id/7190987/auburn.

Beinart, Peter. "The New McCarthyism of Donald Trump." *Atlantic.* July 21, 2015. www.theatlantic.com/politics/archive/2015/07/Donald...mccarthy/399056.

Berger, Zack. "Judge in Corman Lawsuit Criticizes NCAA, Elaborates on Landmark Case." *Onward State,* 2 April 2015. onwardstate.com/2015/04/02/judge-in-corman-lawsuit-criticizes-ncaa.

Berger, Zack. "Kaidanov, Penn State Resolve Wrongful Termination Suit." *Onward State*. 12 December 2015. onwardstate.com/2015/12/12/kaidanov.

Bérubé, Michael. "Why I Resigned the Paterno Chair." *Chronicle of Higher Education*. 15 October 2012. chronicle.com/article/Why-I-Resigned-The-Paterno/134944.

Bochlert, Eric. "Judging Louis Freeh." *Salon*. 4 June 2002. www.salon.com/2002/06/04/freeh.

"Bombing of Dresden." *History*. www.history.com/topic/world-war-ii/battle-of-dresden.

Conlin, Bill. "The Grand Experiment." *Beaver Stadium Pictorial*. 25 November 1967.

Connelly, Steve. "Sue Paterno Releases Statement on Family's Decision to Drop Lawsuit Against NCAA." *Onward State*. 30 June 2017. onwardstate.com/2017/06/30/sue-paterno-releases-statement.

Cummins, John and Kirsten Hextrum. "The Management of Intercollegiate Athletics at UC Berkeley: Turning Points and Consequences." November 2013. *Center for Studies in Higher Education*. University of California, Berkeley. www.eshe.berkeley.edu/sites/default/files/shared/publictions/docs/ROSP.CSHE_12.1.

Despain, Joshua J. "From Off the Bench: The Potential Role of the U.S. Department of Education in Reforming Due Process in the NCAA." *Iowa Law Review* 100 (2015): 1285-1326.

Dodd, Dennis. "Joe Paterno's Loyal Son Refuses to Let His Father's Legacy Wilt." *CBS Sports*. 14 May 2013. www.cbssports.com/collegefootball/story/222437678.

Dodd, Dennis. "No Bluffing—NCAA Has Lost All of Its Credibility with Penn State, USC, etc." *CBS Sports*. 7 November 2014. www.cbssports.com/collegefootball/writer/dennis-dodd/247888247.

Dohrman, George. "An Inside Look at the NCAA's Secretive Committee on Infraction." *Sports Illustrated*. 18 February 2010. www.si.com/more-sports/2010/02/18/suc-coi.

Edison, Maxwell. "Sara Gamin and Sally Jenkins at ASPE." *Black Shoe Diaries*. 11 April 2012. www.blackshoediaries.com/2012/4/11/29400213/sara-gamin-and-sally-jenkins.

"Estate of Paterno, J., v. NCAA, No. 877 MDA 2015" *The Supreme Court Reporter*, 25 July 2017. www.pacourts.us/courts/superior-court/court-opinions.

Fink, Steven. "Say It Ain't So, Joe!—The Penn State Crisis" in his *Crisis Communications: The Definitive Guide to Managing the Message*. New York: McGraw Hill, 2013.

Flanagan, Caitlin. "Death at a Penn State Fraternity." *Atlantic*. November 2017. www.theatlantic.com/magazine/archive/2017/11/a-death-at-penn-state/540657.

Flandez, Raymond. "Penn State Grapples with Angry Donors." *The Chronicle of Philanthropy*. 21 November 2011. philanthropy.com/article/penn-state-grapples.

Fowler, Jeremy. "Teflon Tide: Examining Alabama's Recent NCAA Concerns." *CBS Sports*, January 28, 2014. www.cbssports.com/collegefootball/writer/jeremy-fowler.

Gailey, Caitlin. "Julie Del Giorno: The Life Behind the Athletics Integrity Officer." *Onward State*. 19 March 2015. onwardstate.com/2015/03/19-julie-del-giorno.

Garrett, Michael. "Freeh Investigator: NCAA Had No Influence on Investigation or Content of Freeh Report." *StateCollege.com*. 31 January 2015. www.statecollege.com/news/local-news/freeh-investigator.

Grasgreen, Allie. "At Last, Storm Settles at Miami." *Inside Higher Ed*. October 23, 2013. www.insidehighered.com/news/2013/10/23/ncaa-ends-miami.

Grasgreen, Allie. "New Day for Division I Athletes." *Inside Higher Ed*. October 28, 2011. www/insidehighered.com/news/2011/20/28/ncaa-board.

Griffin, Andrew W. "Will Freeh Bungle Penn State Child-Sex Abuse Investigation Too?" *Red Dirt Report*, 21 November 2011. www.reddirtreport.com/red-dirt-grit/will-freeh-bungle.

Hammel, Bob. "Student-Athletes: Tackling the Problem." *Phi Delta Kappan*. 62 (September 1980): 7-13.

Horne, Kevin. "International Emails Show NCAA Questioned Authority to Sanction Penn State." *Onward State*. 5 November 2014. onwardstate.com/2014/11/05/international-emails-show-ncaa.

"Jackson State: A Tragedy Widely Forgotten." 3 May 2010. www.npr.org/templates/story/story.php?storyId=12646361.

Jacobi, Adam. "The NCAA's Many Problems: Perception Clouds Alabama Issue." *SB Nation*. October 9, 2013. www.sbnation.com/college-football/2013/100/9/4819820/alabama.

"Joe Paterno to Retire; President Out?" *ESPN.com*. 9 November 2011. www.nytimes.com/2012/01/19/sports/ncaafootball/penn-state-trustees.

Jones, David. "Sandy Barbour Far From Perfect Fit as New Penn State AD But Has Personal Tools to Adapt." *Penn Live*, 5 August 2014. www.pennlive.com/sports/index.ssf/2014/08/sandy_barbour.

"Joyner Retires." *Penn State News*. 17 June 2014. news.psu.edu/318567/2014/06/17/allIV.

"Busted: Behind the Sandusky Arrest." *Yardbird*. 22 January 2014. www/yardbird.com/busted_narcotics_agent.

Kercheval, Ben. "What the Paternos' Critique of the Freeh Report Didn't Do, and What It Did." *NBC Sports*. 10 February 2013. collegefootballtalk.nbcsports.com/2013/02/10/what-the-paterno.

Kleban, Patty. "Open Letter to Mark Emmert." *StateCollege.com*, 5 December 2016. www.statcollege.com/news/sports/wp/2017/06/02.

Kletchen, David J. Jr. "How Penn State Turned a Crisis Into a Disaster: An Interview with Crisis Management Pioneer Steven Fink." *Business Horizons* (2014): 673.

Knaub, Kelly. "NCAA Says Paterno Can't Elbow in to Penn State Sanction." *QLA360*. 7 May 2014. www.law360.com/articles/535435/ncaa-says-paterno.

Lawrence, Marta. "Penn State's Paterno Wins Ford Award: NCAA Honors Advocate for Intercollegiate Athletics During Career." *NCAA News*. December 30, 2010. www.ncaa.com/news/football/2010-12-22/penn-states-paterno.

Lewis, Jerry M. and Thomas R. Hensley. "The May 4 Shootings at Kent State University." *Ohio Council for the Social Studies Review*. 34 (Summer 1998): 9-21.

Liautaud, Marian V. "Success, Honor, and the Legacy of Joe Paterno." *Christianity Today*, 16 November 2011. www.christianitytoday.com/omen/2011/november/success-honor.

Looney, Douglas S. "A Lot of People Think I'm Phony and Now They Think They Have the Proof." *Sports Illustrated*. 52 (17 March 1980). www.si.com/vault/1980/03/17/824489/there-are-a-lot-of-people.

Mallon, William T. "The Alchemist: A Case Study of a Failed Merger in Academic Medicine." *Strategic Alliances in Academic Medicine* (2003): 26-37. journals.lww.com/academicmedicine/documents/mallon.pdf.

McCormack, Aidan M. "Seeking Procedural Due Process in NCAA Infraction Procedures. States Take Action." *Marquette Sports Law Review*. 2 (Spring 1992): 100-177.

Mitchell, Max. "Defamation Suits Tied to Freeh Report Heating Up." *The Legal Intelligencer*. 30 March 2016. www.thelegalintelligencer.com/id=1202753674045/defamation.

Mitchell, Max. "NCAA-Penn State Settlement Turned on Court Ruling." *The Legal Intelligencer*, 17 February 2015. www.conradobrien.com/news/ncaa-penn-state-settlement.

Murphy, Jan. "Paternos Gave Another $100,000 Donation to Penn State in December." *Penn Live*. 14 January 2012. www.pennlive.com/midstate/index/ssf/2012/01/paternos-gave.

Newhall, Kristine E. and Erin E Buzuvis. "Sexuality and Race, Law and Discourse in Harris v. Portland." *Journal of Sport and Social Issues*. 32 (November 2008): 345-368.

Nix, Elizabeth. "What Was the Dreyfus Affair?" *History*. 14 January 2015. www.history.com/news/ask-history/what-was-the-dreyfus-affair.

"Paternopaterfamilias," *Quest*. September/October, 1978. Joe Paterno Vertical File, Penn State University Archives.

"Paternos Pledge $3.5 Million to Penn State." *Penn State News*. 15 January 1998. Joe Paterno Vertical File, Folder "2000s," Penn State University Archives.

Paterno's [sic.] Drop Lawsuit vs NCAA. *BlueWhite Illustrated*, 30 June 2017. bwi.forums.rivals.com/threads/paternos-drop-lawsuit.

Petchesky, Barry. "When Current PSU President Rodney Erickson Bent the Rules for Jerry Sandusky." 12 July 2012. deadspin.com/5925561/when-current-penn-state.

"Posts Tagged 'Paul Silvis.'" *The Penn Stater*. 7 March 2014. www.pennstatermag.

com/tag/paul-silvis.

Potter, James. "The NCAA as State Actor: Tarkanian, Brentwood, and Due Process." *University of Pennsylvania Law Review*. 155 (2007): 1269-1304.

Price, S. L. "How Did Carolina Lose Its Way?" *Sports Illustrated*. 122 (March 16, 2015: 67.)

Price, S. L. "We Are Still Penn State." *Sports Illustrated*. 5 November 2012. www.si/com/vault/2012/11/05/106252298/we-are-still-penn-state.

"Q&A: Emmert on Presidential Retreat." *NCAA News*, August 10, 2011. www.ncaa.com/news/ncaa/2011-08-10/qa-emmert-presidential-retreat.

Quirk, Charles E. "NCAA v. Tarkanian, 488 U.S. 179(1988). In John W. Johnson (ed.). *Historic U.S. Court Cases: An Encyclopedia*. New York: Routledge, 2001. Vol 1, 233-236.

Ramos, Ronnie. "Talk of Change Continues at Summit." *NCAA News*. August 10, 2011. www.ncaa.com/news/ncaa/2011-08-10/talk-change-continues-summit.

Reilly, Rick. "Joe Paterno's True Legacy." *ESPN*. 23 January 2012. espn.go.com/espn/story/_/id/7492873/rick-reilly-paterno-true-legacy.

Reilly, Rick. "Not An Ordinary Joe," *Sports Illustrated*, 22 December 1986. www.si.com/vault/1986/12/22/114570.

Reilly, Rick. "The Sins of the Father." *ESPN*, 13 July 2012. espn.go.com/espn/story/_/id/8162972/joe-paterno-true-legacy.

Rowell, Darren. "Penn State's Attendance Down Again." *ESPN*. 25 November 2012. Espn.go.con/college-football/story/_/id/8671564.

Scolforo,Mark. "Lawyer Says Defense Attorney Helped Penn State Edit Release." 18 October 2016. www.wrex.com/story/33418176/lawyer-says.

Sievert, Justin. "Revamping the NCAA's Penalty Structure Through Sentencing Guidelines." *Law Insider*. 22 December 2011. www.thelawinsider.com/insider-news-ncaa-penalty-structure.

Smith, Rodney K. "A Brief History of the National Collegiate Athletic Association's Role in Regulating Intercollegiate Athletics." *Marquette Sports Law Review*. 11 (Fall 2000): 8-22.

Smith, Ronald A. "Far More than Commercialism: Stadium Building from Harvard's Innovations to Stanford's 'Dirt Bowl.'" *International Journal of the History of Sport*. 25 (September 2008): 1453-1472

Smith, Ronald A. "Football, College." In Stephen Riess (ed). *Sports in American Colonial Times to the Twenty-First Century*. Armonk, NY: M.E. Sharpe, 2011. Vol I, 355-361.

Smith, Ronald A. "The Rise of Basketball for Women in American Colleges." *Canadian Journal of History of Sport and Physical Education*. 1 (December 1970): 140-149.

"Statement from President Spanier." *Penn State News*. 5 November 2011. news.psu.edu.story/story/153819/2011/11/05.

"Story of the 1881 and 1887 Teams." *Penn State Alumni News.* 10 (December 1923): 10-12.

Thompson, Charles. "Penn State Trustees Ken Frazier Fires Back at Freeh Report Critics." *Penn Live*, 14 March 2013. www.pennlive.com/midstate/index. ssf/2013/03/penn-state_trustees-Ken_Frazier.html.

Van Natta, Don, Jr. "Docs: NCAA, Freeh Worked Together." *ESPN.* 12 November 2014. espn.go.com/espn/tol/story/_/11863293/court.

Van Natta, Don, Jr. "Fight on State: In Wake of Scandal Power Struggle Spread from Penn State Campus to State Capital." *ESPN Magazine.* 4 April 2012. espn.go.com/espn/tol/story/_/id/7770996/in-wake-joe-paterno.

Van Natta, Don, Jr. "Inside the Negotiations that Brought Penn State Football to the Brink of Extinction." *ESPN Magazine.* 4 August 2012.

VoxMediaUser136261. "The Monday Morning Wash—Contemplating the Death Penalty." *SB Nation.* 12 December 2011. www.uwdawgpound. com/2011/8221275653/the-monday.

"'We Are' Sculpture Spells It Out for Penn State Community." *Penn State News.* 1 July 2015. news.psu.edu/story/362033/201/15/07/01.

Wolverton, Brad. "Freeh Group Member Criticizes NCAA's Use of Investigative Report." *Chronicle of Higher Education.* 27 July 2012. www.chronicle. com/article/Freeh-Group-Member-Criticizes/133213.

Wojciechowski, Gene. "Paterno a Study in Contradictions." *ESPN. 22 January 2012. espn.go.com/college-football/story/_/7488723/former-penn-state.*

Wong, Glenn, Kyloe Skillman, and Chris Deubert. "The NCAA's Infractions Appeals Committee: Recent Case History, Analysis and the Beginnings of a New Chapter." *Virginia Sports and Entertainment Law Journal.* 9 No. 1 (2009): 47-153.

Wright, Jerry Jaye. "Irish, Edward Simmons 'Ned'." in David L. Porter, ed. *Biographical Dictionary of American Sports: Basketball and Other Indoor Sports.* Westport, CN: Greenwood Press, 1989): 140-142.

Wushanley, Ying. *Playing Nice and Losing: The Struggle for Control of Women's Intercollegiate Athletics, 1960-2000.* Syracuse, NY: Syracuse University Press, 2004.

Newspapers

Albergotti, Reed. "A Discipline Problem: Paterno Fought Penn State Official Over Punishment of Players. *Wall Street Journal*, 22 November 2011. www.wsj. com/articles/SB100.

Associated Press, "Paterno Says He Should Have Done More." *Scranton Times-Tribune.* 9 November 2011. thetimes-tribune.com/paterno-says-he-should-have-done-more.

Bachman, Denise. "The Truth About Joe: A Saint He Certainly Ain't. [Penn State] *Daily Collegian.* 21 March 1980. Joe Paterno Papers, Box 07594, Folder "Newspaper Clippings, 1980-1989," Penn State University Archives.

Bachman, Denise and Joe Saraceno. "Meiser Wonders, 'Why Penn State?'" [Penn State] *Daily Collegian.* 9 April 1979, pp. 1, 10-11.

Beard, Aaron. "NCAA Hits UNC Football with 1-Year Postseason Ban." *USA Today.* March 20, 2012. usatoday.com/sports/college/football/2012-3-20.

Berkland, Linda. "Letter to the Editor." *Centre Daily Times.* 8 July 2017, p. 6A.

Berkowitz, Steve. "NCAA Nearly Topped $1 Billion in Revenue in 2014." *USA Today*, March 11, 2015. www.usatoday.com/story/sports/college/2015/03/11/ncaa-financial.

Bernstein, Adam. "Richard A. Jewell; Wrongly Linked to Olympic Bombing." *Washington Post.* 30 August 2007. www.washingtonpost.com/wp-dya/content/article/2007/08/09.

Bonesteel, Matt. "Joe Paterno's Son Says Newly Revealed Allegations Are 'Bunk.'" *Washington Post.* 6 May 2016. www.washingtonpost.com/news/early-lead/wp/201605-06/joe-paterno.

Boston, Alison and Lori Falce, "Corman Announces End to Penn State Sanctions; Paterno Wins Restored." *Centre Daily Times.* 16 January 2015. www.centredaily.com/news/local/education/penn-state/jerry-sandusky/article42901299.html.

Bracken, Ron. "Nittany Lions Not Used to Off the Field Turbulence." *Centre Daily Times*, 18 August 1992, p. D1.

Bracken, Ron. "Paterno Refuses to Answer Questions About Phillips." *Centre Daily Times*, 27 March 2003, p. B1, B4.

Bracken, Ron. "Ron Bracken: Climate of Secrecy Led to Crumbling of Camelot." *Centre Daily Times.* 11 November 2011. *www.centredaily.com/news/special-reports/joe-paterno/article42806880.html.*

Centre Daily Times, 16 January 1983, p. D2. 20 February 2012, p A1. 1 March 2012, p. A1. 20 April 2012. 9 May 2012, p. A1, A6. 26 May 2012, p. 16. 12 June 2012, p. A3. 13 June 2012, p. A1, A6. 12 June 2012, p. A3. 13 June 2012, p. A1, A6. 5 August 2012, p. A8. 14 March 2017, p. 1A, 3A. 25 March 2017, p. 1A, 3A. 3 June 2017 p. 1A, 3A.

Cook, Ron. "Paterno's Legacy at Penn State Long Will be Debated." *Pittsburgh Post-Gazette.* 9 May 2016. www.post-gazette.com/sports/ron-cook/2016/05/09/Ron-Cook.

Cowell, Alan. "After 350 Years, Vatican Say Galileo Was Right." *New York Times*, 31 October 1992. www.nytimes.com/1992/19/31/world/after-350-years.

Dent, Mark. "Paterno Family Granted Standing to Challenge NCAA Consent Decree with Penn State." *Pittsburgh Post-Gazette.* 11 September 2014. www.post-gazette.com/local/region/2014/09/11/paterno.

Eder, Steve. "N.C.A.A. Admits Mishandling Miami Inquiry." *New York Times*, January 23, 2013. www.nytimes.com/2013/01/24/sports/ncaa-admits-misconduct.

Everson, Darren and Hannah Karp. "The NCAA's Last Innocents." *Wall Street Journal*. 22 June 2011. www.wsjcom/articles/SB10001424057000521286339O.

Ferraro, Thomas. "In the World of College Athletics. . . : He is Not an Average Joe." *Los Angeles Times*, 17 May 1987. articles.latimes.com/1987-05-07/sports/sp-774_I_Joe-Paterno.

Figel, Bill. "Lesbians in World of Athletics." *Chicago Sun-Times*, 16 June 1986. www.clubs.psu.edu/up/psupride/articles/chicago%20times.

Ganim, Sara. "Former Centre County DA Ray Gricar's Reasons for Not Pursuing Case Against Jerry Sandusky." *Harrisburg Patriot-News*, 6 November 2011. www.pennlive.com/midstate/index.ssf/2011/11/former_centre_county.

Ganim, Sara. "Penn State Athletic Director Tim Curley, Senior Official Charged in Jerry Sandusky Investigation." *Penn Live*, 5 November 2011. www.pennlive.com/midstate/index.ssf/2011/11/sandusky_investigation_sources.html.

Gamin, Sara. "Sandusky Faces Grand Jury Probe." *Harrisburg Patriot-News*. 31 March 2011. www.pulitizer.org/files/2012/local-responding/local01.pdf.

"Joe Paterno Interview: Sally Jenkins Discusses Her Talk with Ex-Penn State Coach." *Washington Post*, 16 January 2012. live.washingtonpost.com/joe-paterno-speaks-to-sally-jenkins.html.

Henneberger, Melinda. "What Paterno Admitted He Knew: Sandusky Couldn't Have Done Without Him." *Washington Post*. 3 July 2012. www.washingtonpost.com/blogs/she-the-people/post/what.

Hobson, Will. "Former Penn State President Graham Spanier Sentenced to Jail for Child Endangerment in Jerry Sandusky Abuse Case." *Washington Post*. 20 June 2017. www.washingtonpost.com/news/sports/wp/2017/06/02.

Johnt, Carol Ross and Marisa M. Kashino. "Who Ya Gonna Call? Joe Paterno Looks to Washington for Legal Counsel, PR Help." *Washingtonian*. 8 July 2017. www.espn.com/college/football/story/_id/7834352/penn-state-pays.

"Justices Uphold N.C.A.A.'s Right To Demand Suspension of Coach." *New York Times*, December 13, 1988. www.nytimes.com/1988/12/13/sports/justices-uphold-ncaa.

Longman, Jere. "A Boost from the State Capitol Helped Penn State Escape N.C.A.A. Penalties." *New York Times*. 4 February 2015. www.nytimes.com/2015/02/05/sports/ncaafootball/how-one-legislator-helped.

Luna, Tarum. "Penn State Hires PR Firm to Address Scandal." *Pittsburgh Post-Gazette*, 26 April 2012. www.post-gazette.com/news/education/2012/04/26/penn-state.

MacAskill, Ewen. "Edward Snowden, NSA Files Source: 'If They Want to Get You in Time They Will.'" *The Guardian*. 10 June 2013. www.theguardian.com/world/2013/jun/09/nsa-whistleblower.

Mahler, Jonathan. "Student-Athlete Equation Could be a Win-Win." *New York Times*. 10 August 2011, B13.

Mataconis, Doug. "Joe Paterno Struck Lucrative Contract Deal Months Before Sandusky Story Broke. *Outside the Beltway.* 14 July 2012. www.outsidethebeltway. com/joe-paterno-struck-lucrative-contract.

McAllister, Ray. "Paterno Brought a Million Dollar Night." [Penn State] *Daily Collegian*, 2 April 1973, p. 13.

McCollough, J. Brady. "Death of Joe Paterno Created Deep Void for Penn Staters." *Pittsburgh Post-Gazette.* 29 January 2012. www.post-gazette.com/ frontpage/2012/01/29/Death-of-Joe-Paterno.

Miller, Matt. "Judge Slams Paterno, McQueary as He Sends Spanier, Curley and Schultz to Jail Over Child-Sex Case." *Penn Live*, 3 June 2017. www.pennlive. com/news/2017/06/judge_slams_paterno.

Minemyer, Chip and Chris Rosenblum. "'Joe's Legacy': Almost a Year After His Death, Paterno's Image Still Debated, Defended." *Centre Daily Times.* 19 January 2013. www.centredaily.com/news/special-reports/joe-paterno/ article4285778.html.

Murt, Katie. "Through the Storm: Rodney Erickson's Career at Penn State." [Penn State] *Daily Collegian*. 2 May 2014. wwwcollegian.psu.edu/news/campus/ article_24dc6288-d18f-11e3-acad-0017a43b2370.html.

New York Herald. 12 October 1905. p. 1.

New York Times. 21 January, 1947, p. 19.

New York Times. 19 January, 2012. www.nytimes.com/2012/01/19/sports/ ncaafootball/penn-state-trustees.

New York Times. 20 December 1996. www.nytimes.com/1996/12/20/us/ head-of-fbi.

"Ohio State Football: Jim Tressel Had Poor History of Reporting Violations." *Telegram Chronicle Online.* July 16, 2011. chronicle.northcoastnow. com/2011/07/16/ohio-state-football-jim-tressel.

"Paterno Violated Rule in Signing of Quintus McDonald." *Los Angeles Times*, February 28, 1985. www.articles.latimes.com1985-02-18/sports/sp-128900.

"Penn State is Placed on Year's Probation: Damage to Reputation Feared." *New York Times*. April 5, 1979. www.nytimes.com/1979/04/05/archives/penn-state-is-placed.

Persons, Sally. "Trump Slams Merck CEO for Quitting Manufacturing Council Over Charlottesville Reaction." *Washington Times*. 14 August 2017. www. washingtontimes.com/news/2017/aug/13/donald-trump-slams-ken-frazier.

Poorman, Mike. "Penn State Football: What is the Future of Beaver Stadium." *Statecollege.com*. www.statecollege.com/news/columns/penn-state-football-what-is-the-future.

Puskar, Gene J. "Paterno's Wife to Receive $13.4 Million Pension from Penn State." *USA Today*. 22 May 2012. www.usatoday30.usatoday.com/sports/ college/football/story.

"Rutgers Coach Kyle Flood Suspended Three Games, Fined $50,000." *USA Today Sports*, September 16, 2015. www.usatoday.com/story/sports/ncaa.

Salzman Avi. "UConn Basketball Then and Now," *New York Times*, 18 April 2004. www.nytimes.com/2004/04/18/nyregion/uconn-basketball.

Schrotenboer, Brent. "Digging into the Past of NCAA President Mark Emmert." *USA Today*. 3 April 2013. www.usatoday.com/story/sports/ncaa/2013/04/02/ncaa-president.

Shutz, Eric. "Fencer Reveals More Information Surrounding Kaidanov's Departure." [Penn State]*Daily Collegian*. 10 September 2013. www.collegian.psu.edu/sports/fencing.

Sisak, Michael R. "Joe Paterno's Dying Secret." *Citizens Voice*. 10 June 2012. citizensvoice.com/news/joe-paterno-s-dying-secret-1.1327633.

Snyder, Audrey. "Penn State Athletic Director Sandy Barbour Backs Off 409 Sticker Stance." *Pittsburgh Post-Gazette*. 20 January 2015. www.post-gazette.com/sports/psu/2015/01/20.

"Sue Paterno Defends JoePa in Letter to Former Penn State Players." *Huffington Post*. 8 February 2013. www.huffingtonpost.com/2013/02/08/sue-paterno-defends-joe.

Thamel, Pete. "For Paterno, Lover of Classics, Tragic Flaw to a Legacy." *New York Times*. 22 January 2012. www.nytimes.com/2012/01/23sports/ncaafootbll/joe-paterno-leaves-a-complicated-legacy.html.

Thamel, Pete. "N.C.A.A. Begins Penn State Inquiry." *New York Times*, 18 November 2011. www.nytimes.com/2011/11/19/sports/ncaafootball/ncaa.

Thamel, Pete. "Sanctions Decimate the Nittany Lions Now and for Years to Come." *New York Times*, 23 July 2012. www.nytimes.com/2012/07/13/sports/ncaafootball/penn-state-penalties-incude-60.

Thammel, Pete and Mark Viera. "Penn State's Trustees Recall Painful Decision to Fire Paterno." *New York Times*. 19 January 2012. www.pennstatesunshinefund.org/results/download/2012011922 15letter.

Thomas Jefferson's Reputation Settles Lawsuit Brought by Owners of Monticello." *P R Newswire*. 5 September 2000. www.prnewsire.com/news-releases/group-of-defenders.

Thompson, Charles. "Joe Paterno's New Record: $13.4 Million in Pension from Penn State." *Penn Live*. 23 May 2012. www.pennlive.com/midstate/index.ssf/joe_paternos_new_record.

Thompson, Charles. "Penn State Trustee Ken Frazier Fires Back at Freeh Report Critics." *Penn Live*, 14 March 2013. www.pennlive.com/midstate/index.ssf/2013/penn-state-trustees-Ken_Frazier.html.

Thompson, Charles. "NCAA Responds to Senator Jake Corman's Accusations of 'Manipulation and Deception' Regarding Penn State Sanctions." *Penn Live*. 11 February 2015. www.pennlive.com/midstate/index.ssf/2015/02/ncaa_respond.

Tracy, Mark. "N.C.A.A.: North Carolina Will Not be Punished for Academic

Scandal." *New York Times.* 13 October 2017. www.nytimes.com/2017/10/13/sports/unc.

Weber, Paul J. "NCAA Convention: New President Mark Emmert Calls for Tougher Parent Rules, . . ." *Columbus* (Georgia) *Ledger-Enquirer.* January 14, 2011. www.ledger-enquirer.com/sports/college/sec/auburn-university.

Whiteside, Kelly. "Paterno Isn't All Smiles in Happy Valley." *USA Today.* 19 April 2003. Joe Paterno Papers, Box 07594, Folder "Newspaper Clippings, Magazine Articles," Penn State Archives.

Wilner, Jon. "Cal Stadium Plan Financially Flawed." *San Jose Mercury News.* 24 June 2013. www.mercurynews.com/ci_23528258/cal-stadium-plan-financially-flawed.

Wogenrich, Mark. "A Look at Penn State's Athletic Budgets." *The Morning Call.* 16 March 2015. blogs.mcall.com/nittany_lines/2014/03/a-look.

Wogenrich, Mark. "Penn State Attendance Up 6 percent for 2017." *The Morning Call.* 19 November 2017. www.mcall.com/sports/college/psu/mc-spt-penn-state.

Wright, James. "10 Years After 'Mission Accomplished,' the Risks of Another Intervention." *Atlantic,* 1 May 2013. www.theatlantic.com/international/archives/2013/05/10-years.

Reports, Documents

"Arbitral Award Delivered by the Court of Arbitration for Sport." CAS1011/A/2625 Mohamed Bin Hammam v. FIFA, Lausanne, Switzerland. 19 July 2012. www.taqs-cas.org/fileadmin/user_upload/Award20262520-FIN.

"Athletics Integrity Agreement Between the National Collegiate Athletic Association and the Big Ten Conference, and the Pennsylvania State University." 28 August 2012. www.psu.edu/ur/2012/Athletics_Integrity_Agreement.pdf.

"Binding Consent Decree Imposed by the National Collegiate Athletic Association and Accepted by the Pennsylvania State University." 23 July 2012. www.ncaa.com/content/penn-state-conclusions.

"Critique of the Freeh Report: The Rush to Injustice Regarding Joe Paterno." February 2013. ESPN.go.com/pdf/2013/espn_OTL_FINAL%KING&Spaulding.

DePasquale, Eugene. "Performance Audit Report: The Penn State University, June 2017. www.paauditor.gov/Media/Default/Reports/PSU%Audit%20 Report.pdf.

"Due Process and the NCAA," Hearings Before the Subcommittee on the Constitution of the Committee on the Judiciary. House of Representatives, 108th Congress, 2nd Session, 14 September 2004.

Emmert, Mark, to Rodney Erickson, 17 November 2011. www.psu.edu/ur/2011/ncaa.pdf.

"Engagement to Perform Legal Services on Freeh Sporkin & Sullivan by Penn

State University Board of Trustees." 2 December 2011. ps4rs.files.wordpress.com/2015/03/freehsporkinsullivanengage.

English Standard Bible.

Enteen, George. "A Penn State Dialogue." Email to friends. 30 November 2011. In possession of author.

"Equity in athletics." (2011, 2012, 2013, 2014) Penn State Survey. publicaccess.psu.edu/docs/financial_year.

Frazier, Kenneth. "Update on Special Investigations Task Force Activities." 4 May 2012. www.pennstatesunshinefund.org/results/download.20111.

"Freeh Report." 12 July 2012. www.nytimes.com/interactive/2012/07/12/sports/ncaafootball/13penn state.

"Hearing Before the Committee on Commerce, Science, and Transportation, U.S. Senate, 113th Congress, 2nd Session, 9 July 2014.

"Hearings Before the Subcommittee on the Constitution of the Committee on the Judiciary House of Representatives, 113th Congress, 2nd Session,September 14, 2014.

Holy Bible, King James Version.

"Intercollegiate Sports." Hearings Before the Subcommittee on Commerce, Consumer Protection and Competitiveness of the Committee on Energy and Commerce. House of Representatives, 102d Congress, 1st Session, 19 June 1991.

Moulton, H. Geoffrey, Jr. "Report to the Attorney General on the Investigation of Gerald A. Sandusky." 30 May 2014. www.scribd.com/doc/230973065/Report.

Murrow, Edward R. "See It Now," March 9, 1954.

"NCAA Division I Manual, Constitution and Bylaws, 2011-2012." www.ncaapublications.com/productdownloads/D112.pdf.

"NCAA Legislative Services Database—LSDBi." wwbl.ncaa/exec/miSearch.

"NCAA Reaches Proposed Settlement in Corman Lawsuit." 16 January 2015. www.ncaa.org/about/resources/media-center/news/ncaa.reaches.

National Collegiate Athletic Association *Proceedings.* 1939, 1941, 1949, 1951, 1952, 1953, 1955, 1956, 1963, 1964, 1965, 1966, 1967, 1984, 1985.

"Paterno Report, The Critique of the Freeh Report." 10 February 2013. *Centre Daily Times*, 11 February 2013.

"Report of the Factual Findings of the Investigation into Alleged Improper Contact by the Rutgers Head Football Coach with a Faculty Member." September 15, 2015. president.rutgers.edu/sites/president/files/Final%Report.pdf.

"Report of Special Committee to Confer with Pittsburgh Alumni," ca. 1929-1930. John Oswald Papers, Box 10290, Folder "Athletics Relating to Admission, Policies, Etc. 1979-1982," Penn State University Archives.

"Report of the Special University Faculty Committee to Review President Thomas' Proposed Amendment to the University's Non Discrimination Policy."

19 March 1991. Penn State Board of Trustees Minutes, 16 May 1991, Penn State University Archives.

"Sandusky Press Conference." 7 November 2011. cumberlink.co/sports/penn-state-ib/sandusky-press-conference.

Schreffler, Ronald L. "Penn State Department of University Safety Incident Report." 3 June 1998. notpsu.blogspot.com/2013/07/when-did-ray-gricar-close-his-sandusky.

"Senate Bill 187, Regular Session 2013-2014." Pennsylvania General Assembly. www.legis.state.pa.us/cfdocs/billinfo.cfm?syear-203&sind=0&bo.

"Statement of Findings." Senator Corman News Release. 11 February 2015. www.senatorcorman.com/files/2015/02/News-Release-Statement-of-Findings-pdf.

"Text of Louis Freeh Response to Paterno Report." *Centre Daily Times.* 10 February 2013, p. A3.

"Title IX, Education Amendments of 1972." United States Department of Labor. www.dol.gov/oasam/regs/statues/titleix.htm.

"University Concludes Investigation of Claims Against Women's Basketball Coach." Penn State Press Release. 18 April 2006. www.clubs/psu.edu/up/psupride/articles/press%20release%404 182006.pdf.

U. S. Department of Education. "Final Program Review Determination." 3 November 2016. www.studentaid.ed.gov/sa/sites/default/files/fsawg/datacenter/cleryact/pennstate.

University Concludes Investigation of Claims Against Women's Basketball Coach." 18 April 2006. www.clubs/psu.edu/up/psupride/article/press$release%404182 006.pdf.

Wainstein, Kenneth L., A. Joseph Jay III, Colleen Depman Kukowski. "Investigation of Irregular Classes in the Department of African and Afro-American Studies at the University of North Carolina at Chapel Hill." October 16, 2014. cqh929iorux33fdpl53203kg.wpengine.netdnacdn.com.

Lawsuits

Commonwealth of Pennsylvania v. Graham B. Spanier, Court of Common Pleas of Dauphin County Criminal Division at No(s): CP-22CR-00e615-2013, Superior Court of Pennsylvania, No. 304 MDA 2015.

Commonwealth of Pennsylvania v. Timothy Mark Curley. Court of Common Pleas, Dauphin County, Pennsylvania, No. CP-MD-1374-2011.

Corman v. NCAA. www.senatorcorman.com/legal-documents-corman-vs-ncaa.

Estate and Family of Joseph Paterno v. NCAA, Mark Emmert, and Edward Ray. Docket No. 2013-2082, Civil Division, Court of Common Pleas of Centre County, Pennsylvania.

Graham B. Spanier v. Louis J. Freeh and Freeh Sporkin & Sullivan,LLP. Docket No. 2013-2707, Court of Common Pleas of Centre County, Pennsylvania, Civil

Action, 14 October 2016.

Graham B. Spanier v. Penn State University, No. 2016-0571, Court of Common Pleas of Centre County, Pennsylvania, Civil Action-Law, 9 November 2017.

Jennifer E. Harris v. Maureen T. Portland, et al., Civil Action No. 1:05-CV-2648, U. S. District Court, Harrisburg, PA. 33 January 2006.

Kaidanov v. Pennsylvania State University, Pennsylvania Eastern District Court, Case No. 2:14-cv-03191, District Judge Gene E K. Pratter presiding.

NCAA v. Tarikanian. 488 U.S. 179 (1988).

Pearsoll v. Chapin, 44 Pa 9 (1862) Assumpsit, Action of, III. Grandes (E) Torts.

Penn State v. Pennsylvania Manufacturers' Association Insurance Co., No. 131103195.

Solesbee v. Balkcom. 339 U.S. 16 (1950).

Todd McNair v. NCAA, 6 February 2015, Court of Appeals of the State of California, Second Appellate District, Division 3.

Speeches, Correspondence, E-works, and Unpublished Works

Anonymous. "A Curious Assignment—Hiring Public Relations Firms to Manage Communications with Faculty?!" Monitoring University Governance blog. 27 April 2012. lebpsusenate.blogspot.com/2012/04-curious-assignment-hiring-public/html.

Anonymous. Email to Ron Smith, 5 September 2017. Author's possession.

Booher, Dennis Alan, "Joseph Vincent Paterno, Football Coach: His Involvement with the Pennsylvania State University and American Intercollegiate Athletics." Ph.D. dissertation, Penn State University, 1985.

Campbell, Anthony C. "An Impact Analysis of the NCAA's Handling of the Pennsylvania State University's 2011-2012 Case." Ph.D. dissertation, Creighton University, 2014.

Chambers, Alycia A. to Ronald Schreffler, 7 May 1998. www.msnbemedial.msn.com/msnbc/sections/news/chambers_sandusky_report.

Cohen, Andrew. "Thus Begins the Rehabilitation of Joe Paterno." 15 January 2012. www.pennstatesunshinefund.org/results/download/2012011649.

"Director of Intercollegiate Athletics Appointment Terms." Press release, 26 July 2014. www.psu.edu.ur/2014/Barbour.pdf.

"Dunham Named as Vice President and General Counsel." Press release. 23 May 2012. www.pennstatesunshinefund.org/results/download/20111.

Edelman, Richard. "Richard Edelman Public Relations Strategy for Penn State-Sandusky." *YouTube*, 30 June 2014. www.youtube.com/watch?v=t3KDnaLr50.

"Football Fans Boost Home Attendance by 5,000." Penn State news release, 2 December 2014. news.psu.edu/story336808.

Harvey, Paul. Discussion with author, 22 January 2014.

"Hoover Legacy, The, 40 Years After." 4 May 2012. www.fbi.gov/news/stories/the-hoover-legacy.

"Joe Paterno's Speech to the BOT Following His First National Championship." 22 January 1983. docs.google.com/document/d/Lvm/vpkrt7KrmyZlqjisepf8.

"John Cappelletti Heisman Acceptance Speech. 13 December 1973. Penn State University Archives.

Jones, David. Discussion with author. 6 May 2016.

Kwiencinski, Chris. "Big Ten Schools Enjoy High Attendance." www.landof10.com/big-ten/big-ten-football-home-attendance.

Loizides, Antonios. "Draco's Law Code." *Ancient History Encyclopedia.* www.ancient.eu/dracos.

Mark Emmert to Rodney Erickson, 17 November 2011, Author's possession.

Monsieur Verdoux (1947) "Movie Script." www.springfield.co.uk/movie_script.php/movie+monsieur-verdoux.

Oldsey, Bill. "Letter of Intent to Maribeth Roman Schmidt and PS4RS Board of Directors, 18 January 2016. PS4RS.files.wordpress.com/2016/02/2016-bill-oldsey-letter.

"Paterno Family Abandons All Claims Against NCAA." NCAA press release, 30 June 2017. www.ncaa.org/about/resources/media-center/news/paterno-family-abandons.

"Penn State Commencement Speech by Head Football Coach Joe Paterno." 16 June 1973. www.pennstatemag.files.wordpress.com/2012/01/paterno1973commencementspeech.

"PS4RS—Penn Staters for Responsible Stewardship." www.ps4rs.org.

"Rene Portland Named 2005 Renaissance Person of the Year." Penn State press release. 23 July 2005. www.clubs.psu.edu/up/psupride/article/press%20release%2072 32005.pdf.

Ron Smith, email to Jan Bortner, 30 August 2013 and Bortner to Smith, 3 September 2013. Author's possession.

Statement from President Donna E. Shalala." February 18, 2013. www.miami.edu/index/php/news/release.

"The 100 Richest Universities: Their Generosity and Commitment to Research 2017." www.thebestschools.org/features/richest-universities-endowments.

Triponey, Vicky, email to Ron Smith. 13 January 2016, Author's possession.

Weber, Jodi. "Joe Paterno in the NCAA." Ex Sci 444 paper, 21 April 1992, Penn State University Archives.

Welch, Susan. "Farewell to Joe Paterno, a Legendary Liberal Arts Leader." College of the Liberal Arts News Release. Ca. February 2012. www.la/psu/edu/news/farewell-to-joe-paterno-a-legendary-liberal-arts-leader.

"Wick Sollers." www.kslaw.com/people/JSedwick-Sollers.

Interviews

Frank, Russell. "Oral History Interview with Ron Bracken." 16 June 2009. comm.psu.edu/assets/uploads/brackeninterview.pdf.

Jenkins, Sally. "Joe Paterno's First Interview Since the Penn State-Sandusky Scandal. *Washington Post.* 14 January 2012. www.washingtonpost.com/sports/college/joe-paterno.

Spanier, Graham. Interview by author. Lincoln, NB. April 12, 1995.

Swisher, John. Discussion with the author, Lemont, PA. 11 November 2014.

Thiel, Glenn "Nick." Author interviewed by Thiel, State College, PA. April 1968.

Archival Collections

Bernie Asbell Papers, Penn State University Archives.

Chancellors' Central Files, University of Nebraska, Lincoln, Archives.

Dougherty, N W. Collection, University of Tennessee Archives.

Joe Paterno Vertical File, Penn State University Archives.

John Cappelletti Heisman Acceptance Speech, Penn State University Archives.

Office of the Vice President for Student Affairs Papers, Penn State University Archives.

Office of the Senior V.P. for Finance Records, Penn State University Archives.

Papers of George W. Atherton, Penn State University Archives.

Papers of Joe Paterno, Penn State University Archives.

Papers of Rip Engle, Penn State University Archives.

Penn State Board of Trustees Executive Committee Minutes, Penn State University Archives

Penn State Board of Trustees Minutes, Penn State University Archives.

President Joab Thomas Papers, Penn State University Archives.

President John Oswald Papers, Penn State University Archives.

Ridge H. Riley Papers, Penn State University Archives.

INDEX

A

Academy of Physical Education and Kinesiology, ix

AIAW. See Association of Intercollegiate Athletics for Women

Alcindor, Lew (Kareem Abdul-Jabbar), 15

All-Sports Museum, 113

Ancient Greek storyteller, 122

Anderson, Sherwin (basketball), 19

Anouilh, Jean, 44

antitrust, 14, 157

Aristotle, 56

Association of Intercollegiate Athletics for Women (AIAW), 18-19

Athenian lawgivers, 141

athletic coup, 66-70

"Athletics Integrity Agreement," 79, 81, 82

athletic isolation, 17-29

athletic scholarships, 5-7, 10, 12, 18, 71, 78, 85, 100, 135, 144, 146

athletic violations at Penn State, xii, 8, 17-20, 27, 70-74, 82, 83, 148

Atkinson, Heather (field hockey player), 19

Atlanta Olympics bombing (1996), 37

Atlantic Monthly article (2017), 140

Auriemma, Geno (Connecticut), 105

B

Bachman, Denise (Daily Collegian reporter), 114

Baldwin, Cynthia (Penn State chief counsel). See also Fina, Frank (prosecutor)

    2010 Jan. 22: General Counsel for Penn State, appointed, 151

    2011 Dec.: NCAA created list of questions from Donald Remy; interviewed Baldwin and Spanier, along with 400-plus individuals with knowledge of athletics, 42-43

    2011 Jan. 12: Tim Curley, Gary Schultz, and Joe Paterno testified before the Grand Jury, "represented" by Cynthia Baldwin, 152

    2011 April 13: Spanier testified before Grand Jury, "represented" by Baldwin, 152

The Joe Paterno statue overlooking Mt. Nittany *Photo: Ronald Smith*